THE DEMOCRACY
DEVELOPMENT MACHINE

The Democracy Development Machine

Neoliberalism, Radical Pessimism, and Authoritarian Populism in Mayan Guatemala

Nicholas Copeland

Cornell University Press
Ithaca and London

Publication of this open monograph was the result of Virginia Tech's participation in TOME (Toward an Open Monograph Ecosystem), a collaboration of the Association of American Universities, the Association of University Presses, and the Association of Research Libraries. TOME aims to expand the reach of long-form humanities and social science scholarship including digital scholarship. Additionally, the program looks to ensure the sustainability of university press monograph publishing by supporting the highest quality scholarship and promoting a new ecology of scholarly publishing in which authors' institutions bear the publication costs.

Funding from Virginia Tech made it possible to open this publication to the world.

www.openmonographs.org

First published 2019 by Cornell University Press

Library of Congress Cataloging-in-Publication Data

Names: Copeland, Nicholas, author.
Title: The democracy development machine : neoliberalism, radical pessimism, and authoritarian populism in Mayan Guatemala / Nicholas Copeland.
Description: Ithaca [New York] : Cornell University Press, 2019. | Includes bibliographical references and index.
Identifiers: LCCN 2018045106 (print) | LCCN 2018046018 (ebook) | ISBN 9781501736070 (pdf) | ISBN 9781501736087 (epub/mobi) | ISBN 9781501736056 | ISBN 9781501736056 (cloth) | ISBN 9781501736063 (pbk.)
Subjects: LCSH: Mayas—Guatemala—Politics and government. | Mayas—Guatemala—Government relations. | Guatemala—Politics and government—1985– | Guatemala—Economic conditions— 1985– | Democracy—Guatemala.
Classification: LCC F1435.3.P7 (ebook) | LCC F1435.3.P7 C67 2019 (print) | DDC 972.81—dc23
LC record available at https://lccn.loc.gov/2018045106

For Mildred Copeland

Contents

Acknowledgments

It is a miracle that this book was ever written, and the fact that it was is a result of tremendous debts. My decision to do research in Guatemala was heavily influenced by the enthusiasm of colleagues at the University of Texas at Austin, especially Irma Alicia Velázquez-Nimatuj, Ramón Ponciano Gonzales, Ven de la Cruz, and Ajb'ee Jimenez. Thank you for your patience and generosity over the years. UT Austin presented a truly unique and wonderful place and time to study political anthropology in Latin America and the borderlands. I am fortunate to have met and shared ideas with an unusually large number of committed scholars and activists: Mark Anderson, Melissa Biggs, Ronda Brulotte, Vania Cardoso, Ben Chappell, Emiliana Cruz, Richard Flores, Melissa Forbis, Jen Goett, Pablo Gonzalez, Ted Gordon, Pete Haney, Scott Head, Keisha Khan-Perry, Cale Layton, Liz Lilliott, Chris Loperena, Korinta Maldonado, Mariana Mora, Courtney Morris, Vivian Newdick, Brandt Peterson, Nadjah Ríos, Gilberto Rosas, Apen Ruíz, Lynn Selby, Dan Sharp, Fernanda Soto, Shannon Speed, Angela Stuesse, Heather Teague, Mike Trujillo, and Jackie Zahn. It will always be humbling to be among this generation of luminaries. Teresa Velasquez has been a constant collaborator whose combination of commitment, brilliance, and sense of humor is without equal. I am also thankful to the staff of the Benson Latin American Collection, who curate the many treasures stored there.

Notable among the many other dear and talented individuals I was privileged to meet at Texas were Can Aciksoz, Mohan Ambikaipaker, Matt Archer, Whitney Battle, Jamie Brandon, James Brow, Beth Bruinsma, Peggy Brunache, Jenny Carlson, Galeet Dardashti, Adriana Dingman, Bob and B. J. Fernea, Kaushik Ghosh, Dan Gilman, John Hartigan Jr., Deborah Kapchan, Jennifer Karson, Ward Keeler, Ritu Khanduri, Mathangi Krishnamurthy, Ozlem Okur, Hisyar Ozsoy, Alisa Perkins, Leighton Peterson, Jemima Pierre, Jacqueline Polvora, Junaid Rana, John Schaefer, Ruken Sengul, Nathan Tabor, Leela Tanikella, Francis Terry, Faedah Totah, Linta Vargese, Maria Velásquez, Kamala Visweswaran, Scott Webel, Anthony Webster, Mark Westmoreland, and Casey Williamson. I am especially grateful to Nell Barker, Leah Ferguson, Celeste Henery, Ken MacLeish, Shaka McGlotten, Diya Mehra, Joel Page, Rachael Pomerantz, Nadjah Ríos, Ken Rubin, Liz Smith, Raja Swamy, and Halide Velioğlu for helping me keep life and school in perspective. And it is hard to imagine a kinder and more thoughtful person than Mubbashir Rizvi. I was fortunate to receive sage advice from Charlie Hale, Katie Stewart, Kamran Asdar Ali, Virginia Garrard, and Polly Strong. Begoña Aretxaga was a truly formidable mind and mentor whose intensity will be forever missed. Ron Greene and Mel Tapper shaped my thinking in a thousand ways.

I was blessed to have had a large group of nonanthropologist but equally brilliant friends over several iterations of Austin life, including Billy O'Leary, Natalie Vallot, Darren Jones, Tamara Goheen, Jacob Childress, Chris McNett, Anne Merrill, and Karla Steffen, many of whom happened to later staff the anthropology department. I was in a vibrant intellectual world inhabited by Stapp Beeton, Dave Breshears, Jon Brody, Chris Burk, Nikheel Dhekne, Eric Emerson, Jeni Emerson, Blake Eno, Michelle Gajda, Ryan Goodman, Penelope Gonzalez-Marks, Derek Jenks, Yuri Kostun, Kevin Kuswa, Brian McBride, Georgette Oden, Megan O'Neil, Joel Page, Jay Reed, Judd Renken, Joel Rollins, Bill and Kim Shanahan, Kate Shuster, Stephen Stetson, Sammi Whitmire, and Dave Wyrick. They set me on a path of ethical and political development that led me to anthropology.

I had encountered Brian Ragsdale, Orion Auld, Chris Carty, Seth Ulrich, and Andy Graan even earlier.

My family—Marian, Bud, Mildred, Bill, Scott, and Catherine—is a truly eclectic group and has been a constant source of support and perspective over the years, including offering some suggestions with which I completely disagree. The Jimenez family—Blanca, Mary, Fabi, Luis, Romelia, José, Miguel, Julio, Victor, Eva, German, and Marvin—welcomed me into their lives in San Sebastián, taught me many things, and showed me the true meaning of hospitality. My *compas* from *Asociación* Ceiba were Luisa Morales, Erick Monroy, Pepe Maldonado, Anna Maria Ramos, Alfonso Morales, Chepe Díaz, Chepe Ros, Elías Raymundo, Marina Domingo, Candelaria Gabriel, Fabiana Ortíz, Carolina Floren, Tom Feyaerts, and Francisca Velasquez. Without the guidance of the indomitable Isabel Sáenz, whose work for women's rights knows no limits, I would have never gotten very far. The team at the *Centro de Estudios y Documentación de la Frontera Noroeste de Guatemala* (CEDFOG) provided a tremendous resource. It is a true loss for the region that their doors have closed. Pedro Camajà and Aníbal Salazar from FUNDEBASE have been central to my current understanding and research.

Anthropologists working in Guatemala and Central America are a model for dedication and intellectual generosity, among them Santiago Bastos, Jennifer Burrell, Manuela Camus, Ted Fischer, Liza Grandia, Carlota McAllister, Ellen Moodie, Diane Nelson, Debra Rodman, and Finn Stepputat. The following kind and wise individuals read and commented on parts of the manuscript: Abigail Adams, Aaron Ansell, Ted Fischer, Carol Greenhouse, Akhil Gupta, Matt Heaton, Eric Jenkins, Stuart Kirsch, Christine Labuski, Chad Lavin, Tania Li, David Nugent, Peter Potter, Barbara Ellen Smith, Steve Striffler, and Janell Watson, along with several anonymous reviewers. All errors are mine alone.

My time at Arkansas was graced with many superb colleagues and friends, especially Rob Brubaker, Jesse Casana, Lisa Corrigan, Kirstin Erickson, Stuart Fulbright, Troy Gittings, Andy Horowitz, Hamsa and Moshe Newmark, Kelly O'Callaghan, Karon Reese, Laurent Sacharoff, Kathryn Sloan, and Sergio Villalobos-Ruminott. Brittany Philips and Erin Von Feldt were my family. Ted Swedenburg is a dear friend, wise mentor, and devotee of international pop culture who will absolutely not relent. Steve Striffler is a giant whose shoes at Arkansas I could never fill. The members of the Workers' Justice Center in Springdale have my full respect. I was lucky to have known and taught the banjo-playing, bike-riding, antiwar veteran hillbilly Jacob George. Rest in power.

I am fortunate to be an anthropologist in Virginia Tech's remarkably eclectic Department of Sociology and to have so many wonderful colleagues and friends in Blacksburg, especially Aaron Ansell, Mark Barbour, Sabrina Barry, Shannon Bell, Jen Bondy, Daniel and Margaret Breslau, Brian Britt, Toni Calasanti, Mauro Caraccioli, Katie Carmichael, Maria Elisa Christie, Sam Cook, Cara Daggett, Zach Dresser, Tom Ewing, Ted Fuller, Matt and Rachael Gabriele, Ann Genova, Laura Gillman, Tish Glosh, Ellington Graves, Saul Halfon, Johnny Hall, Dennis Halpin, Kwame Harrison, Jim Hawdon, Rebecca Hester, Mike Hughes, Brenda Husser, Trevor Jamerson, María del Carmen Jiménez, Sharon Johnson, Sitinga Kachipande, Lindsay Kahle, Rohan Kalyan, Melanie Kiechle, Neal King, Devon Lee, Elizabeth Mazzolini, Erin Mckelvy, Erika Meitner, Jesse Meltsner, Corey Miles, Marian Mollin, Lipon Mondal, Shelton Norwood, Phil Olsen, Sarah Ovink, Anthony Peguero, Karl Precoda, Mindy and Paul Quigley, Pallavi Raonka, Wornie Reed, Ryan Rideau, Petra Rivera-Rideau, Claire and Nick Robbins, Jack Rosenberger, John Ryan, Suchitra Samanta, Emily Satterwhite, Pam and Peter Schmitthenner, Helen Schneider, Donna Sedgwick, Eric Sindelar, Amy Splitt, April Stapp, Ken Surin, Anthony Szczurek, Steve Trost, Vinodh Venkatesh, Abby Walker, and Dale Wimberley. Barbara Ellen Smith is a mentor and role model, kind friend, and brave leader who always wants to talk about what is most important.

My research received funding from the University of Texas, from the H. F. Guggenheim Foundation, and from the University of Maryland Center for Latin American and Caribbean Studies, where I enjoyed conversations with Janet Chernela, Shane Dillingham, Saúl Sosnowski, Mary Kay Vaughan, and Daryle Williams. Thank you to Jim Lance from Cornell University Press for believing in this book. It would never have been possible without the help of so many friends in San Pedro Necta. My deepest gratitude goes to feminist killjoy, fashionista, and Walmart slayer Christine Labuski for walking the path with me.

Portions of chapter 3 were previously published in "Regarding Development: Governing Indian Advancement in Revolutionary Guatemala" (*Economy and Society* 44, no. 3 [2015]: 418–44). Portions of chapter 4 were previously published in " 'Guatemala Will Never Change': Radical Pessimism and the Politics of Personal Interest in the Western Highlands" (*Journal of Latin American Studies* 43, no. 3 [2011], 485–515) and in "Mayan Imaginaries of Democracy: Interactive Sovereignties and Political Affect in Postrevolutionary Guatemala" (*American Ethnologist* 41, no. 2 [2014], 305–19.

ABBREVIATIONS

ALMG: *Academia de Lenguas Mayas* (Academy of Mayan Languages)

ANACAFE: *Asociación Nacional del Café* (National Coffee Association)

ANN: *Alternativa Nueva Nación* (New Nation Alternative)

ASODESI: *Asociación del Desarrollo Integral* (Association for Integrated Development)

ASP: *Asamblea Sociál y Popular* (Social and Popular Assembly)

CA: *Acción Católica* (Catholic Action)

CACIF: *Comité de Asociaciones Agrícolas, Comerciales, Industriales y Financieras* (Coordinating Committee for Agricultural, Commercial, Industrial, and Financial Associations)

CAFTA: Central American Free Trade Agreement

CASA: *Centro de Acción Social* (Center for Social Action)

CC: *Corte Constitucional* (Constitutional Court)

CEH: *Comisión de Esclaramiento Histórico* (Commission for Historical Clarification)
CICIG: *Comisión Internacional Contra la Impunidad en Guatemala* (International Commission against Impunity in Guatemala)
COCODE: *Consejo Comunitario de Desarrollo* (Community Development Council)
COMUDE: *Consejo Municipal de Desarrollo* (Municipal Development Council)
CONAVIGUA: *Coordinadora Nacional de Viudas de Guatemala* (National Coordinator for Guatemalan Widows)
CPO: *Consejo del Pueblos del Occidente* (Council of the Peoples of the West)
CSJ: *Corte Supremo de Justicia* (Supreme Court of Justice)
CUC: *Comité de Unidad Campesina* (Peasant Unity Committee)
DC: *Democracia Cristiana Guatemalteca* (Guatemalan Christian Democracy)
DECOPAZ: *Programa de Desarrollo Comunitario para la Paz* (Community Development Program for Peace)
DIGESA: *Dirección General de Servicios Agrícolas* (General Directorate of Agricultural Services)
EGP: *Ejército Guerillero de los Pobres* (Guerrilla Army of the Poor)
FCN: *Frente de Convergencia Nacional* (National Convergence Front)
FENACOAC: *Federación Nacional de Cooperativas de Ahorro y Credito* (National Federation of Cooperatives for Savings and Credit)
FIS: *Fondo de Inversión Social* (Social Investment Fund)
FNDG: *Frente Nueva Democratica Guatemalteca* (New Guatemalan Democratic Front)
FODIGUA: *Fondo de Desarrollo Indígena de Guatemala* (Indigenous Development Fund of Guatemala)
FON: *Frente de Oposición Nacional* (National Opposition Front)
FONAPAZ: *Fondo Nacional para la Paz* (National Fund for Peace)
FRG: *Frente Republicano Guatemalteco* (Guatemalan Republican Front)

FUNDEBASE: *Fundación por el Desarrollo y Fortalecimiento de las Organizaciónes de Base* (Foundation for the Development and Strengthening of Grassroots Organizations)

FUR: *Frente Unido de la Revolución* (United Front of the Revolution)

GANA: *Gran Alianza Nacional* (Grand National Alliance)

IDF: International Development Foundation

ILO: International Labor Organization

LIDER: *Libertad Democrática Renovada* (Renewed Democratic Liberty)

MAGA: *Ministerio de Agricultura, Ganadería y Alimentación* (Guatemalan Ministry of Agriculture, Livestock, and Food)

MIFAPRO: *Mi Familia Progresa* ("My Family Progresses")

MLN: *Movimiento Liberación Nacional* (National Liberation Movement)

NTX: Nontraditional Export

ORPA: *Organización Revolucionaria del Pueblo en Armas* (Revolutionary Organization of the Armed Populace)

PAC: *Patrulleros de Autodefensa Civil* (civil self-defense patrols ["ex-PACs"])

PAN: *Partído de Avanzado Nacional* (National Advancement Party)

PAR: *Partído de Acción Revolucionario* (Revolutionary Action Party)

PGT: *Partído de Trabajadores Guatemaltecos* (Guatemalan Workers' Party)

PR: *Partído Revolucionario* (Revolutionary Party)

RCDP: Rural Cooperative Development Project

RDP: Rural Development Plan

REDSAG: *Red Nacional por la Defensa de la Soberanía Alimentaria en Guatemala* (National Network for the Defense of Food Sovereignty in Guatemala)

REHMI: *Recuperación de Memoria Histórica* (Recuperation of Historical Memory)

SEGEPLAN: *Secretario General de Planificación Nacional* (Secretary General of National Planning)

SFEI: *Sociedad para el Fortalecimiento de la Economía Indígena* (Society for the Strengthening of the Indigenous Economy)

STEG: *Sindicato de Trabajadores de la Educación de Guatemala* (Guatemalan Educational Workers Union)

TLC: *Tratado de Libre Comercio* (Free Trade Treaty)

TSE: *Tribuno Supremo Electoral* (Supreme Electoral Tribunal)

UCN: *Unión de Cambio Nacional* (Union of National Change)

UNE: *Unidad Nacional de Esperanza* (National Unity of Hope)

UNOPS: United Nations Office for Project Services

URNG: *Unidad Revolucionaria Nacional Guatemalteco* (Guatemalan National Revolutionary Unity)

USAID: United States Agency for International Development

THE DEMOCRACY
DEVELOPMENT MACHINE

INTRODUCTION

A Transition to Misery

Guatemala's armed conflict was one of the longest and bloodiest in modern Latin American history. It spanned decades of organizing by peasant, indigenous, student, religious, and workers' organizations, along with several armed revolutionary groups—motivated by anti-imperialism, land reform, equality, and social democracy—that were all violently opposed by a fascistic military dictatorship backed by national elites and the US government. Its nadir was a brutal scorched-earth campaign in 1981–1983, during which the army killed tens of thousands, displaced over a million, and committed hundreds of massacres in order to divide guerrilla organizations from their civilian base in the indigenous western highlands.[1] With the internal enemy defeated, and confronted with economic disarray and international condemnation, the army pursued limited democracy in 1985 while permanently occupying rural towns and forcing village men to participate in antiguerrilla civil defense patrols (PAC).[2] With great courage, civil society organizations fought to expand the democratic opening as human rights advocates risked their lives to denounce state violence and to search for loved ones who had been forcibly disappeared.[3] The most storied protagonist of Guatemala's transition was the Pan-Mayan movement, which pursued cultural revitalization, self-determination, and a pluri-national state.[4] Throughout the 1990s, indigenous organizations took power in rural towns across the western highlands—a tectonic shift in local racial hierarchies—just as state decentralization raised the stakes of local control. In 1992, the 500th anniversary of Columbus's voyage, Rigoberta Menchú was awarded the Nobel Peace Prize for her *testimonio* depicting life as an Indian girl, her family's struggle for land and experiences with state violence, and indigenous support for resistance movements, as well as for her global advocacy for indigenous rights (Burgos-Debray, 1985).

Pressure from a coalition of popular and Mayan movements and business elites led to the signing of peace accords in 1996.[5] The left found more success in UN-brokered negotiations than on the battlefield. Hailed internationally as a historic transition to multicultural democracy, the accords' call for structural reforms alongside the official recognition of human and indigenous rights inspired hope for lasting change. Although the accords were limited and many remained skeptical,[6] they were a watershed in Guatemalan history, their significance marked by the return of refugees from Mexico and mountain hideouts, the dismantling of rural paramilitaries and army garrisons, the legalization of leftist parties and movements, the recognition of indigenous identity, and the arrival of UN monitors and a phalanx of national and international organizations promoting development and human, indigenous, and women's rights.[7]

Two truth commissions cut through army propaganda and silence about the causes, extent, and perpetrators of the violence, and they wove a new narrative of Guatemalan history. The UN Commission for Historical Clarification (CEH), established in the peace accords, found the army and paramilitaries responsible for 93 percent of nearly 200,000 estimated deaths, including 626 massacres, and revealed that the vast majority—83 percent—of those killed were Mayas, members of Guatemala's majority indigenous underclass. They also concluded that the army had committed "acts of genocide" during the scorched-earth campaign. The CEH further framed the violence as an expression of racism and inequality at the heart of Guatemalan society: an agro-export economy founded on indigenous dispossession, the 1954 overthrow of a democratically elected president who was implementing land reform, and deeply rooted patterns of violence and racism. Testimony catalogued by the Recuperation of Historical Memory Project (REHMI 1998), a separate truth commission directed by Catholic Church's Office for Human Rights, corroborated and added depth to these findings.

Democracy was marketed in Guatemala as the path to peace and to the economic and political inclusion of the indigenous majority, a clean break from a history of internal colonialism, dictatorship, and war. As President Clinton apologized for US complicity, Guatemalans were rethinking their ethnic and gender identities and rebuilding communities and institutions, often with direct assistance from the state they had fought against for decades and international donors whose motives were opaque. Guarded optimism coursed through the programs and workshops of *Asociación* Ceiba, a leftist, human-rights–oriented nongovernmental organization (NGO) in rural Huehuetenango, for which in 2002–2003 I conducted a collaborative investigation of Mayan women's organizations in Colotenango. Ceiba's members—a collection of former revolutionaries, returned refugees, feminists, agronomists, physicians and health promoters, and European and US volunteers—imagined their programs as the leading edge of democratic transformation in a region recently awakened from a long nightmare. My first exposure to this energy was in 1998 as an anthropology graduate student in Austin, Texas, where several Guatemalan activists had come to develop politically engaged research agendas.[8]

Perhaps predictably, democracy has been profoundly disappointing to Guatemalan progressives; their hopes for lasting social transformation have been crushed by persistent poverty, state violence, impunity, rising inequality, and the election of corrupt authoritarian parties.[9] Right-wing parties have blocked the peace accords while pursuing a transition to free market policies of free trade, deregulation, austerity, privatization, and resource extraction that have harmed the majority to benefit the few.[10] Violent crime and femicide thrive in a climate of economic and physical insecurity and impunity that has prompted hundreds of thousands to migrate north since the 2000s.[11] Deregulation, speculation, and rising demand for raw materials have accelerated extractive industries and land grabs, unleashing a new cycle of conflicts.[12]

Rather than expanding in civil society, progressive movements are divided and have an uneven following in rural communities.[13] In 1999 voters rejected a constitutional referendum required to implement the accord on indigenous rights (Warren 2002). Twenty years after peace, no movement or party wields the capacity to force significant economic redistribution, or even implementation of the accords, now a dead letter (Hernández Pico 2005). Violence against indigenous and peasant organizations proceeds routinely in the name of defending the democratic order while army assassins, mobster politicians, and white-collar criminals walk free and while transnational corporations and national elites monopolize national resources, wreck the environment, and pay minimal taxes.[14] Patterns in Mayan politics feed democratic disenchantment. Unlike in Bolivia and Ecuador, where indigenous and peasant coalitions mounted electoral challenges to free market policies, rural Mayas have mostly avoided radical movements and many have voted for authoritarians, most disturbingly for former dictator Efraín Ríos Montt for president in 2003, whose evangelical populist image contrasted starkly with accusations of genocide during the scorched-earth campaign.[15]

The Democracy-Development Paradox

This book confronts the chronic failure, nagging persistence, and deep interrelationship between democracy and development—two pillars of Western modernity—and their implications for rural politics in the age of neoliberalism, especially in post-conflict societies. Liberal democracy—free elections and free markets—is the seemingly self-evident form of government in most of the world, based on an idea of popular sovereignty, celebrated as the ideal, widely understood as synonymous with peace and freedom, and promoted by international institutions as a remedy for a host of social ills. Yet liberal democracy increasingly channels illiberalism, its ostensible opposite, producing war, intolerance, and authoritarianism from within the democratic process itself. Across the world, frustrated multitudes rally behind authoritarian populists who employ violence and other illiberal means alongside claims to defend "the people" against immigrants, economic stagnation, terrorism, corrupt elites, cultural decay, and sometimes their own neighbors. Authoritarian populism is not new but has proliferated alongside the shift to neoliberalism: a philosophy that sees the common good as best achieved by concerted efforts to maximize individual economic freedom and economic growth; restrictions on regulation, redistribution, and labor power; and the global expansion of free markets.[16] More than a set of economic policies, neoliberalism is a political rationality that extends market logic into all domains of social life.

Development is a paramount value in market societies, associated with economic prosperity and progress and encapsulated in the idea of living better. Development is synonymous with economic growth, rebuilding communities riven by war and natural disaster, and improvement in general. Development is the primary responsibility of all states and the metric by which they are judged, the putative motive of much of their activity. In dominant conceptions of the global South, development is further understood as a necessary and inevitable process through which poor and conflict-ridden "third-world" countries become more like the "first world" as their citizens overcome endemic cultural backwardness to become "modern."[17] Democracy and development are widely assumed to be fundamentally compatible and mutually reinforcing. Development exists outside of democracy, but democracy—in the global South especially—depends on development: it is built out of efforts to train individuals to understand the scope and responsibilities of democratic citizenship, participate in free markets, and engage in democratic decision making, the latter largely centered around development. However, democracy and development routinely fall short as neoliberal polices exacerbate poverty and inequality and expose citizens to exploitation, displacement, and environmental harm. Disillusionment with democracy is largely a result of its inability to address the failure of development; their fates are intertwined. Yet the pull of democracy and development remains strong, even among the very people who bear the brunt of their failures.

Anthropologists and cultural critics are decidedly ambivalent about the dangers and possibilities of democracy and development, mirroring divided and increasingly pessimistic perceptions of the political present. Critics on the left point to liberal democracy's violent foundations and features—differentiated regimes of citizenship, border policing, repression of dissent, and assimilationist tendencies—perpetuated through seemingly apolitical procedures.[18] They highlight liberal democracy's disregard for historical struggles for material rights, its affinity with imperialism and free market hegemony, and its remarkable capacity to neutralize critique.[19]

Political theorist Jodi Dean (2009) dismisses democracy as "communicative capitalism": a "neoliberal fantasy" that derails and absorbs dissent.[20] Development is similarly derided as a form of economic and cultural imperialism rooted in neocolonial inequalities that disrupts indigenous economic and political structures and spoils ecologies in the name of progress.[21] James Ferguson (1994) branded development an "anti-politics machine" that reinforces state power and spreads bureaucracy and market rationality while obscuring the structural and political causes of poverty. Development and democracy appear as mechanisms of control rather than liberation.

In a different register, political theorist Wendy Brown (2015) warns of the evisceration of liberal democracy, along with more radical possibilities, by neoliberal political rationality,[22] while the poverty economist Amartya Sen (1999) sees development, understood as the increase of human capacity for the marginalized, as the expansion of freedom. Others look to the potential of "alternative" or "radical" democracy and development to challenge injustice and construct egalitarian futures, either from the bottom up, as with the Zapatistas, or through the state, as in Bolivia.[23] Anthropologists have analyzed multifarious efforts to weaponize and militarize democracy and development and to foster democratic citizens habituated to free markets and resigned to spiraling inequalities. They have also shown how democracy and development are generative, open-source ideals that are reworked and reimagined by various groups to challenge violence and exclusion.[24] Neoliberal and authoritarian varieties of democracy and Eurocentric, capitalist models of development predominate, and they become entangled with both egalitarian and reactionary populist politics on the ground.

How do different combinations of development and democracy operate alongside political and economic violence to transform the terrain of rural politics under neoliberalism? How have democracy and development been imagined, assembled, and securitized to extend counterinsurgency—coordinated action against radical movements—through post-conflict transitions? What are the dangers of pursuing decolonization on the terrain of neoliberal democracy and development? How do the contradictions of "neoliberal" empowerment inform alliances with authoritarian populism? These matters hold great urgency for marginalized populations throughout the global South who over the last several decades have navigated a political terrain defined by post-conflict and post-socialist transitions, indigenous rights movements, neoliberal policies, and progressive and reactionary populisms.

The Democracy Development Machine explores these questions in San Pedro Necta, a Maya-Mam majority town in the rural department of Huehuetenango in Guatemala's western highlands. Huehuetenango is one of Guatemala's poorest departments, and more than 65 percent of its inhabitants are indigenous. Because of its remoteness, poverty, and indigenous peasant majority, Huehuetenango is commonly imagined as a hinterland. The department's indigenous communities rallied behind the democratic revolution of 1944–1954, were the cradle of the guerrilla movement in the 1970s, were devastated by counterinsurgency, and have staged a political resurgence since the 1990s. In 2003 San Pedro joined the ranks of many highland towns where the authoritarian Guatemalan Republican Front (FRG), led by Ríos Montt, gained a strong indigenous following to notch victories after the peace accords.

Throughout the western highlands, democracy was established through development during an ongoing counterinsurgency and a peace process to extend neocolonial order alongside demilitarization and free market restructuring.[25] Organized villagers seized upon democracy and development to extend long-standing struggles for individual and collective advancement, dignity, and basic resources: central elements of decolonized citizenship. Wary of reifying power or romanticizing resistance, I explore Mayan Sampedranos' entanglements with distinct facets and fusions of democracy and development as they took shape over two decades. My analysis is based on seventeen months of ethnographic and historical fieldwork beginning in 2003, spanning all of 2004, and then in subsequent visits through 2014. "Neoliberal" democracy and development disappointed local expectations, brought unintended consequences, and extended counterinsurgency by other means, calling into question their efficacy as vehicles for progressive change even when subalterns try to reclaim them. I attribute the success of authoritarian populism in San Pedro to the ways that it offered ephemeral but material forms of relief from the failures of democracy and development, from within the confines of neoliberal order, while simultaneously reinforcing these limits.

Critical scholars of post-conflict settings question the separation between democracy and war, approaching democracy as a field of power that reproduces wartime antagonisms in altered form.[26] Democracy's politics becomes most evident in post-conflict transitions when its edges line up against competing national projects and histories of struggle. *The Democracy Development Machine* analyzes how democracy and development worked alongside political and economic violence in a context of material deprivation to reorganize indigenous politics on market and electoral terms, and to erode collective solidarity and instill competitive individualism, in part through Sampedranos' efforts to put them in the service of their own struggles. This book also contributes to public and scholarly discussions of political and social transformations in Mayan communities since democratization (1985) and after the peace accords. Specifically, it reframes Mayan support for authoritarian politicians, particularly Ríos Montt, by showing how Sampedrano political alignments were not based on consent, fear, false consciousness, or strategic engagement but were reactions to the deficits and perverse effects of neoliberal democracy and the forms of development at its core.[27]

On the ground, democracy and development interacted with grassroots political imaginaries that were forged through centuries of colonial state formation and most recently by engagements with nationalist governments, religious organizations, revolutionary politics, and counterinsurgency. In San Pedro, under military rule and through the peace process, different forms of development wove local struggles for advancement into market activities and local democratic politics by empowering new kinds of subjects with new outlooks and capacities. Frustration with the limits of these spaces found tragic expression through authoritarian populisms that harvested pessimism, uncertainty, vulnerability, and resentment, only to reinforce the structures that made them inevitable. Authoritarian populism advanced during a transition away from military rule despite the profound misgivings of its own supporters. In these ways, politics in San Pedro blurred distinctions between state and civil society, violence and development, decolonization and counterinsurgency, and democracy and war.

Developing Neoliberal Democracy

The Democracy Development Machine describes the assembly and operation of a "governing assemblage" (Li 2007a)—a network of political regulation—that was composed of political violence, official historical narratives, market-oriented capacity development, infrastructural development, clientelist party politics, and state multiculturalism. These seemingly disconnected and conflicting elements were brought together in the context of extreme poverty and racial inequality to displace radical politics into a severely reduced political field, repressing memories of past struggles, reinforcing pessimism, empowering new political and economic subjects whose desires and politics fit neocolonial and neoliberal parameters, telescoping broader conceptions of development and well-being into "projects" and private advancement, incentivizing participation in divisive party politics, promoting narratives of Mayan neutrality and multicultural inclusion, exacerbating class divisions and resentment, sowing mistrust, aggravating insecurity, fragmenting autonomous organizations, marginalizing traditional governing structures, and blaming indigenous citizens and leaders for poverty, abandonment, corruption, and democratic failure.

Democracy and development reorganized rural society and political culture—landscapes of memory, capacities, livelihoods, self-conceptions, understandings of the politically possible, community relations, and organizational forms—creating new spaces for agency within a constricted horizon. Kathleen Stewart (2011) asks how "circulating forces . . . become the live background of living in and living through things" in a process of worlding (445). Democracy and development constituted a political world defined through privatized experiences of advancement, influence, and access tethered to collective defeat, insecurity, uncertainty, and fragmentation.

Theories that view subaltern reappropriations of democracy and development as resistance treat democracy and biopower as separate from violence, and they draw a line between the "practice of politics . . . the expression, in word or deed, of a critical challenge . . . a refusal of the way things are," on the one hand, and governance—"calculated attempts to regulate conduct"—on the other (Li 2007b: 12). These binaries implode when democracy and development align themselves with local struggles for expanded citizenship in order to reformat them into limited and contradictory spaces of market advancement, ethnic politics, and electoral competition that transform political imaginaries and erode the bases of collective action while political and economic violence foreclose alternatives.

Democracy and development enabled and rationalized trade-offs between victimhood and political agency, national and local change, individual and collective well-being, development projects and self-determination, and indigenous and class politics. Founded in violence and steeped in market rationality, democracy and development have reshaped grassroots politics and shattered community solidarity more insidiously than the official counterinsurgency. Despite historic gains, democratic politics in San Pedro has lost its way. This predicament, and the propensity for authoritarian alliances that it creates, reflects the unmaking and remaking of a political world, not false consciousness.

Anthropologists have countered narratives of postwar liberation by examining how democracy reinforces asymmetrical social relations during post-conflict transitions. Julia Paley (2001) demonstrates how the discourses and practices of democracy in post–Pinochet Chile redefined citizenship on market terms. Strategically framed opinion polling managed public attitudes, while technocratic expertise excluded poor communities from decision making and gave them new roles as "service providers" while the state retreated. Movements became "responsible" for their government, for they had voted for it and had a seat at the table. This reorganization of citizenship, she argues, legitimated free market reforms and contributed to the demobilization of civil society despite major continuities of policy and personnel between democracy and dictatorship that were not up for a vote—a great irony of democratic Chile. In reaction, she describes how some social movements resisted their relegation to service-provider status by asserting expertise and demanding decision-making power.

Charles Hale (2002) describes a continental shift to "neoliberal multiculturalism" as a form of democratic governance in Latin America that departs from assimilationist nationalist projects of *mestizaje* (mixing) by extending a limited package of cultural rights to apolitical (nonconfrontational) indigenous groups while repressing indigenous organizations that directly challenge foundational inequalities or free market policies. This mix of symbolic inclusion and violence aims to produce "permitted Indians" who pursue cultural politics that do not directly confront capital or historic inequalities. Although concerned that partial inclusion might divide and neutralize indigenous politics, he favors pragmatic engagement with multicultural states to strategies of refusal, as exemplified by the Zapatistas.

These approaches reveal the limits of free market democracy and different dimensions of its cultural politics. Paley exposes how power works through democratic discourses and mechanisms that blend with market logic, but she understates the ways in which neoliberal democracy is constituted by violence.[28] Hale contends that authoritarian violence limits indigenous politics to "permitted" multicultural spaces, but he treats democracy as generally neutral and downplays the significance of development and market rationality in mediating indigenous inclusion.[29] Neither approach explains why members of Guatemala's majority indigenous underclass, with a long history of radical politics, would follow ultraconservative populists who oppose human rights and structural reform and embrace criminality and violence. And neither theorizes the interplay between democracy and development or the totalitarian strain of democracy that I encountered in San Pedro.

Instead of comparing Guatemalan democracy to a normative model, I describe how it was assembled, imagined, and experienced in a particular place and connected to processes of state formation.[30] Guatemalan democracy was not simply "a tangle of elements thrown together in a radical composition" (Stewart 2013, 1) but purposefully arranged and linked to existing realities in order to produce or reinforce particular subjects, affects, conceptual horizons, and repertoires of action. The army, state and international development institutions, and political parties established democracy in Guatemala's rural communities on the heels of genocide under intensive militarization, with the aim of completing the counterinsurgency and streamlining neoliberal restructuring by dismantling a radical political culture and cultivating a docile, market-oriented form of indigenous citizenship focused on private advancement and local party politics. Indigenous villagers saw democracy and development as hard-won openings in a rigidly exclusive, racist political order and as a means of changing that system by claiming citizenship and transforming themselves. Governance requires rendering a field of intervention on technical terms, which tends to "exclude the structure of political-economic relations from . . . the diagnoses and descriptions" of planners (Li 2007b: 7). Democracy and development in Guatemala were not depoliticized; they were concrete spaces for advancement that offered immediate material gains within prevailing political and economic structures that were packaged as similar to, but distinct from, revolutionary visions of democracy and development that focused on dismantling structures of oppression. Democracy and development were "boundary objects": ideas and sets of practices that united villagers, the army, state, international institutions, and social movements in a common project and fields of action despite vastly distinct conceptions of democracy and development and political aims.[31] I analyze the dialectic between governance and subaltern reappropriation, paying close attention to the forms composing neoliberal democracy, the different scales at which democracy and development were produced and contested, and corresponding shifts in micro-political relations.

The chapters examine how neoliberal democracy was established in a rural town—specifically, how it was composed out of forms of development focused on "improving" historical memory, individual capacity, and political capacity: efforts that were framed as safe concessions to grassroots demands but that excluded historical struggles as well as desires for far-reaching, national-level redistribution, such as land reform. They also describe how neoliberal democracy and development operated and were experienced in rural villages. Chapter 1 provides background on San Pedro's political history and describes how the army's promotion of sanitized historical memories led to the denial, even after the peace accords, of any trace of local revolutionary politics or radical desire. It analyzes the conditions under which these denials are maintained, in part by helping stake claims to legitimate democratic citizenship while critiquing state violence, and how they set limits on democratic political agency and fostered uncertainty about past struggles that provided political cover for the FRG.

Chapters 2 and 3 bridge critical scholarship on human-capacity development, infrastructure, and democracy by showing how market-oriented capacity development equipped some Sampedranos with the normative skills and outlooks associated with neoliberal democratic citizenship. Capacity development was a new measure of individual value and neoliberal democracy's human infrastructure.[32] Chapter 2 examines how discourses and practices of capacity development promoted by various institutions instilled new desires and forms of self-fashioning, particularly an enterprising individualism that simultaneously challenged, accelerated, and rationalized socioeconomic inequality, created a new method of ranking people, privatized notions of well-being, modified and reinforced gender hierarchies, and promised "deindianization" while informing the adoption of Mayan identities. Chapter 3 describes a model of political development through which villagers were trained to navigate state institutions to obtain development projects and to run political campaigns. It also examines how a development-oriented Mayan leadership inspired by the revolution but wary of state violence channeled collective struggles into capacity development, market advancement, and local electoral politics centered on development projects. These forms of capacity-driven advancement helped some escape poverty and legitimated local Mayan electoral ascendance while eroding radical political imaginaries, blaming poverty on individual choices and backwardness, legitimating interpersonal discrimination, sidelining traditional forms of authority, and empowering a Mayan leadership class disengaged from collective movements for redistribution. However, some locals criticized discriminatory uses of *capacidad* and embraced ways of being human not rooted in individual improvement.

Chapter 4 shows how structural and political violence infuse democratic political imaginaries under neoliberalism, informing engagements with authoritarian parties and (dis)engagements with social movements. It draws on theories of political affect to examine how Sampedranos experienced neoliberal democracy through weakened capacities for collective action, structural violence, everyday suffering, resentment, and uncertainty.[33] It describes how targeted repression, framed as defending the democratic rule of law, echoed counterinsurgency patterns, reinforcing pessimism and chilling participation in radical politics, despite the persistence of radical common sense. What I call "radical pessimism" is part of a global political affect attuned to neoliberal curtailments on collective agency that normalize self-interested politics. Radical pessimism builds on analysis of the decentered performances through which states are constituted as social facts and as objects of fear and desire by examining how Sampedranos engage with interlinked state and corporate sovereigns that they see as violent, indifferent to their suffering, impossible to defeat, and willing to kill indigenous life or offer temporary relief from structural violence in exchange for complicity.[34] Rather than principled refusals of state authority, or hegemony, persistent desire for radical social change in San Pedro was smothered by a history of violence, compromised solutions, uncertainty, and patterns of deceptive complicity that fueled a climate of betrayal and distrust.[35] Nonetheless, new forms of organizing and challenges to state violence, extractive development, party politics, and corruption seek to harness pessimism as a force for radical politics.

Chapter 5 explores how infrastructural development anchored a democratic political world of electoral politics that operated in a machine-like fashion to refocus politics and shatter local solidarity.[36] Narrated as Mayan inclusion, party-led development was a carnival of self-interest that redefined grassroots demands for development in terms of discrete "projects" distributed through exclusionary patronage networks. Clientelist, zero-sum distribution of insufficient projects in conditions of extreme poverty, inequality, and pessimism reinforced powerlessness and insecurity, and it inflamed community divisions while shifting blame for structural inequality and corruption onto individual greed and bad Mayan leadership. Project-led, clientelist party politics turned Sampedranos into agents of sovereign violence: they acquired vital resources by ensuring their neighbors' "slow death" by abandonment (Berlant 2007).[37] Through these politics, Mayas became complicit with structural violence by marking individuals, families, and villages for abandonment, an injustice for which they held one another responsible. These realities complicate recent reassessments of patron-client exchange as consistent with local moral economies and collective action[38] and as vehicles for material rights in what some call a new "politics of redistribution" emerging as a countercurrent to neoliberal austerity.[39] Clientelist redistribution in San Pedro left poverty unchanged, violated moral economies, and fostered a divisive politics of self-interest that further depleted capacities for collective action. It also engendered intense criticism rooted in an ethic of reciprocity.

Guatemala's transition to democracy as part and parcel of a moderately progressive yet still historic peace agreement staved off an electoral revolt against free market policies—such as what happened across Latin America in the 2000s—and instead created conditions for authoritarian populism. As a political discourse that divides "the people" against the powerful, populism is the dominant idiom within democracy for addressing exclusions and grievances.[40] Populisms hail from the right or left, veering into fascism when resentments are channeled into racism, or radical mobilization when it challenges economic and political power.[41] Neoliberals criticize populism as irrational and threatening to democracy, although they often make populist appeals. Many have examined how populist renderings of social antagonisms resonate (or not) with grassroots moral economies across diverse publics. Instead of trying to understand receptions to populism by unraveling the deep meanings of populist symbolism, chapter 6 illuminates populism's materiality and affective force in contexts of political violence, material deprivation, division, and pessimism. More than a mirror of democratic exclusions (Panizza 2005) or a mediating mechanism in "civic governmentality" (Roy 2009), authoritarian populism reinscribed neoliberal democracy's foundational limits as it tapped into wells of insecurity, mistrust, uncertainty, and resentment created by its failures. It appealed to corporeal needs and perceived grievances, gaining followers without ideological resonance and despite revulsion at national candidates and policies.

A Rural Town

Nested in the Cuchumatanes Mountains high above the Inter-American Highway that follows the snaking and turbulent Selegua River, the town of San Pedro Necta sits midway between the Guatemala-Mexico border to the northwest and the department capital to the east, half a day's journey from Guatemala City by bus.[42] Perpetually green, rounded peaks laced in mist rise like giant walls around the small plateau that contains San Pedro's urban center. A bright, multicolored, eye-shaped cemetery sits on a slope overlooking narrow, gray-paving-stone streets that are laid out in a grid around the Catholic church, the municipal building, the market, and a small park. The town houses a police station, several development organizations, two high schools, a cooperative, a state hospital, government offices, various party headquarters, and numerous small businesses, private residences, a few sparse mini-hotels, a bank, and recently an Internet cafe.[43] San Pedro is famous for excellent coffee and is home to several large *fincas* (plantations). Although visually stunning, San Pedro is not a tourist destination. There is a handful of sparse *comedores* (diners), a few bakeries, and more than a dozen grimy cantinas. Older adobe buildings with cracked plaster walls and fading paint press against newer buildings of grey cinder block, many bought with money from *los estados* (the United States). A turbulent river roars through the center of town, its brown water frothing with sewage and agrochemical runoff and choked with plastic waste.

In the evenings, children play *fútbol* on a dusty concrete basketball court where uniformed schoolchildren congregate after class and where vendors sell fried chicken, tacos, and French fries. On Sundays, the court transforms into a loud and pungent market, crowded with people and plastic tarps, as thousands come down from the villages to buy and sell, socialize, exchange news, eat, drink, see a dentist or barber, listen to exuberant street hawkers, or attend Mass at the Catholic church or a *culto* (worship service) at one of nearly a dozen evangelical churches. Roads that twist and climb up the mountainsides to rural villages are paved only at the steepest points to enable the passage of overloaded Toyota pickup trucks. Ordinary marvels of civil engineering, paved roads are potent signs of recent state-funded modernization and increased flows of commerce to and from remote villages, as well as visits from missionaries, teachers, health providers, police, development workers, politicians, and NGO agents of various stripes. A local, indigenous-owned bus service travels to and from Huehuetenango twice daily, and pickups make hourly trips down the steep mountainside to the highway. "Tuk tuks," three-wheeled motor taxis, a recent addition to local transport, sputter as they carry passengers to and from nearby villages.

Seventy-five percent of San Pedro's nearly 30,000 residents are Maya-Mam speakers, and the other 25 percent are monolingual Spanish speakers. The Mam occupied this place long before the arrival of the Spanish; the name "Necta" derives either from the Mam *nej ta* (first father), for Saint Peter, or *nect a* (a place where there is water), for an abundant mountain spring. Indigenous women wear handwoven *huipiles* (blouses) with distinctive red-and-white horizontal stripes, and black *cortes* (skirts) tied with red sashes. Most Sampedranos identify as either Mam or Ladino (nonindigenous), although the more recently introduced terms "Maya" and "indigenous" are gaining ground. Throughout the book, I use both but generally use "Maya" for more-recent events reflecting both the later adoption and political meaning of this term. I reserve the term "Indian" to signal the usage when that racial pejorative was common (pre-1990s). I refer to nonindigenous, monolingual Spanish-speaking residents as "Ladinos," although some prefer the term "mestizo" because of their mixed ancestry and negative associations with "Ladino."[44]

Unlike most rural *municipios,* where Ladinos live almost exclusively in town centers, many also live in San Pedro's villages, where their grandparents settled to grow coffee, gaining private titles to communal indigenous land. The vast majority of indigenous Sampedranos live in one of twenty-two surrounding *aldeas* (villages) located far from the town center, but a rising number of economically mobile families live in town. Villages typically have one small school and two churches (Catholic and evangelical), a few *tiendas* (stores), and a sports field, with small houses, mostly adobe, hidden by coffee and *milpa* (maize fields) and connected by winding paths. Villager livelihoods consist of subsistence farming, cash cropping, day labor, construction, transportation, and other commercial activities. Many poorer villagers migrate annually to work on coastal plantations. Most indigenous households grow their own food—primarily maize and beans—a fact of which they are proud and which they accomplish on steep slopes with hand tools and the help of chemical fertilizers and pesticides. As fertilizer costs rose, many bought cheaper, but less tasty, maize from Mexico. Families supplement modest diets with sugary coffee.

Poverty and illiteracy are endemic and far more prevalent in indigenous villages, where infrastructure remains minimal despite recent improvements.[45] Many families still lack potable water, housing, stoves, sewage, sinks, and electricity, most of which began to arrive in the mid-1990s. Remote villages are accessible only by steep, unpaved roads, some tracts graded with packed gravel, the rest turning to mud during the rainy season (May-October), impeding most trucks. Ladinos are far more likely to be comfortable, educated professionals and to be monolingual (Spanish speaking), but most are poor, with minimal schooling or skills training. Indigenous Sampedranos, especially men, are often bilingual and increasingly literate, and a small number are high-school and college educated and work as teachers, merchants, and professionals. Animosity between indigenous and Ladino groups runs deep, but significant interaction, kinship ties, interdependency, and attachments to place also unite the groups and blur the divide. A strict gendered division of labor and discrimination against women are also dominant in both communities. A significant percentage of local youths migrated to the United States in the 1990s and 2000s seeking work, and many, but not all, sent *remesas* (remittances) to their families back home. Some of those who returned built houses and started businesses.

Inhabitants of villages closer to the town center have easier access to commerce, schools, and development, and show more outward signs

Figure 1. View of San Pedro Necta, 2017. Photo by Esdras Ramírez.
Used with permission.

of socioeconomic differentiation in personal appearance and ownership of commodities such as trucks and cinder-block houses. Closer-in villages have also produced the most successful indigenous entrepreneurs and prominent indigenous political leaders of the last several decades. Youths in these villages are on average better economically positioned to migrate to the United States. San Pedro's massive northwestern slope, on the other side of the mountain from the town center, is a giant *finca*, its endless rows of coffee stretching down the mountainside, disappearing into a bluish mist and Mexico. Villages engulfed by the valuable black-green slopes of the *finca* zone are among the poorest in the *municipio*. Their exclusively indigenous residents work as plantation *mozos* (peons) and farm small plots of maize rented from the owner, who lives in Guatemala City. San Pedro's poorest villagers, also the most remote and the least developed—the farthest from the state—have become increasingly pivotal in local elections and a key constituency in authoritarian populism.

Engaged Anthropology after Counterinsurgency

San Pedro was not a regional revolutionary epicenter, but the guerrillas found significant support in many villages and left an imprint on local imaginaries that persisted through the counterinsurgency. Autonomous indigenous political organization at the village level reemerged after 1983 and took over town politics in 1993 before splintering in the late 1990s and creating an opening for the FRG victory in 2003. Arriving shortly after those elections, I lived in San Pedro until December 2004 and made numerous return visits, the last in 2014.[46] While there, I participated in everyday life and attended numerous events in villages and the town center, had hundreds of conversations with Mayas and Ladinos, and conducted dozens of formal interviews, with emphasis on politically influential individuals or people who were close to important events in town history or whose experiences crystallized broader trends. Observations and inquiries about villagers' perceptions of and interactions with various state governments, religious organizations, the guerrilla movement, the army, political parties, state and nonstate institutions, and social movements shed light on local conceptions of politics and history, as well as the origins of village organizing and divisions before the revolution, during the war, through the transition to democracy, and after the accords. Living for six months in "Los Altenses" (The Heights)—a pseudonym for the local village that had birthed the most influential indigenous political organization since the 1970s—helped me to understand the milieu in which this movement rose to prominence and why it broke down, and revealed the village-level reverberations of the 2003 election. Following various candidates to rural villages during the 2011 election season provided additional insights into local experiences of democracy and engagement with authoritarian populism. Interviews with the directors and village representatives of the main development programs from the 1970s to the 1990s, observation of the planning and implementation of development projects, and review of assorted program documents shed light on the histories and local meanings of development, as did accompanying villagers to work in their parcels and to protests against mining and free trade.[47] These methods further revealed local meanings of indigeneity, historical narratives, perceptions of power and violence, and the dynamics of town/village and indigenous/Ladino relationships. Over time, I became familiar with local livelihoods, home economics, the reality of poverty, and meanings of success and failure, and watched a generation grow into maturity between the United States and Guatemala. Making numerous return visits over a decade enabled me to reinterview key individuals and gave me insight and access unavailable to one-time visitors.

Being a white male *gringo* with an advanced degree lent me credibility and helped me access both indigenous and Ladino communities and male-dominated spaces, but limited my access in various ways. My prior work as a researcher with *Asociación* Ceiba in nearby Colotenango, a revolutionary hotbed, may have lent me some credibility because Ceiba ran projects in several villages in San Pedro, staffed by various national and foreign "experts," but might have given me an aura of radicalism. For this reason, I left Ceiba prior to beginning this research, and such perceptions, if they existed, did not impede my access to villagers from a range of backgrounds and political leanings. I learned key words in Mam but conducted the bulk of this research in Spanish and worked with Mam research assistants. Most adult men and politically influential women spoke fluent Spanish, and many generously translated conversations from Mam. My inability to understand more than basic phrases in Mam significantly limited my participation in everyday life, but I made many friends, had numerous in-depth conversations and interviews, and developed rapport with many influential individuals. Participant observation enabled me to peer beyond campaign rhetoric and reductive frames to apprehend local politics and history as lived experience. Names and details have been altered to protect individual identities, with the exception of elected officials and others connected to well-known events. As a study of only one town, this research is limited, but it does provide intricate details about how democracy and development work at the local level, whose dynamics are hidden beneath framings of state failure. Although there are significant differences among *municipios,* the patterns described here are common in the highlands.

Neutrality in the face of great injustice constitutes complicity, and it contradicted my motivation to pursue research in Guatemala, which was to produce analysis that would be useful to grassroots actors and organizations, and to create a compelling depiction of shifting forms of power and to draw attention to emergent alternatives. My aim was to conduct anthropology "yoked . . . to the service of the poor" (Farmer 2005, 138), which is never a straightforward task, but nevertheless informs the questions I asked and my interpretations. My research questions, methods, and analysis took cues from discussions with Mayas and Ladinos engaged in struggles against interlocking systems of race, class, and gender oppression and regimes of state and corporate power. I was particularly influenced by concerns that Sampedranos expressed about local divisions. Aligning with one group—a hallmark of influential conceptions of activist research—seemed misguided or impossible given the splintering of the indigenous movement and the alignment of one faction with the far-right FRG.[48] Not taking sides allowed me to move between opposing organizations whose members were generous enough to tolerate and trust me. I did my best to listen empathetically and to provide feedback when I could.[49]

This positioning also allowed me to align my research with shared values and concerns beneath divisions and shifting alliances, the basis for previous and possibly future modes of collective action.[50] My aim was to understand the factors and motivations behind local antagonisms, not endorse them, especially as Sampedranos' misgivings about their own political entanglements became clear. This was a kind of "virtual alignment" rooted in the potential for multiple rearticulations of current identities and relationships, rather than alignment with the expressed politics of a particular group. This orientation guided my research into the rise and fall of the most important political coalitions in San Pedro since the 1990s, examining how they formed, their strategies, and the currents that each rode to power. I followed the rise of the first indigenous political organization after the scorched-earth campaign, which became the coalition of José Antulio Morales: the most influential local Mayan politician during and after the transition to peace. I also examined the FRG coalition led by Mariano Díaz, a Mayan shoe salesman who defeated Morales' local candidate in 2003, and the surprising victory of Rony Galicia, a Ladino suspected of narco-trafficking, who took over the Guatemalan National Revolutionary Unity (URNG) in 2011. Slowly and unevenly, moving among villages, the town center, and state institutions past and present, I investigated the world of local democratic politics, tracing the origins of local divisions back to contradictory spaces for indigenous advancement.

Neoliberal democracy presented Sampedranos with sanctioned forms of agency whose realization undermined the possibility for collective struggle against the oppressive conditions that motivated that agency in the first place. While undeniably tragic, framing this predicament as a "double bind" (e.g., Fortun 2009, Cattelino 2008) is too rigid; it treats all options as equally problematic ethically and strategically, when Sampedranos must decide and take action, which they sometimes regret, but always knowing that the only way out of double binds is through them.

Neoliberal democracy, composed of various forms of democratic development, can be a devastating machine for disfiguring grassroots politics even as it opens up new political possibilities. Far from including Mayas as full citizens with distinct rights, neoliberal democracy in San Pedro was founded on the defeat of historic struggles and their reconfiguration in local, ethnic, individual, and market terms. Stripped of material rights, neoliberal democracy drew villagers into complicity with their collective exclusion; it waged "war by other means" (McAllister and Nelson 2013), achieving counterinsurgent goals not only through repression but always against a background of physical and economic coercion. Neoliberal democracy and development wove grassroots desires for material rights into productive and privatized relationships with the state and the market—structures that systematically victimize Mayas in the collective—in ways that undermined their collective dreams and organizational capacities. Authoritarian politics offered piecemeal solutions to the failures of this democratic assemblage that ensnared people who passionately opposed authoritarian policies, only to reproduce those failures, which reflected deep contradictions in Guatemalan society. At the same time, grassroots reconceptualizations of democracy and development rooted in material rights, reciprocity, and antipathy to state and corporate power emerged in reaction to the failures of neoliberal democracy, animating alternative politics.

Daniel Jordan Smith (2008) describes a confounding situation in which "Nigerians are active participants in the social reproduction of corruption even as they are also its primary victims and principal critics" (5). In a similar vein, years of violent manipulation did not foster a new imaginary in which Sampedranos consented to neoliberalism and authoritarianism or saw Ríos Montt as a populist hero;[51] authoritarian engagements were "atmospheric attunements" to a pathological political world built on the wreckage of past struggles (Stewart 2010). This was a maddening democracy in which Mayas forged alliances with hostile forces and enacted violence on their neighbors in a climate of uncertainty, insecurity, pessimism, and mistrust. Such attention to the micro-practices though which evolving patterns of violence and governance were lived and contested illuminates how neoliberal democracy "literally accretes" and distributes "energies . . . across a field of subjects-objects-bodies-affects" (Stewart 2013).[52] This ethnography assesses the dangers of neoliberal democracy and development as paths to advancement after armed conflict, and possibilities for rearticulation. In pointing to unmet desires for alternative ways to organize economic and political life, it underscores the violence of the international capitalist order and shows how, "even in resisting the modernizing project that is imposed upon them, the subaltern classes embark on a path of internal transformation" (Chatterjee 2005, 96).

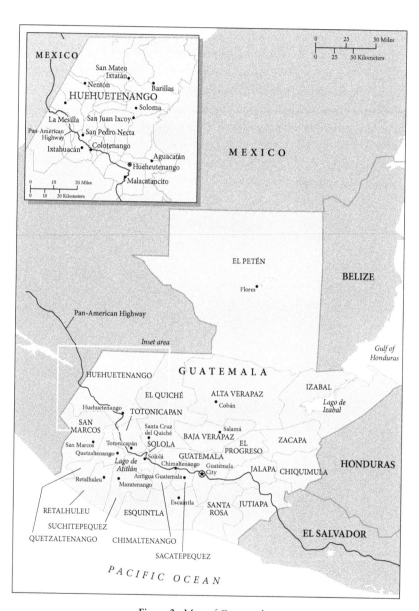

Figure 2. Map of Guatemala.

1

"They Committed No Crime"

Developing Democratic Memories

It hurts a lot to carry [these bones]. It's like carrying death. I'm not going to bury them yet. Yes, I want him to rest, and I want to rest myself, but I still can't. They are the proof of my declaration. I will not bury them yet. I want a paper that tells me "they killed him, and he had not committed any crime, that he was an innocent . . . ," then we will be able to rest.

Testimony to the Commission for Historical Clarification
(CEH, 1999, my translation)

Kill me if you want, but I know that I haven't done anything.
They're going to kill me, and I am an innocent.

Sampedrano villager's speech at
the military base in 1982

Postwar elaboration, working through an event after the fact, is necessary to stay sane and is always political, an effect of struggle, an assumption of identity.

Diane Nelson, Reckoning

One morning in September 2004, several hundred Sampedranos convened in the town salon, a large, sparsely constructed event space atop the market building with unevenly affixed, rusted *lamina* (corrugated zinc sheeting) walls. They had come to witness the inauguration of a local development organization, Maya-Mam Nej-Ta, whose title evoked the indigenous name of the town, signaling the recent interest in Mayan identity. Mariano Díaz, the newly elected Mayan FRG *alcalde* (mayor), had been invited to speak. We all listened as his address, delivered through a microphone with the energy and cadence of a campaign speech, wandered into historical narrative:

> For thirty-five years there was war. We ruined this country. And why? [pause] I don't know! But now we are at peace. How do we achieve peace? Being at home, with the family. As parents we give good educations to our children, and they develop in the future. San Pedro Necta has a hospital, it has a bank, it has various development associations—now it has one more—there will be a road with asphalt. Everything is going to bring more money, more business to San Pedro.

In this framing, whatever happened in the past is irrelevant in the present. Peace is embodied in private acts, such as in raising children, in "business," and in an NGO whose bland mission statement was a vague desire for "projects," undoubtedly destined to be a political vehicle for its founder, an educated indigenous dentist from the town center who was respected for good works but not taken seriously as a candidate. No one in the audience reacted publicly to this display of what appeared to be a case of either historical ignorance, a willful whitewashing of the past, or some mix of both.[1]

Soon after the inauguration, I met with Paola, a Mayan woman in her late fifties who was visiting from Mexico, where she had fled in 1982 after the army kidnapped several of her family members whom she maintained were innocent. I wanted to talk to her about what had been happening in San Pedro between 1978 and 1982. Closing her eyes, as if preparing to feel something intensely painful, she began to tell me about her former best friend, Natividad Ramírez, a young, educated indigenous woman:

> She worked with the nuns. . . . We went to school together. She was from here in the town center. She got married, and I did not. She was very beautiful. They [the army] killed her. Why? "I don't know!" as Mariano Díaz says! And why are you here, an indigenous man as mayor?! Why are people paid a decent wage now on the *finca* (plantation) if you don't know?

Paola had attended the meeting where Díaz spoke earlier that day. She snapped with disgust at his comment, which she recalled spontaneously as she remembered the murder of her dear friend. Linking Natividad's death to better wages on the *finca* and to indigenous political power spoke to deep interconnections between indigenous and revolutionary struggles. To her mind, Díaz had trivialized Natividad's death, one of a multitude of extreme sacrifices that had improved conditions for indigenous people and that he had benefited from personally. She continued, "I was very mad [at Díaz]. Some of [the people] don't know why. 'I know why' I would have said. I should have stood up. *Cae mal* [I don't like it]." Although she saw his discourse as inexcusable ignorance, it reflected the different narrative worlds in which they had lived since 1982. Her reticence at the meeting spoke to the continued difficulty of expressing her beliefs in public.

We know that memories fade, but can they die or be replaced? What is the connection between memory and political agency? How does memory become a target of development during a transition to neoliberal democracy, and what happens when activists, historians, and ordinary people try to bring alternative memories back to life? This chapter examines the politics of memory in San Pedro and in so doing wades into polarized polemics about memory in postwar Guatemala, particularly regarding the nature and extent of indigenous participation in the revolutionary movement. After a brief review of indigenous politics in San Pedro from 1944 to 1983, I examine the conditions under which depoliticized versions of this past circulated as truth, how other narratives of collective politics became marginalized, and how these patterns of remembering and forgetting informed Sampedranos' orientation to neoliberal democracy. I show how the discourse claiming that indigenous Sampedranos were neutral during the war and "trapped between two armies" was a critical reaction to state violence that was then selectively promoted by the army in the name of development and became embedded in postwar identities, affects, and forms of reasoning. This quasi-resistant, postrevolutionary "landscape of memory" (Kirmayer 1996) was the result of heterogeneous efforts to develop proper democratic subjects and a central component of neoliberal democratic governance. It opened space for Mayan criticisms of state violence but excluded radical demands from postwar political thought and sowed uncertainty that rationalized support for the FRG. I also examine emerging possibilities for an encounter with the past not restricted by counterinsurgency truth.

A History of Struggle

Indigenous Sampedranos have a long history of acting in concert, locally and nationally, succumbing to and overcoming intra- and intercommunal divisions, and forming alliances with and against external groups, fighting simultaneously to be included in a political and economic system based on racial domination and violence and to transform it, often in contradictory ways and with uneven results.[2] Elderly indigenous Sampedranos, men and women, described their childhood as a time of "slavery" when indigenous people were treated "like animals" by Ladinos, planters, and state officials. They did what they could to avoid the tax and labor demands of the colonial state, often seeking protection from the Catholic Church. Since the 1870s, the dawn of Guatemala's liberal era, Creole elites who wanted to plant coffee and have it harvested for a pittance forced villagers off fertile land and instituted mandatory labor drafts.[3] In the 1930s, the dictator Jorge Ubíco ended an interlude of reform and mass politics in the 1920s and instituted debt-peonage systems and vagrancy laws to coerce villagers to work on coastal plantations and in infrastructure projects—such as cutting a path for the Inter-American Highway—for starvation wages in wretched conditions.[4] Some joined labor organizations to fight for better wages and working conditions on the South Coast.[5] After the revolution of 1944, indigenous Sampedranos and many working-class Ladinos rallied behind nationalist governments that abolished forced labor and enacted social democratic policies. In the early 1950s, numerous villagers joined peasant leagues that pressured President Jacobo Arbenz into passing a far-reaching land reform law.[6]

Fearing a communist revolution, the CIA fomented a coup in 1954 that toppled Arbenz, reversed land reform, ended democracy, and unleashed death squads in the countryside. With land activism criminalized, a modernizing stratum of indigenous Sampedranos opted for incremental advancement in their own communities, bucking the will of town Ladinos and villagers employed as labor contractors. Many found a chance in Catholic Action (CA), a church organization formed to promote economic development in Indian communities as an alternative to communism and to undermine *costumbre* (folk Catholicism). Maryknoll priests preached development and the new Catholicism to indigenous catechists who were drawn to the idea that all of God's children are equal, and who were seeking relief from the economically burdensome *cofradía* (religious brotherhood) system. Religious conversion and market production empowered younger, modernizing leaders to displace age-based community hierarchies and curtail dependency on town Ladinos.[7] Development was also marked by rising class divisions among villagers.

The decline of the traditional hierarchies and new conceptions of development and equality incited local challenges to Ladino dominance in the 1960s and 1970s. Educated indigenous leaders ran for mayor in progressive parties, ended municipal labor drafts, and fought against the Ladino takeover of communal land.[8] Indigenous activists found further encouragement from Maryknoll priests who, after 1968, were influenced by liberation theology, a political reading of the New Testament as a message of advancement for the poor. Politics in San Pedro after 1975 cannot be understood without appreciating the influence of the guerrilla movement. The Guerrilla Army of the Poor (EGP) was the first guerrilla organization to arrive in San Pedro, followed soon after by the Revolutionary Organization of the People in Arms (ORPA).[9]

I knew that it was impossible to measure precise levels of participation or sympathy almost twenty-five years after the fact, but through persistent and patient questioning it became clear that large numbers of indigenous Sampedranos across class and social divisions and some Ladinos saw the guerrillas favorably, at least at first, although more for their aims than their tactics.[10] This was most pronounced among the CA activists and developmentalists who saw the revolution as consistent with new Catholic teachings. Many Sampedranos interpreted the revolution as a continuation of the *lucha de los pobres* (the struggle of the poor) from the 1940s. Sampedranos with little or no land could not meet their subsistence needs or access the cash economy, and who thus depended on annual labor migrations to plantations on the South Coast, were enthusiastic about guerrilla demands for higher wages and land reform. The guerrillas tapped into a burgeoning "will to improve" to expand their following among rural villagers (Li 2007b). As the guerrillas held *charlas* (chats) about capitalist exploitation and plans for a socialist government, sympathetic villagers hid combatants, served as their lookouts, helped dig underground shelters, and prepared them food. Sampedranos favorable to the guerrillas were mainly sympathizers, not combatants, but many joined the Peasant Unity Committee (CUC), an indigenous-led peasant organization formed in 1977 that was linked to the guerrillas.[11] By 1980, the poorest and most remote villages, especially those in the northern *finca* zone, where most villagers only rented land from *patrones* (bosses) to grow corn, had become *territorio libre* (liberated territory) where the guerrillas held open meetings. In villages nearer the town center, organizing remained more secretive. The guerrillas carried out several major actions in San Pedro, most notably a shootout with police in the marketplace that left one EGP combatant dead; the execution in 1979 of Gilberto Herrera, a *finquero* and local leader of the reactionary National Liberation Movement (MLN); and the burning of the municipal building in 1981.

Local perceptions of the guerrillas were never uniform and were shaped by class, religion, and livelihood. Certain evangelicals were notably critical of guerrilla rejections of state authority, and many otherwise sympathetic villagers objected to the use of violence, some fearing reprisals based on their experiences after 1954. Moreover, some indigenous military commissioners spied for the army, and *contratistas* (labor contractors) sided with the planters, as did some relatively well-off villagers who had gotten ahead growing, buying, or reselling coffee and who worried that the guerrillas would take their land or business. Landowning Ladinos, in general, saw the guerrillas as a threat to their property and workforce, if not their lives. Certain guerrilla actions, such as destroying electricity posts and bridges, strained their relationship with otherwise sympathetic villagers. But the largest criticism was of violence. One evangelical indigenous critic of the guerrillas was assassinated after threatening to report neighboring families to the army, hardening his extended family's opposition to the movement.[12] Divisions between guerrilla factions further worried sympathetic villagers, and local combatants chafed about Ladino dominance and misallocation of resources in the organization.[13] Despite this uneven reception, the guerrillas' message and presence transformed local political imaginaries, even among some detractors, and injected new energy into local struggles that preexisted and aided their arrival.

Considering democratic movements in twentieth-century Latin America, Greg Grandin (Grandin and Klein, 2011) identifies an "insurgent individualism . . . deeply rooted in the institutions and experiences of mass radical politics" (182):

> Mid-twentieth century democracy offered a venue in which individuality and solidarity could be imagined as existing in sustaining relationship to

one another through collective politics directed at the state to demand justice. . . . Local political struggles related to other global conflicts and historical events allowed many to experience the world not in its illusionary static present but as evolving, as susceptible to change through action. (196)

This passage captures the zeitgeist in San Pedro, where revolutionary organizing was galvanized by modernizing indigenous leaders whose individual reputations were forged in collective struggles for empowerment. This amplification of agency was evident in indigenous challenges to a Ladino mayor's effort to sell communal land: an issue that exceeded guerrilla objectives and that guerrilla commanders likely viewed as a distraction or a strategic error. In 1978, for the first time since Arbenz, optimism for local and national struggles converged, at least momentarily, at the ballot box. Restive energies focused on the presidential campaign of Manuel Colom Argueta, who was the popular former mayor of Guatemala City and an advocate for labor rights and land reform who founded the United Front of the Revolution (FUR), a reformist party associated with the revolution.[14] Their hopes shattered with Colom Argueta's assassination prior to the elections. As regional guerrilla organizing and activity steadily increased in Huehuetenango from 1979 to 1981, driven in large measure by the intensification of death squad violence under the dictator Lucas García, many Sampedranos imagined themselves on the edge of a revolution, a perception heightened by the Nicaraguan revolution in 1979 and CUC's massive 1980 strike in the cane fields on the southern coast. This moment would not last.[15]

General Ríos Montt took power by coup in March 1982, announced amnesty for guerrillas willing to surrender, and started a "scorched-earth" campaign. Hoping to drive a wedge between the guerrillas and their civilian base, the army targeted entire villages for massacres that made no distinction between civilians and combatants. Dozens of massacres in Huehuetenango in 1982–1983 killed and displaced thousands. Army attacks in San Pedro increased dramatically in March 1982.[16] In addition, Ríos Montt ordered all male villagers ages 16–60 to join self-defense patrols (PAC). Resisters were doused in frigid water, imprisoned, tortured, and even killed.[17] Round-the-clock patrols instilled panoptic control, pressed fear into the minute crevasses of daily life, and forced villagers to take sides.[18] Rather than fight it out, local sympathizers abandoned the guerrillas and joined the patrols for protection.

Intense repression instilled fear and uncertainty as the army extended its tentacles by establishing permanent deployments in every highland town and continued to terrorize villagers. The army set a curfew, ran a village dragnet, tortured suspects to "confess" and name names, and ordered townspeople to dump disfigured bodies in the Selegua River. Many family members of the deceased fled, fearing for their lives.[19] Some Ladinos took advantage of the situation to denounce as guerillas indigenous leaders who threatened their authority; others were denounced over land disputes and personal grievances. The army installed a Ladino *alcalde* in 1982 and began to saturate villages with counterinsurgency dogma. Although local violence was ghastly, several Sampedranos felt lucky to have avoided the harsher atrocities suffered by other *municipios,* where a stronger guerrilla presence led to intra-village violence and more army massacres.[20] At the time, most indigenous Sampedranos hated Ríos Montt, both for the massacres and for establishing the patrols. The army commanded respect but was the embodiment of terror and racial oppression in the eyes of most villagers.

Memory Politics in Postrevolutionary Guatemala

Control of the truth surrounding armed conflict, particularly Mayan memories of their role in this history, was a central aim of the counterinsurgency.[21] According to the army, Mayas never wanted the guerrillas in the first place; supporters were either coerced or tricked. Very few villagers were involved in guerrilla organizations, and those who were, for the most part, were the ones who were killed. In addition, army violence was the guerrillas' fault for placing Mayas between "two armies." In this version of the narrative, after inviting military repression the guerrillas, true cowards, fled, leaving the population defenseless. The army also claimed that the guerrilla movement never had a prayer of changing power at the national level, and even if they had, their goal of communism was utterly bankrupt. Killing subversives was thus deemed necessary to protect Guatemala from becoming "another Cuba." Democracy and human rights were reframed as *babosadas* (stupid ideas) that would "bring consequences." The army called guerrillas "subversives," "terrorists," "atheists," and "delinquents" who stole and vandalized. Moreover, the civil patrol was completely voluntary, an expression of popular repudiation of the revolution. The army "defended" Mayas from ideological manipulation, moral perdition, wrongheaded policies, and crime. Ladinos often voiced these sentiments, as did many Mayas.

In completely disqualifying revolutionary desire or demands, this framing ignores the popularity of guerrilla demands among indigenous villagers while normalizing the social and economic conditions that led many to entertain or embrace these politics. Furthermore, it blames illegitimate violence on the guerrilla presence and frames army attacks on Mayan communities as legitimate, ignoring that the violence often made no distinction between civilian and combatant, followed no due process of law, and involved torture, kidnapping, rape, and the killing of children and the elderly. It also depicts Mayas as infantile, weak-minded creatures who were easily misled and unable to make responsible decisions about their future. It portrays them as having no politics at all.

During over a decade of counterinsurgency, the army used the civil patrol system to hammer these resolutely depoliticizing and contradictory "truths" about political reality and history into the hearts and minds of indigenous villagers, a form of psychological development to prepare villagers for democracy.[22] One former village-level patrol captain showed me the book used to record the minutes of the village civil patroller meetings. The ledger recounted how villagers were routinely forced to denounce the guerrillas and to repeat admonishments about the dangers of human rights, communism, and democracy. Military officers and Ladino patrol captains from the town lectured them that under communism everyone would have to give up half of their land, no matter how much or little they owned, and they would be forced to bring everything they produced to the *alcalde,* who would ration out everyone's food.

Traumatized villagers were reluctant to discuss not only the guerrillas but also the democratic revolution in the 1940s: the "silence on the mountain" was deafening (Wilkinson 2004). When they did speak, as with many Mayan communities the majority of Sampedranos publicly narrated their position during the armed conflict as having been "caught between two armies" and spoke publicly about people killed by the army, especially indigenous leaders, as having no relationship to the guerrilla movement. Even the most strident and moving public criticisms of the military erased any trace of local politics.

David Stoll (1993, 2009) takes Mayan expressions of the "two armies" discourse at face value. In *Between Two Armies* he describes the Ixiles as "dedicated neutralists," and he provides Mayan testimony about guerrilla extortions of aid, recruits, information, and other forms of loyalty. His later work criticizes Rigoberta Menchú's *testimonio* as guerilla propaganda and scolds solidarity scholars who assert widespread popular support for resistance movements. Yves Le Bot (1995) similarly attributes Mayan reticence toward revolutionary politics to their communal orientation. Stoll concludes that in Ixil territory a small guerrilla presence led to military attacks, which led to increases in guerrilla support, forcing the military to resort to extreme violence.[23]

Human rights activists and scholars have criticized Stoll for blaming the violence on the guerrillas, echoing army discourse, and contradicting the Truth Commission's core conclusion that colonial inequality, state violence, and racism sowed the seeds of conflict.[24] Most galling is Stoll's refusal to acknowledge any influence of extreme violence and Orwellian social control on public memories of the revolution.[25] Recent historical and ethnographic research affirms widespread indigenous participation in the guerrilla movement, even if this participation was later disavowed.[26]

But even some criticisms of Stoll inadvertently rehearse some aspects of the "two armies" frame. For example, Sanford (2003) denounces Stoll and Le Bot for blaming the guerrillas for attacks on Mayan communities, an interpretation that she sees as an act of symbolic violence complicit with military attempts to whitewash genocide as the "killing of communists" (202–3). Alliances with the guerrillas, she contends, are not sufficient to explain the army's targeted killing of civilians, including the elderly and children.[27] Sanford argues that Mayan "survivors who give testimony are speaking truth to power—whether the power of the army, guerrillas, local and national governments or the international community" (181). In framing Mayas as occupying a pure space outside of and in opposition to power, this formulation coincides with Stoll's, especially when Mayas echo the "two armies" discourse.

McAllister (2003) describes how Maya Chupolenses fought hard for the guerrillas but disavowed their participation after their military defeat. Hale (2006b) also examines the conditions under which these "official" memories took root and continue to flourish among Mayas. He adopts a framework advanced by Rolph-Trouillot (1995), who distinguishes between two types of historicity: what "actually happened"—"historicity one"—and the narrative frames through which past facts are organized and interpreted—"historicity two." Events do not present themselves in narrative form with meanings intact; their contours and meanings are constituted in the present through different narratives and memorial practices that are constrained and enabled by power relations. Rolph-Trouillot further sees historical narrative as an important condition of possibility for political agency.

Hale (2006b) locates the ascendance of the "two armies" frame in relation to the rise of neoliberal multicultural governance. Around 1983, the military, eager to establish a veneer of legitimacy in the newly razed highlands in preparation for democratization, opened space for criticism of military excesses. Maya survivors, he argues, had a strong desire to process the terrifying experiences of the violence:

> Many civilians—Mayans and Ladinos alike—find in the *dos demonios* image a resonance with previous experience and a source of solace: as victims rather than protagonists, they have less burden of responsibility for the problems spawned by the violence, greater claim for redress and more room for maneuver in the present. (108)

However, according to Hale, framing Mayas as victims rather than revolutionary agents also fulfills the desire for managed inclusion of indigenous groups within existing political economic structures. Although San Pedro was not a revolutionary stronghold like Chupol, a certain disavowal nevertheless approximates processes in San Pedro after the violence and through the peace accords. However, it does not fully capture the forces through which these denials were maintained almost a decade after. As I will recount below, I found a number of factors—fear, shame, investment in "innocent" identities, depoliticized conceptions of human rights, evangelical historical narratives, and campaign rhetoric—that fostered an atmosphere of public amnesia and uncertainty and new forms of agency that reinforced individual and collective disavowals, not only of participation in the guerrilla movement but of any traces of revolutionary or radical desire or politics in San Pedro's past. I also encountered incipient challenges to this frame.

What are the implications of these denials for contemporary Mayan politics? McAllister argues that only by recognizing the prevalence of

Chupolense investments in the revolution can we appreciate them as full, historical agents. She sees the contemporary dilemma confronting Mayas as the question of how to affirm their role as both protagonists in and victims of the armed struggle in a political culture in which admitting involvement justified violence. The price of innocence is high indeed. Hale concurs. He identifies three dominant narrative frames through which Mayas encounter the past—"Mayanista," "two armies," and "revolutionary triumphalism"—and argues that none of these explain the heterogeneity and fluidity of Mayan political participation that he uncovered in Chimaltenango. The revolutionary frame, now "anachronistic," glosses over substantial problems with the guerrillas, especially divisions between indigenous intellectuals and leftist groups that grew as the war raged on. The Mayanista frame affirms Mayan agency after the conflict but not before or during, a move that Hale (2006b) calls a "Faustian bargain that runs the risk of undermining points of substantial overlap between these two political vectors, as well as some of the credibility, complexity and wisdom of these same Mayan actors in the present" (107). These narrative frames undermine the possibility of imagining how Mayas can pursue radical politics and still be Mayan, and under which Mayas and Ladinos can work together in a unified movement for common class interests without marginalizing ethnic concerns.[28] The solution for many politically engaged anthropologists and historians has been to recover obscured histories of Mayan revolutionary agency in order to reinvigorate postwar politics.[29] To *not* recover this history would be to treat the fruits of a genocidal counterinsurgency as untainted. In the end, there is no neutral way to talk about historical memory. But what about Mayas who did not identify with the guerrillas for a variety of reasons but nonetheless shared many of their demands? Treating revolutionary agency as a sine qua non of radical desire conflates rejection of the guerrillas with rejection of their objectives: a central goal of the counterinsurgency deployment of the "two armies" frame.

Diane Nelson (2009) warns against rigid categories of victim and victimizer that oversimplify fluid and multiple identities assumed by indigenous Guatemalans, especially in light of forced collaboration. She highlights emerging postwar identifications that transcend wartime binaries (the evil state versus good civil society) and open new spaces for political agency. Likewise, many Sampedranos have developed powerful attachments to the "two armies" narrative and its associated denials of revolutionary agency and desire precisely because of the spaces that it opened. But these spaces were highly compromised.

The Slow and Uneven Thaw of Imposed Memory

After the scorched earth and the establishment of the civil patrols, the simple accusation of guerrilla involvement carried a death sentence. The most ardent supporters fled or were killed, and many sympathizers fell into despair. Terrified villagers, regardless of prior involvement, began to publicly and desperately denounce the guerrillas and their demands in order to survive, even within their own families. Clandestine support for the guerrillas lingered in a few villages, then disappeared completely. Although some succumbed to the army's pressure to *delatar* (betray one another), most villagers bound together in silence. One evening I listened on as male village leaders with different religious and political affiliations, including a former military commissioner, recounted proudly how they told the military nothing and kept their neighbors alive. One put his finger over his lips, said *"Shhh,"* and smiled.

Nevertheless, most community members became to some degree complicit in the violence against neighbors and even relatives who did not follow army orders. Some were more zealous and enthusiastic, but even those who harbored an ideological allegiance with the guerrillas and patrolled with *doble cara* (two faces) became agents of repression. Some revised past allegiances or sympathies toward an interpretation within which their actions caused less cognitive dissonance. These revised feelings were reinforced by the sense that the PAC was defending villagers from the army as well as the guerrillas, maintaining unity and organizing villages in pursuit of development.[30]

Fear continued to play a significant role in shaping public memories, even a decade after the peace accords. Many villagers worried that their names would appear on a list that could fall into the wrong hands.[31] Some were unwilling to discuss wartime events and told me so in no uncertain terms, having been accused for decades of guerrilla involvement, their lives repeatedly threatened, and having witnessed the torture and murder of friends and family. One person who eventually agreed to talk after avoiding me for months told me that there were still townspeople—mostly Ladinos but also indigenous *orejas* (ears) and former military commissioners—who continued to spy for the army. He warned that my digging into local history would bring problems. Members of Antulio Morales' political coalition had formed a partial alliance with Ladino patrol leaders who enjoyed impunity and were still feared.[32]

The state monopoly of the truth and imposition of silence was never absolute, however, and peace negotiations heightened public desire to clarify the past. The exhumations of massacre sites and truth commissions that followed prompted numerous local memorializations of the victims and denunciations of victimizers. Although these have been publicized internationally by numerous human rights organizations as well as via postwar ethnographic accounts,[33] most towns in the indigenous highlands, San Pedro among them, have not carried out a public confrontation with the past. Nevertheless, postwar political transformations allowed new historical narratives to germinate and gain ground in a fledgling public sphere, provoking significant challenges to counterinsurgency understandings of politics and history. With the local military apparatus dismantled, fear was not the factor in shaping public memory that it once was. Privately and in hushed tones, some individuals told different stories.

Adherence to official narratives was noticeably slipping, not reverting to previous forms of thought but loosening the hold of imposed truths on public discourse. One sign of this change was that a growing number of Sampedranos who were opposed to the guerillas in the 1970s had begun to believe that the guerrilla movement had been integral to the signing of the peace accords, an event that almost all Maya Sampedranos saw in a positive light.[34] Pedro Lopez, an evangelical and a former village leader of the civil patrols who had been steadfastly opposed to the guerrillas because he believed they murdered his father, expressed his reappraisal of the guerrilla movement succinctly. He stopped short of endorsing the guerrillas completely but recognized some positive outcomes of their struggle: "Today we can see that the guerrillas did something good. Everything is backward. Today things are better for indigenous people. There is space for us. Before, there was a lot of discrimination. Now there is more respect."

Although most Maya Sampedranos did not see the guerrilla movement or revolutionary ideology as a viable political position in the present, there was a growing appreciation of the gains they made for indigenous people, particularly regarding treatment by Ladinos. Several individuals, including some who had vehemently denied guerrilla activities previously, later admitted privately, often proudly, their participation in or sympathy for the guerrillas, an indication that a different historical narrative might emerge. Nevertheless, revalorizations of the left outside of leftist parties and organizations typically provided a selective memory of revolutionary goals, conflating them with the far-more-moderate peace accords. And most "alternative" postwar visions of history—such as those echoed by many human rights and Mayan organizations and the Catholic Church—stayed within the "two armies" narrative frame.

Next to the truth commission reports, the most radical challenge to official history during the postwar period was the URNG (Guatemalan National Revolutionary Unity), formed in 1982 and now a legal political party. The URNG was a significant political force in San Pedro, as evidenced by its third-place finish in the 2003 elections. An unabashedly revolutionary version of history was central to this party's identity. It affirmed local support for the guerrillas, criticized the fundamental injustice of the state, denounced and sought retribution for state violence, and opposed mining concessions and the Free Trade Amendment. However, the leftist counter-narrative had not, by 2009, come close to displacing the denials that saturated the public sphere. If such denials were not empirically accurate and the guerrillas now constituted a legal political party, what other factors sustained these denials in the face of postwar challenges? Disavowals of the revolutionary past *and* the demands associated with that past found sustenance in a new landscape of memory marked by trauma, guilt, and humiliation; a desire for legitimate victimhood; depoliticized conceptions of human rights; and evangelical narratives.

The Democratic Landscape of Memory

After living in the town center for several months and making extended trips to various villages, I took up residence in the village of Los Altenses, the birthplace of the first post-1982 indigenous political coalition. Before my arrival, I was informed about its political divisions, which followed largely along the lines of the three largest extended-family groups and were related to, although not reducible to, different stances toward the guerrillas. I was told that one evangelical family, the Lopezes, had opposed the guerrillas; one Catholic family, the Ruízes, had supported, housed, and hid them, and recruited fellow villagers; and another Catholic family, the Bravos, most associated with development, had remained neutral (I later learned differently). All families publicly denied any participation in the guerrilla movement in 2004, and as far as I know continue to do so until today. Conflict between families during the war abated somewhat after the violence but had reemerged in a different form through party politics. All three families were united with José Antulio Morales' coalition since its emergence in the mid-1980s until 1999, when the family rumored to have had the strongest connection to the guerrillas split to join the FRG. Members of Antulio Morales' coalition criticized Ríos Montt as an assassin and could not understand why so many of their neighbors could support a man who had done so much violence to indigenous people and who they themselves had once hated so fervently.

One afternoon I arranged a meeting with the patriarch of the Ruíz family, who was an active member of Mariano Díaz's FRG coalition in the 1999 and 2003 election cycles. Upon my arrival to Rodrigo Ruíz's house, I was surprised to find all the adult male members of this family seated together. The sons, two of whom were teachers, were waiting for me and told me that they wished to participate in the interview alongside their father. I was excited that they were so eager to participate but was concerned that the interview might stay at the surface level in a group this size. They began the discussion by describing recent political divisions in the village. Although their candidate had won, electoral wounds were still fresh, and tempers were hot. After that discussion, I asked the question that had baffled their neighbors from a rival political coalition: why it was that this family, which had once supported the revolution, now supported Ríos Montt and the FRG? They quickly and testily informed me that the premise of my question was inappropriate. The eldest brother, a farmer in his late thirties, responded defensively:

We didn't have any part in the guerrillas. At least my uncle didn't participate. My father, no, he didn't participate either. They didn't carry a weapon. Those that did participate only gave them [the guerrillas] tortillas. But to go and fight? Not at all. Why are they in favor of Ríos Montt now, those that

participated? In that time, a person doesn't forget. When a person participates, they never forget. We're talking about the URNG and those that are
still around. They are never going to help Ríos Montt. They had weapons.
They already did that. But in our particular case here, we didn't have anything. What I mean is that we didn't take it [the revolution] into account.
And then later, like my uncle said, it calmed down after Ríos Montt. [The
PAC] was a good thing for the people. And then Ríos Montt himself thought
about paying the people a little for their work. We gained our compensation. Who doesn't want money? That's why we wanted that candidate.

In the same breath, he denied his family's sympathy for the guerrillas, defined "participant" as "combatant," and praised Ríos Montt for "calming down" the violence with the PAC and now for paying them for their
service. A few weeks later, one of the other sons, who was at that meeting
but had not spoken, approached me privately. He told me that not only
his family but also the other Catholic families had all participated in the
guerrilla movement, not as combatants but as village-level collaborators
and sympathizers, and that they had suffered greatly as a result. Chok-
ing back tears, he wanted me to know that his family had lived through
fear of assassination, torture, and ridicule by their neighbors even though
they too were collaborators. His family had borne the shame, and it was
all for nothing.

Perhaps the most determinative element in the Ruíz family's contemporary denial was the then-obvious fact of the military defeat of the guerrillas: military criticisms of the guerrillas as doomed to fail seemed like
indisputable facts. Another villager told me that the people had been
"traumatized and humiliated" by the army and that they now refused to
talk about the past. Much like what McAllister (2003) saw in Chupol,
many villagers felt foolish for having ever having believed in the first place
and felt guilty about the tragedy that ensued. Such sentiments relied on
reading history backward, as if violence and failure were the only and
inevitable results of revolutionary desire. Bitterness, recriminations, and
shame stifled meaningful discussions about what the guerrilla movement
or its signature demands meant to villagers at the time; misgivings calci-
fied into long-standing rifts.

One of the most emphatic discourses of revolutionary disavowal came
from family members and friends of individuals who were killed by the
military; these emblematic deaths were key sites for the construction of

public memories. Surviving family members denied any involvement that their loved ones might have had with the guerrillas, insisting that they were innocent of the crime for which they had been assassinated. This was evident in the way that Juana Solares, a war widow, mourned her deceased husband, Raúl, a locally famous and respected indigenous leader who was killed by the military in the early 1980s. "She's a widow, a victim. Go talk to her!" one prominent Ladino told me when I told him I was interested in town history during the war. Juana had a good-natured, somewhat irreverent humor. As we began to meet and talk about town politics and history, our conversations often turned toward her husband. I had already heard of Raúl from others and hoped Juana might tell me more about what he had hoped for and believed in.

One of the first indigenous primary school teachers in the town, Raúl was well-known throughout San Pedro as an outspoken and fearless indigenous leader. He had a strong personality and was fairly intimidating because he was tall and spoke with a booming voice. As a teacher and in public life, Raúl adamantly and vocally supported the then-radical idea that indigenous people were equal to Ladinos: that they could become just as smart and educated as Ladinos and should be treated and carry themselves accordingly. After normal school hours he stayed on and taught men from the village to read and write, always encouraging them and talking about politics and advancement.

Unsolicited, Juana told me how the army grabbed Raúl and that neighbors heard his screams all night emanating from the military base in middle of town. She described in unsettling detail how the soldiers cut out his tongue and lacerated his broken body. His terrified and heartbroken siblings fled to Mexico and Canada, but Juana remained. As she lamented the cruelty and arbitrariness of Raúl's fate, she insisted that *"El no tenía delito"* ("He had committed no crime"), in reference to his involvement in the revolution. That this statement was intended to give an additional emotional charge to her story was evident in her trembling speech and the silence that always followed. In Juana's narrative, powerful Ladinos had Raúl killed to keep control over town politics. In her telling, Raúl was a martyr, "working for the community," the opposite of Antulio Morales, who was a *chucho por pisto* (a dog for money).

Many Mayan Sampedranos I spoke with deviated from Juana's narrative. Several insisted that Raúl had been with the guerrillas and that he was in fact a local guerrilla leader. One young man personally blamed Raúl for ordering the assassination of his grandfather, a military commissioner and labor contractor. As a widow, it was Juana's obligation, and perhaps compulsion, to uphold the reputation of her deceased husband, to defend him as a good person. This caretaking proceeded according to her estimations of community expectations about proper behavior. It was not simply his memory at stake; her identity and honor were deeply entangled in her deceased husband's reputation. Like many Guatemalan war widows, Juana was incredibly brave. She had at the time publicly denounced the killing to the authorities, to no avail. Central to her claim was that the state had no evidence and that Raúl never had a trial; they had violated due process. Since the peace accords, she sought compensation from the state. At first she was denied his teacher's insurance policy, but she eventually received it. She tried repeatedly to get a *resarcimiento* (restitution) payment and asked if I could help take her case to an institution. She seethed at the state's reneging on its promise of *resarcimiento* and the politicization of the process—the latter being a key point of contention among leftist organizations in the post-accords period.

Regardless of whether or not Juana was willfully obscuring aspects of Raúl's past, if one were to believe the denials of all those whose family members were killed by the military, one would have to conclude that no indigenous leaders supported the guerrillas. There were certainly many reasons why Juana might have wanted to deny Raúl's revolutionary past. One was a conception of legitimate victimhood that formed during the period of intense violence and was transformed by the threat of violence and the postwar associations sutured to the idea of the guerrilla movement. These new meanings required the deceased be understood as "innocent" when killed in order to be legitimate and worthy of mourning, and focused on the state's negligence according to standards of evidence and procedure. Conceding the army's logic of criminality enabled family members to speak of the injustice of their loved ones' deaths. Insistence on innocence subtly balanced the peculiar needs of this situation: it allowed public criticisms of the military but avoided state reprisals, it avoided recrimination for local guerrilla excesses, and it maximized the possibility of material benefits for the family members. Most importantly, denying Raúl's participation allowed Juana to remember him as a martyr for indigenous rights and a hero, not a "criminal" who "deserved" to die.

The emergence of human rights discourses during militarization and their rise in prestige after the peace accords and truth commissions gave official weight to criticisms of state violence. Quite controversially, human rights offered the only available language with which to criticize state violence in the decade between 1985 and 1996. Although associated with the left, the dominant human rights discourse, at least as it was articulated in San Pedro, reinforced the "two armies" narrative and a restrictive, ahistorical conception of politics. Human rights denunciations of both factions on the grounds that each committed abuses, while technically true, obscured significant differences regarding the extent and nature of acts committed by each group. Human rights criticisms focused more on the army, especially after the truth commissions, but typically erased the historical causes of the armed conflict and replaced the political project of the revolution with an appeal to proceduralism. Human rights often had no politics except human rights.

The goal of human rights was not political transformation but the marking and punishing of offenders to bring their actions into accord with a norm of conduct that was nonviolent and democratic: disagreements, in this project, should be resolved through nonviolent democratic means. Violence was justified in this conception *only* in the name of defending legal procedures and the rule of law, and such violence was not seen as political. Violence became a problem *only when it exceeded reasonable and necessary limits or did not follow legal procedure.* Poverty, social suffering, inhumane conditions—these ordinary features of a political system based on class and race hierarchies—were not marked as violence or as problematic, but as ordinary background without history. Violence became political, antidemocratic, and illegal when it was used to change these background conditions and challenge the legitimacy and sovereignty of a political order that defined them as normal and legal. The dominant focus on political rights ignored social or material rights entirely and did not recognize a relationship between structural and political violence, a core conclusion of the Commission for Historical Clarification (CEH).

Rather than a wholesale critique of political violence, human rights discourse in San Pedro dovetailed with the military definition of guerrillas as criminals. This was made clear by Arnulfo Bravo, a community leader and former candidate for mayor, in response to my question about whether the army's actions during the war were justified. Answering slowly and deliberately with a gravitas honed by serious consideration, Arnulfo said that human rights should have guided military violence:

> [The violence] was not justified. Because the people they killed, some of them had not committed a crime. One time in Chemiche [a village] there was a man from Santiago Atitlán [a town in the department of Sololá]. He was mentally ill. He would go house to house asking for food, clothes, somewhere to sleep. Who knows how the army found him? They said he was a guerrilla and hung him under the bridge. He wasn't a guerrilla, and that was unjust. Neither the government nor the guerrillas alone are responsible for the violence. Neither was justified. Figure out who are the people involved in the guerrillas. They should have done it like that. Make a diagnostic. Who are those who are most involved with the guerrillas? Look closely; justify it well. In the same way that they do it in *derechos humanos* (human rights). Look clearly at the individuals who are the guiltiest and pull them up by the roots. But [the army] grabbed whomever—those who had committed crimes, those that didn't—the same.

Instead of assuming their guilt, Bravo thought there needed to be a trial and a process of gathering evidence until incontrovertible proof was found. This was an explicit critique of the indiscriminant tactics deployed by the army for decades but not of counterinsurgency in general. In his view, human rights were needed to accurately identify people to kill! Bravo thought that the guerrillas should have used reason: "How great it would have been if [the guerrillas] had gone directly to the government to debate in order to improve the situation. . . . No one worried to say, 'Look, men, let's not kill anymore. It would be better if we quit.'"

This notion that moral individuals calling for a parley could have prevented this tragedy is undercut by the fact that the Guatemalan army murdered thousands of nonviolent dissidents without remorse. It also asserts that the point of war was violence itself rather than a struggle between incompatible alternatives. Bravo's adoption of a "neutral" human rights stance equated guerrilla and army violence, bracketed their political projects, and merged democratic and counterinsurgency definitions of illegality. Local interpretations of human rights such as Bravo's summarily excluded guerrilla demands from legitimate democracy and justified the routine violence of the state to preserve order, provided that it followed procedure, using democratic means to fulfill counterinsurgent ends. Assessing the toll of decades of state and para-state violence against working-class politics in Barrancabermeja, Colombia, Lesley Gill argues that "a limited conception of individual 'human rights' has replaced more ambitious dreams of social transformation. More generally, political terror has led to the atrophy of working class consciousness and solidarity, while individual rights and actions have become the new, narrower political horizon for working people" (2016, 24). Narrow conceptions of human rights enacted similar antipolitics to reinforce counterinsurgent and neoliberal aims in San Pedro.

Protestant missionary work in Central America has its roots in the mid-twentieth century and was driven in large part by conservative US evangelicals, many of whom were supportive of militaristic foreign policy, adhered to a prosperity gospel, and sought converts among poor peasants, often with CIA assistance.[35] After the extreme violence, and with the Catholic Church tainted by association with the guerrillas, many Mayas joined evangelical churches for protection. Virginia Garrard-Burnett argues that villagers were drawn to protestantism because it "promised solace and peace and helped reorder the lives of people whose families, communities, and psyches had been ruined by violence" (2010, 136). Most Pentecostal sects in Guatemala were independent and had a decentralized, lightly institutionalized model focused on personal revelation and Bible study that spread rapidly after the worst of the violence. Pentecostals were usually united around a more apocalyptic vision born out of wartime desolation, beliefs that were "congruent with the existential reality of the era" (134). Pentecostalism also fit Ríos Montt's narrative, which cast the counterinsurgency as a trial out of which will emerge a new Guatemala based on morality, law and order, and respect for God.[36]

I found echoes of this discourse among protestants in San Pedro, especially Pentecostals. Ernesto Rivas was a lay indigenous preacher who led Sunday worship services at a small new Pentecostal church in his village. A learned man who had studied the Bible, he had a self-assured attitude about his faith. He was also a FRG supporter in 2003. When I asked him how he rationalized, as a Christian, supporting Ríos Montt, given the allegations of violence, he made recourse to Biblical prediction:

> Doesn't the Bible say that there is going to be war, nation against nation, and neighbor against neighbor? The only thing that people can do in times

of war is to try not to get involved and to pray to God for it to end. Ríos Montt is not responsible. It was his job. He had no choice. This is going to happen. He should not be judged. They can't do anything to him any way. Ríos Montt is *fuerte* [strong]. This case [his indictment for genocide] is political.

This perspective on history removes agency from the actors and places it in the hands of God. Everything is a part of God's plan, in which his son would return after a cataclysm. For Ernesto, this divine agency operated through Ríos Montt, exonerating him for his actions, however evil. From this perspective, dwelling on the violence or prosecuting Ríos Montt was pointless, as was avoiding the FRG based on his role in prior events. This nihilistic stance engaged in a kind of "two armies" narrative in that it depicted both sides as equally flawed players in a preordained end-time drama whose specific outcome was of no real consequence in relation to planetary cataclysm.

Guided by such perceptions, the vast majority of evangelicals participated in worldly politics for the same mundane reasons as their neighbors: to get "projects" and personal assistance. In fact, condemnations of the worldly wickedness of all politics and politicians doubled as a blanket response to accusations of hypocrisy leveled against any participants in electoral politics, not just evangelicals. Although I expected that Ernesto and other Pentecostals would be particularly loyal to Ríos Montt, they were scattered among various parties, and the ones I spoke with did not view his candidacy as the path to a New Guatemala. Instead, evangelical discourses shaped political conceptions in that refusal to make exceptions between people gave moral force to criticisms of the unequal exchanges and unfair distributions of development and other resources associated with party politics. They formed part of an emergent democratic imaginary that was a reaction to the failures of neoliberal democracy and development.

Amnesia, Uncertainty, and Opportunism

Sampedranos were quite aware of the monumental changes in the decade after the peace accords. The violence had touched nearly every family, and they had endured immense suffering. But many indigenous Sampedranos, especially younger ones, were less clear about specifics: What had caused the war? Who killed who and why? How had Sampedranos participated? Such topics were rarely discussed publicly, and when they were it was often in a contradictory fashion on this new landscape of memory. A sustained critical public confrontation with events in the recent past had never happened in San Pedro, and perhaps never will. I attempted to coordinate a public memory project there in 2009, soliciting collaboration from villagers and rural teachers with the assistance of the director of the local high school, a Ladino in his thirties. The idea was to gain a more comprehensive view of events in each village and to share the information with the town. We quickly abandoned the plan when he began receiving death threats over his cell phone.

This silence contributed to widespread confusion and uncertainty about the past, the sowing of which had been a core counterinsurgency objective.[37] One example of the implications of this lack of historical information was Jeremías Lopez, a young Maya who was finishing high school in 2004. He was a quiet but serious person, a good student who had been active in party politics with the right-wing PAN Party. We spoke on September 15, 2004, Guatemala's National Independence Day. That morning, schoolchildren had paraded through town, marching to military-sounding drumbeats; carrying posters with images of the national flag, the *quetzal* (the nearly extinct national bird, also the name of the national currency); singing songs; and reading poems. When I asked what Independence Day meant to him, he said that he only recently learned about indigenous dispossession from reading a book assigned in a high school history class:

> Five hundred years of exploitation and slavery!? When I read this, it was like the mountain fell on top of me. Five hundred years? Why hadn't anyone ever told me? We never studied anything like that in *primeria* or *basica* [elementary or middle school]. I was so angry. I think they should teach these things at a younger age. And then we read poems about Guatemala Linda [a nationalist poem]. We don't even know what Guatemala is. It's terrible.

It was jarring to see someone as mild-mannered as Jeremías so incensed, but his sense of having been cheated and betrayed was understandable.

In our subsequent conversations, I found that he was equally uninformed about the armed conflict and its local manifestations.

Following the dominant human rights narrative of the post-accords period, few Sampedranos believed that the violence of the early 1980s was justified. Most felt strongly that it was a grave violation of human dignity and a manifestation of deep-seated racism against indigenous people, but locals seemed divided on the question of who was responsible. Many voiced considerable anger toward Ríos Montt. The Catholic Church echoed this critique, along with many human rights organizations and social movements, and argued that carrying out multiple crimes against humanity rendered him unfit to be president of a democracy that supposedly respected human and indigenous rights.

Anticipating these allegations, and assisted by irreconcilable interpretations of the past, the FRG circulated a whitewashed version of Ríos Montt's historical role. They portrayed Ríos Montt as a benevolent leader who ended the violence by forming the civil patrols and later remembered to pay the patrollers, not as the general who gave the order for genocide.[38] They instead blamed the massacres on the previous dictator, Lucas García. The FRG campaign thus blended Ríos Montt's counterinsurgency discourse with military concessions to critiques of excessive violence. While accurate for some places, this chronology did not fit events in most of the highlands, or events in San Pedro, where the most intense wave of military violence happened after Ríos Montt took control of the state by coup in 1982 and where villagers at the time blamed him for the violence. Non-FRG supporters denounced this exculpatory narrative as craven opportunism, whereas FRG supporters denounced allegations against Ríos Montt as political smears. It was a testimony to the central role of historical memory and political identity that disputes about tragic events from twenty years before figured centrally into heated debates about party alignments. Although both criticisms and defenses of Ríos Montt assumed that killing Mayas en masse during the war was immoral, neither asserted that these massacres thwarted a political movement in which their town had played a part.

Uncertainty regarding the past left many young politically active Sampedranos with few tools to discern between competing claims swirling about Ríos Montt during the campaign season. I asked Rogelio Martínez, a thirty-four-year-old Maya who was a soldier in the late 1980s and later a local organizer for the FRG, what he thought about Ríos Montt's alleged involvement in genocide. He spoke while his wife nodded and smiled in agreement, turning her head to make eye contact while she also cooked, served us coffee, and entertained their three young children:

> In that time there was war. The military and the guerrilla. When Ríos Montt was governing Guatemala, the thing was calming down. When he made the law that the people patrolled, so that they took care of themselves, of each other. And that is where the war went calming down. But the people say that that was by Ríos Montt's doing when many were killed. I had a very young age in that time, but I have learned many things—that it wasn't Ríos Montt; it was Lucas García. When Ríos Montt came in, the thing calmed down. Perhaps some people were killed in this time, but it wasn't his doing. Rather sometimes between themselves. There are times they sell us out in another *municipio,* and from there they come and grab us. They say it was Ríos Montt, but I don't believe it, with the little opportunity that I have. The other thing is that I didn't see it. The one who knows the most is our God. I could perhaps easily say that it was [Ríos Montt]. But I didn't see anything. We don't have any proof. How are we going to judge our neighbor?

Rogelio was a true believer in Ríos Montt. I found it interesting, however, that although he had served in the army several years after the peak of the counterinsurgency, he did not defend the army's use of violence. Like others in the FRG, he blamed the violence on Lucas García and credited Ríos Montt for "calming things down" with the civil patrols. He added that the media invented lies about Ríos Montt, saying that he had personally attended a rally where the press had falsely reported that Ríos Montt had been booed. Martínez echoed the official party discourse while professing ignorance about the actual events of the past, claiming that they were beyond knowing. In the absence of a clear, disinterested truth, he subscribed to the standard army-FRG propaganda line. Ultimately, his response to allegations against Ríos Montt devolved into extreme skepticism and abdication: "But I didn't see anything. We don't have any proof. How are we going to judge our neighbor?" Obviously, he had a personal interest in this whitewashed interpretation, but the fact that he could publicly adopt this perspective, believe it, and not be subject to constant ridicule was a testimony to widespread uncertainty about the past, generated in part by the counterinsurgency, reinforced by ongoing denials of revolutionary politics and through party politics.

Many party members believed in this narrative, others were unsure, and some cynically toed the line to win the election. Confusion about the past, enhanced by the politically motivated rehabilitation of counterinsurgency psyops, gave Martínez and many others plausible deniability regarding Ríos Montt's past actions, a convenient agnosticism that figured into their democratic decision making. Several years later, Edgar Velásquez, a young, college-educated Maya and high-ranking FRG supporter, told me that "after the violence, the people were scared into silence, and that same silence helped the FRG." This "public amnesia" designed to sever grassroots connections to the guerrilla movement was an important condition under which participation in authoritarian populism became thinkable, at least publicly defensible with a claim to a legitimate and democratic social identity.

Involvement in politics created a significant personal interest in circulating certain narratives about the violence. After meeting and interviewing Mariano Díaz in 2009, I realized that he knew more than he let on in public and that he had been too involved with governing and later too invested in a future in politics to disengage from calculated impression management. It was hard to say if he was unaware of the stakes of past political struggles or if he simply thought that they were irrelevant in the present and that invoking them could jeopardize his relationship with party bosses. Several years after this campaign, Edgar Velázquez, an FRG leader, confessed to me that he had willingly misrepresented what he believed to be the truth of Ríos Montt's past on the campaign trail, explaining that national politics was irrelevant, adding that you never see the truth of a person's heart in politics. Lying, even about something so tragic and consequential, was a prerequisite for democratic success.

The Moral Function of Memory

Counterinsurgency discourses about "two armies" continued to play a major role in shaping public memory in San Pedro, where, in addition to fear, they were supported by investments in identities that took shape after the violence. Denial of leftist politics—including support for leftist demands—allowed criticisms of the military in dangerous times and were crucial to the reconstitution of valorized subjectivities among victims and survivors. These denials, configured by the landscape of memory in San Pedro since the 1980s, stunted the reappraisal of the guerrilla movement that was taking place after the peace accords and significantly limited indigenous democratic agency. For younger FRG supporters especially, public denials and uncertainty gave plausibility to a sanitized narrative about Ríos Montt's role in the violence.

Reflecting on the psychological dimensions of the army's political-military project, Jennifer Schirmer (1998, 24) writes the following:

> Yet the very reason for the need for psychological warfare and social intelligence gathering is the military's implicit understanding of both their responsibility for the massacre campaign and their subsequent scurrilous image in highland communities brutally ravaged by the early 1980s campaigns. Given this legacy, gaining their hearts and erasing the minds of the Sanctioned Mayan may prove to be a more difficult task than the military bargained for.

Indeed, the "two armies" discourse was the supreme Mayan act of wartime resistance, a refusal of army denunciations of Mayas as guerrillas who deserved to die. It was based in part on real experiences; most of those killed during decades of counterinsurgency violence were indeed innocents, even by the army's own twisted standards, and certainly in the minds of most villagers at the time they were murdered. Moreover, the guerrillas made many errors, and many Sampedranos dissented from their methods and goals, misgivings that grew as the war went on and the defeat of the guerrillas became inevitable. With their enemy vanquished, the army shifted its discourse in response to local criticisms of the violence alongside efforts to reestablish legitimacy through providing development.

The "two armies" discourse drew from real experiences, but the counterinsurgency reduced and modified the memories of the past, cutting out the moment before the violence when villagers were emotionally connected to the revolution or at least in broad agreement with its central demands. Mayan efforts to construct socially approved but resistant identities under these restricted conditions smothered a more complicated understanding of the affinities and overlaps, both historical and possible, between indigenous and revolutionary politics. The codification of a sanitized critique of violence and its promotion through the civil patrol system were understood as a process of development. These counterinsurgency memories and the identities invested in them revealed deep complicities between counterinsurgency and neoliberal democracy; legitimated sanctioned forms of resistance as democratic but disqualified more radical visions; and constituted a powerful relay within neoliberal governance. The army's deliberate production of uncertainty further impaired villagers' ability to discern among rival historical claims. Truth commission reports attempted to clear up this confusion, but their findings were not well-known at the local level and were often filtered through depoliticized notions of human rights that also excluded revolutionary politics without question.

Having conceded that guerrillas were criminals and claiming that no one participated in their movement made advocating political demands that seemed "revolutionary" exceedingly difficult even after the peace accords. While resistant to state violence, these new identities were forged within a narrative space of neoliberal democracy that excluded national political transformation. In 2004 and years later, discourses that explicitly linked local desires for well-being to change political and economic structures were marginalized to the point of indecipherability within official democratic spaces. Even the public criticisms of Ríos Montt in San Pedro focused only on the fact of his killings, not the *intentions* or *effects* of those killings, which were to crush rural political organizations and grassroots hopes for radical social transformation. Uncertainty about the past did more than elide potential alternatives; it also contributed to the conditions under which some villagers considered Ríos Montt a legitimate candidate.

Laurence Kirmayer writes that "it is a paradox of freedom that the moral function of memory depends on the constraints of social and cultural worlds to provide a limited range of narrative forms with which to construct coherent stories of ourselves" (1996, 193). All narratives entail situated perspectives and desires, and contain erasures and dangers. It is not a question of whether or not to adopt a perspective on the past or how to find a neutral truth, but which inevitably constrained perspective will prevail and to what effect. Counter-memories that challenged core tenets of counterinsurgency truth were emerging in San Pedro's indigenous villages alongside political discourses that questioned imbalances of political and economic power at the heart of Guatemalan society. For many Ladinos, however, maintaining a positive identity required narratives that downplayed their complicity (enthusiastic or reluctant) in repression or discrimination. For their part, many Mayan Sampedranos sought narratives that captured important parts of their experience, especially experiences with violence, while shielding them from reprisals and protecting them from criticism for their complicity.

Nelson (2009) asks what forms of commemoration might be appropriate for "the complexity of identifications and the agency of those killed and wounded" (109). While recognizing the importance of official memory projects, she warns against delving into the past to assign blame, to fix a stable image of victims and oppressors in order to punish the wrongdoers, noting that "struggles against impunity . . . alone . . . cannot fix Guatemala, or any other place" (113). Remembering the past differently may disrupt these identities, may reopen old wounds, and could lead to new conflicts—even violence—and should ideally happen in a way that allows space for individuals and collectives to rethink their identities. But forgetting may be no less painful than remembering, and the "two armies" narrative does its own violence, consigning communities to silence and shame while denying the existence of movements toward social democracy and redistribution for which many fought and died and whose defeat is part and parcel of their current malaise.

Recognizing widespread indigenous investments in the guerrilla movement does not imply that all supported it—they did not—and were thus responsible for or deserving of what followed—they were not—nor is it a call to return to violence. But acknowledging their historical connection to indigenous politics underscores the indispensability of revolutionary demands to any meaningful conception of democracy or indigenous autonomy. Repairing connections between indigenous and leftist politics need not involve fixing identities, drawing bright lines between good and bad actors, or imposing a "correct" politics from the outside, but it is folly to assume that all historical narratives are equally valid, ethical, or politically fertile. New thinking about the past in the process of contemporary struggles should not be limited to the confines of the revolutionary left, but excluding all trace of radical or revolutionary desire reflects and reinforces the foundational violence of Guatemalan democracy.

2

NOS FALTA CAPACIDAD

Training Enterprising Selves

General Analysis of Attitudinal Development: As the last
Progress Achievement Report concluded regarding the South
Coast Federation: "They are essentially aware of their long range
objectives; however, they still have not settled down to a realistic
understanding of the long road ahead." It was during this reporting
period that leaders of the Federation confronted the question of a
"realistic understanding." They became aware of the fact that an
adequate economic base of their own to finance their ambitious
planning could not be developed overnight, and that the rank-and-
file members in the local associations still did not identify them as
their leaders. But most importantly, they learned that the discipline
(not so much the capacity) of maintaining effective administration
of their organization was alien to them. Most of them have not
understood that the details of bookkeeping, micro-planning
and documentation are a very necessary part of organizational
development. Their life styles are essentially ones of independence
with large spans of leisure time; they do not have to account for
their work and time to other persons. Some are willing to make the
necessary adjustments implied by the "value system" of organization
and some are not. Some understand that these adjustments have to
be made in order to gain the objectives of economic betterment, a
greater voice for themselves as a "people," and the development of a
broader understanding of the world in which they live.

PROGRESS ACHIEVEMENT REPORT: RURAL ORGANIZATION
DEVELOPMENT PROGRAM, PILOT PROJECT—GUATEMALA, 1970

Indeed the very idea, the very possibility of a theory of a discrete
and enveloped body inhabited and animated by its own soul—the
subject, the individual, the person—is *part of what is to be explained,*

the very horizon of thought that one can hope to see beyond. . . .
Our inquiries would pursue the lines of formation and functioning
of an array of historically contingent *"practices of subjectification,"*
in which humans are capacitated through coming to relate to
themselves in particular ways: understand themselves, speak
themselves, enact themselves, judge themselves in virtue of the
ways in which their forces, energies, properties, and ontologies are
constituted and shaped by being linked into, utilized, inscribed,
incised by various assemblages.

NIKOLAS ROSE, *INVENTING OUR SELVES* (ITALICS MINE)

Capacitation isn't just a talk; rather it is that in which you can
achieve a quality of life and changes in people's behavior.

FORMER DEPARTMENTAL DIRECTOR OF DIGESA
(INTERVIEW, 2015)

When I arrived at Juan Jiménez's house early one morning for a scheduled meeting, his wife informed me that he was around back. I walked not far down the trail to find him waiting for me in a recently tilled empty field. After greeting, he explained that his friend, an *ingeniero agrónomo* (agronomical engineer), grows papaya and told him how to make money from it. Jiménez wanted to grow Hawaiian papaya because they are smaller and sweeter tasting and also because, hopefully, based on his research, they would grow in Los Altenses. "I cut all the coffee plants down. My neighbors—the people here—thought it was crazy. But they do not understand. Now I don't want anything to do with coffee." Jiménez was gambling, in an educated way, that papaya sales would earn him much more than simply growing coffee. His reasoning followed that of international development agents and policy makers involved in promoting nontraditional agricultural exports (NTX) to raise the living standards of small farmers.[1] Earlier that year, Jiménez had calculated days worked and fertilizer and transportation costs, and reasoned that he was losing Q150 ($20) per quintal growing coffee. "Coffee doesn't pay," he announced decidedly. After the prices recovered, some people profited, he explained, but so little that NTX sounds better all the time, especially because "coffee requires so much work."

Jiménez already kept bees and sold their honey to a local NGO that exported it. When I asked about the possibility of exporting local varieties of wild mushrooms, some of which were quite unique and delicious, he said that he had also discussed it with the *agrónomo,* proudly informing me that he knew many *ingeniero* whom he had met in his travels to other towns. The same man, Jiménez informed me, *"ya se superó"* ("already made it") selling papaya, and he intended to do the same. As he showed me the new plot, he explained that last week he had invested Q425 ($60) on papaya seeds, a discounted price he arranged through his friend. He can get eighty trees per *cuerda* (20 square meters), each of which bears fruit every six months. He figured he could sell the papaya for Q5 each, regardless of their somewhat small size. "The problem," he said, grinning, "is that no one knows what they are yet." He nodded and laughed at my suggestion that he slice one open and offer samples. He also expressed admiration for the production on large *fincas,* describing how they used tools to level the rows to make sure that no water escaped: "Perfectly even!" They also use two applications of chemical fertilizers and another organic fertilization every two or three years: "Very scientific!"

I first met Jiménez at the village assembly, where I asked permission to live there and conduct research. He sat in the front row and made direct eye contact with an intent expression. He was relaxed and not at all timid about speaking to people from outside the community. He had served on various village development committees and, in 2004, was head of the *padres de familia* (parents) committee, responsible for improving communication between the villagers and the director and staff of the village school, almost all Ladinos from the town center or Huehuetenango. He had inherited a great deal of productive land from his father-in-law, a former leader active in the first development committees in the village.

Jiménez and I spoke on numerous occasions. I enjoyed his quick wit and irreverent attitude, and he seemed interested in hearing my perspectives. One of the first things he told me about himself was that he had taken several courses with the Association for Integrated Development (ASODESI)—San Pedro's most prominent local development institution—and currently worked for it as a health promoter, a job that required travel to different *municipios.* Facts and details learned in courses taken with development institutions in hopes of gaining particular certificates were the standard fare in my conversations with Jiménez and others who had earned such credentials. Villagers trained in such a manner were a distinct minority and were generally less timid and more willing to engage me and to seek out my company than others who were not.

Jiménez took calculated risks experimenting with new crops and used scientific knowledge and technologies to take utmost advantage of his land. He enjoyed learning new things. These traits earned him an elevated status in the community; he was regarded as an intelligent person, one of the most *capacitado* in the entire village. One hot Sunday afternoon, I ran into him at a local cantina where I sometimes went after the market died down to find men when they had free time to talk and to enjoy a beer myself. Jiménez, who had a reputation for sometimes imbibing too much, was drinking beer with two young men from his village. The youths were sipping more slowly than he was, despite his prodding, but listened patiently as he told them about the importance of having "vision" and a "mission." Vision was the goal, and the mission included the concrete steps one would need to take to get there; both were necessary for success. These were lessons he had learned working for ASODESI. As the young men—both high school graduates—listened, it appeared they were humoring him by sitting quietly and nodding at appropriate intervals. I got the impression that they had heard this talk before but enjoyed or at least tolerated it. He continued for several minutes, repeating several times how he traveled to different *municipios,* knew experts, and was always learning new things. He exuded confidence that often veered into arrogance born out of his conviction that he possessed *capacidad.*

Some villagers had evidently grown tired of Juan's self-importance, which also made me uncomfortable on several occasions. One evening I was sitting on a log conversing with one of his neighbors who lived near the unpaved road that runs through the village. Without speaking, the men exchanged an angry glare. I later discovered that the man had been teasing Juan, saying he was from the neighboring town of San Juan Atitán. Juan was actually from a distant *aldea* in San Pedro. The joke was about the name Juan and Juan's mustache, which resembled those typical among Mayan *Sanjuaneros.* The teasing seemed intended to take Jiménez down a notch, as was the disrespectful nickname, "Juan Papaya," mocking his interest in fruit. I interpreted his difficulty in taking these jokes as a sign of his self-perception as someone who should be taken seriously. *Capacidad,* it seemed, did not render a person ethical or immune from criticism, and it was also a source of jealousy.

Juan's close friend Arturo Bravo exemplified similar characteristics, and to a higher degree. When I first met with the development committee

Figure 3. ASODESI offices in San Pedro, 2011. Photo by author.

in Los Altenses, Bravo spoke the most. He proudly described how this was his second time to serve as president of the committee and that the community had recently asked him back because the prior leader had failed in his duties. Although it was a lot of work, Bravo said he had agreed in hopes of promoting development in the village and to build on previous accomplishments. He recounted that during his term as president, the committee got funding for the school we were sitting in, the road, and a potable water project in one zone, among other improvements. Other committee members, two women and another man, the young *alcalde auxiliar,* nodded quietly.

At the meeting where I presented my research plan to the village, it was Bravo who spoke on my behalf, arguing that my research would be good for community development. Bravo was an active and capable participant in village and church meetings and even at town-level meetings with Ladinos. After decades of involvement with a range of development programs, starting as an adolescent in the 1970s, he had no fear of giving his opinion in front of groups, and he seemed to enjoy it. He always tucked a clean shirt in beneath his belt and had a full mouth of clean, straight teeth: a rarity in the villages. As one of very few men in the village with visibly protruding bellies, Bravo had earned the nickname *"Gordo"* ("Fat"). Like Juan Jiménez, he had a tendency to brag about his *capacidad,* but his main focus was on projects he had attained for the village. One evening, a few months after my arrival, and after a few drinks, Bravo reminded me that "if it were not for me, you wouldn't be here." This assertion of dominance and status led into a larger discussion of his skills and credentials: traits that marked him as a leader. Their training, as well as their orientation to self-improvement, market activity, and the acquisition of development projects, made Jiménez and Bravo the ideal subjects of neoliberal democracy. Both men were part of José Antulio Morales' political coalition, and Bravo was a trusted lieutenant.

Capacidad: A New Norm

Stacy Leigh Pigg (1993) describes how categories from development discourse percolate into heterogeneous settings, influencing the way that the subjects of development understand and construct their social worlds. The history of colonial population management is crowded with myriad attempts to instill a "will to improve" among marginal populations (Li 2007b). Akhil Gupta (1998) argues that the preponderance of development discourses has given rise to "underdevelopment" as a dominant form of identity: a pervasive discourse of inferiority and rationalization for inequality that is a defining characteristic of the postcolonial condition. Guatemalan elites have long blamed national underdevelopment on "Indian backwardness" and inferiority even as they repressed indigenous efforts to improve their material conditions. Only in the second half of the twentieth century were policies adopted to promote "Indian" advancement, and only then to contain the threat that extreme poverty and inequality posed to national stability. Yet these programs had left an unmistakable trace. The most significant manifestation of the will to improve in San Pedro was the discourse of *capacidad,* referring to individual capacity development. The description of Jiménez and Bravo shows the manner in which Sampedranos had woven discourses and practices of *capacidad* into their lives and shared conceptual frameworks.

Capacidad, which translates most generally to capacity or ability, is a blanket term commonly used by rural Mayas and Ladinos alike to refer to a person's level of individual capacity *development,* specifically the technical skills and knowledge received through involvement with institutions and experts. This included schooling—the ability to read, write, and do basic math—as well as skills gained through participating in the various kinds of workshops offered by development institutions and NGOs. A person could be capacitated in distinct ways, independently and in combination, but institutional knowledge imparted by experts was always key. For example, the difference between being more or less capacitated as a farmer was based on the extent to which one was fluent in "modern" and "scientific" agricultural practices and agronomical knowledge as defined by agronomists. *Capacidad* was the kind of knowledge or skills attained through training that enabled individuals to perform technical actions that were otherwise impossible. The term was used more broadly to refer to a "modern" or "scientific" outlook, a way of carrying one's person, and one's relationship to economic and political life.

Capacidad was framed as a transcultural universal in that each person could theoretically be assigned an accurate location on a neutral scale of achievement and ability. However, there was no precise consensus on how to rank individuals; this was an ongoing topic of discussion. Still, *capacidad* was thought to be a "principle true in every country" (Mitchell 2002, 55), superior to autochthonous ways of knowing and acting, which from the point of view of *capacidad* were arbitrary, parochial, and pathological: destined to disappear. *Capacidad* was Eurocentric: Western knowledge and behavior were privileged, and white North Americans and Europeans occupied the top place on the scale, followed by Ladinos. European and American experts, prototypically male, were the high priests and priestesses of *capacidad.* But *capacidad* was liberal in the sense that it was theoretically open to everyone willing to undergo the process, which is part of why it was interesting to indigenous villagers in the first place: attaining *capacidad* opened up the practical possibility of becoming equal to Ladinos, materially improving their life conditions by transforming their minds and themselves.

In this chapter I examine how discourses and practices of *capacidad* had taken hold and reorganized the conditions of possibility for subjectivity in San Pedro. I describe the introduction of *capacidad* by an array of institutions over several decades and unpack what *capacidad* consisted of for indigenous Sampedranos and its effects. How did these new values, narratives, conceptions, practices, and desires suffuse their economic, social, and political lives and open up new forms of thought and action? How did *capacidad* alter the patterns and logics of social differentiation? To what extent was *capacidad* gendered and racialized? What possibilities for forming alliances did it make possible and impossible? How and under what conditions did differently positioned Mayas appropriate, resignify or resist *capacidad*?

I began with an understanding of development as a discourse and set of techniques engaged in the formation of new subjects and spaces deployed within diverse schemes of governance and processes of state formation. Reading program documents and secondary sources enabled me to understand how *capacidad* was promoted by a range of institutions for several decades. Living for an extended period of time in rural villages revealed a multiplicity of ways that villagers incorporated notions of development and *capacidad* into the warp and weft of their everyday lives. *Capacidad* was an important way for rural villagers to think about who they were and to grasp a foothold in a chaotic world so patently lacking in justice, compassion, and reason. I describe the poetics of *capacidad*: the ways that Sampedranos used the term and its correlates to mark certain kinds of subjects as possessing, or lacking, a particular kind of quality or status (Clifford and Marcus 1986). *Capacidad* was a way of "narrativizing the local cultural real" (Stewart 1996, 4), infused with the desire to make oneself smarter, more effective, more skilled, and more able to live a healthier, happier, and wealthier life.

Discourses of *capacidad* have generated a new poetics of self by fostering a new way of being in the world, specifically, a market-oriented, rational, calculating individualism. In speaking about sense of self, I am concerned with connections between how people identified socially; who they thought they really were; their personal habits and beliefs, including their notions of intelligent, moral, or normal behaviors; and the ethical and political relationships that they cultivated with themselves and with others. Deeply related to the self is a notion of well-being: the conceptions of the material goods that one needs to survive and be comfortable as well as the ability to make a living. I am particularly interested in emergence of an individualized self that plans and calculates the future and conceives of the acquisition of capabilities as an ongoing project of improvement and as a means of attaining individual and familial well-being through market activities.

Capacidad was the dominant paradigm of advancement and neoliberal democratic self-fashioning that I encountered in San Pedro. It focused on the individual as the target and object of improvement and deployed an array of practices of self-mastery and knowledge. From its arrival, *capacidad* was tangled up with existing narratives, identities, habits, social relations, and political struggles. Rather than depoliticizing poverty (e.g. Ferguson 1994), *capacidad* was presented and taken up as a way of escaping a "backwards" Indian identity by learning the skills, habits, outlooks, and forms of self-discipline required to advance in a market society.[2] *Capacidad* opened new spaces for social and political agency but exacerbated inequality among villages and rationalized discrimination and poverty in a different frame.

New Selves

Capacidad is of recent origin in Guatemala's indigenous communities. For generations, the notion was part of the assumed biological difference between Mayans and Ladinos: Ladinos could attain it; Indians could not. In the traditional community hierarchy, status was granted to men based on age, not *capacidad*. Economic stratification has long existed among indigenous villagers alongside small-scale participation in the market economy.[3] Class divisions intensified with the advent of cash cropping in the 1960s and 1970s, a change that led individuals to challenge community hierarchies and *cargos* (community service responsibilities), mainly because these structures inhibited the accumulation of personal wealth and perpetuated Ladino dominance.[4] Through *capacidad,* villagers came to think of themselves as substantially different types of persons, possessing different personal qualities and status based on the extent of individual subjective transformations and forms of self-mastery offered by institutions.[5]

Capacidad in San Pedro attained universal status as a result of its existence as a common thread between various programs that aimed to improve local conditions. Inspired by Catholic Action's vision for the development of the whole person through education and training, bilingual promoters from the urban center tried to convince villagers to build schools in the 1950s and 1960s. They met stiff opposition from locals who were suspicious of education and who needed their children to work. It was not until the 1970s and after some persuasion that schools were established in all villages and basic education became routine, although for boys more often than for girls.[6]

Throughout the 1970s, Maryknoll priests trained catechists and encouraged economic development among their followers. One founded the Santa Teresita cooperative, which was part of the National Federation of Savings and Credit Cooperatives (FENACOAC), a cooperative network that was closely associated with the moderate reformist Christian Democracy Party and that aimed to lift rural Indians out of poverty.[7] *Capacidad* was a key theme in cooperatives that introduced chemical fertilizers and pesticides at low cost and trained farmers how to use them, helped their members market their crops, educated them on savings, and spoke about politics, even land inequality: a taboo subject after 1954.[8] Cooperatives espoused an inclusive vision of community development and were one of the few spaces where Ladinos and Mayas worked together for a common goal, although only a small percentage of villagers participated actively and the co-op hardly satiated local demand for credit or extension services.[9]

Several state programs that promoted rural development in the 1970s and 1980s helped consolidate an authoritative understanding of *capacidad* that they made available to a large number of villagers alongside agricultural techniques, new technologies, market-oriented pedagogy, and credit.[10] The most significant state-led, USAID-funded agency was the General Directory for Agronomical Services (DIGESA). With superior funding, organization, personnel, and reach, DIGESA promoted market-oriented development as the path to Indian advancement and generalized the use of chemical inputs, credit, and cash cropping.[11] These programs, as I describe in the next chapter, were guided by a vision of political development and a securitized vision of democracy capable of safeguarding Guatemala's asymmetrical social order. They were official responses to grassroots pressure for broader conceptions of development.

Participating villagers, for their part, viewed DIGESA as similar to the guerrilla movement, and safer, even though the army initially opposed it along with all forms of village organization. Development was slow and painstaking but eventually freed some indigenous villagers from exploitative and racially discriminatory work situations either on *fincas* or for local Ladinos.[12] State investment in rural development was minimal; training and credit programs closed during the war, and most of the Public Agrarian sector, including DIGESA, ended during Structural Adjustment in 1996. By then, *capacidad* had become established as a nearly universal value.

As a result of the program closing, despite the prevalence of these discourses of development and *capacidad,* only a small number of individuals—maybe fifteen adult men and fewer adult women in a village—were seen as having truly attained a high level of *capacidad,* and even they wanted to attain more.[13] To be considered *capacitado* did not require a complete high school education, which was largely unavailable to the previous generation, but a high school education would count, and literacy—the ability to speak, read, and write in Spanish at a basic level or better—was almost always necessary. Those who had attained a high level of *capacidad* were generally well-known beyond their home villages and occupied various leadership positions.

In addition to the *capacitados,* some people were labeled as "not wanting to develop." Another group was the *superados*—people who had "already made it" economically. In what follows, I provide ethnographic examples of people who either identify or are identified by others as exemplifying each of these categories in order to demonstrate their salience in people's lives. These categories were interrelated and mutually dependent. They constituted one another and formed a complete and coherent reality.

Los No Capacitados

One way that I came to appreciate what discourses of *capacidad* meant to rural villagers in Los Altenses was by spending time with people who did not embody these norms. Most people, while not overtly critical, did not jump at the chance of receiving a *capacitación* or assuming the responsibilities that come with *capacidad,* such as a position on a village development committee. This was especially evident among the generation of men who had never attended school and who had participated in only a minimal way in DIGESA and subsequent programs. I observed several characteristics of the "less capacitated" type. In making this comparison, I do not intend to reproduce a discourse that makes one into the norm and constitutes the other as "lacking"—although this was exactly what most villagers expressed—but rather to bring into view different categories of personhood.

One of these individuals whom I came to know best and fell into the category of "less capacitated" was Pedro Bravo, whose sense of self and well-being made an interesting comparison because he was Arturo Bravo's older brother. He was only ten years older, but his manner of carrying himself was quite distinct. Both were considered upstanding community members and actively participated in communal events such as weddings, funerals, and work projects. He rarely missed a church service in the village and usually attended Mass in the town. But the differences stood out clearly. Pedro never went to school, and his Spanish was somewhat sparse, although sufficient for basic conversation. Because of this, Pedro had received little direct training in agricultural programs and relied instead on his siblings for critical information. He was very easygoing and secure interpersonally, and did not attempt to manage his impressions according to what he perceived my expectations of "capacitated" behavior to be. Image-managing practices were common to the point of overcompensation among villagers who either had *capacidad* or wanted to, such as Juan Jiménez, who was always worried that others should perceive him as an intelligent leader. Moreover, Pedro Bravo did not engage in much long-term calculation or preoccupation about agricultural production. He had a choice piece of land that he planted with maize, and he never seriously considered diversifying his crop beyond the beans, squash, and herbs that were common to *milpa* agriculture. Nor had he given thought to the oft-repeated warning given by agronomists regarding long-term risks to subsistence production. When I asked if he worried about the diminishing returns of chemical fertilizers, he replied that if his land "is burnt by chemicals, I'll apply a remedy." He was far more concerned about the increasing cost of inputs than their side effects. He was not interested in learning to read or write, and seemed content with the little Spanish he could speak. One of his cousins told me that "of course Pedro is less intelligent. But he has learned. We taught him certain things, about planning and taking care of his money." He voted in elections and participated moderately in political campaigns but was never considered for a leadership position in party politics or on development committees. Compared to his brother, he was significantly less well off, but he was not engaged in concerted efforts to improve his condition.

Superados

Most Sampedranos I talked to expressed a desire to *superarse:* "to get ahead" economically.[14] This concept existed before *capacidad,* dating back to the advent of cash cropping and merchant activities. Over time, more successful farmers purchased more land and hired other villagers as workers. Some opened shops. There were numerous nearly identical *tiendas,* diners, and pharmacies of varying sizes, each animated by a similar dream and using the same business model: buy in bulk in Huehuetenango or La Mesilla and sell at a small markup. Over time, a few of these businesses succeeded and grew to have more selection and lower prices. But their space to grow was limited, and they never expanded beyond the town. They also faced some outside competition. Although *superación* did not necessarily require *capacidad,* it was the preeminent end goal of training and market-oriented development. Participants in DIGESA; the National Coffee Association (ANACAFE), a private promoter of coffee production; and later NTX programs were assumed to be following a path to *superación* through credit, saving, investment, and training. For the vast majority, *superación,* like *capacidad* itself, was elusive, an ever-receding horizon. Communities were rife with stories of individuals who had made a fortune and then lost it, careening back into poverty. But the small number who had "made it," almost all of whom were men, were known as *superados.*

To attain *superado* status was almost to become legendary. One archetypical figure of Mayan *superación* in San Pedro was José Martín. Martín was reportedly the richest individual in town, even wealthier than any Ladino. He owned the *transportes Sampedranos,* a three-bus line that trekked to Huehuetenango twice daily. Many villagers told me his Cinderella story, which was presented as an example of the possibilities of hard work. When he was young, José Martín came to San Pedro from another town; he sold dried fish, walking village to village. He then upgraded his stock to include kitchenware, and, little by little, as he saved his pennies, his wealth multiplied. The narrative of *superación* through *capacidad* framed individual success as a product of personal effort and spark, something that was available to everyone who put in the effort. Once the status was achieved, *superados* were supposedly set for life, but people often fell from grace. The former mayor Natanael Aguilar was one example. When he was mayor, he lived in Huehuetenango, but years later, when he had run out of money, he returned to his village to grow coffee, a clear step down. Newcomers to this group were those who had come back from living in the United States with a nest egg earned in dollars. Individual *superación* was the narrative frame for class divisions that were becoming steadily more pronounced among villagers.

The *superados* were distinguishable by their consumption patterns, which could seem ostentatious relative to the threadbare conditions in which most Sampedranos lived. They built new houses, sometimes in villages, usually in the town center, and sometimes in Huehuetenango, but always with *terraza* (a flat, cement ceiling, or terrace), more expensive and durable than the more common adobe and *lamina* construction. The wealthiest Mayas lived in the town center, some in houses with multiple levels. *Superados* also engaged in significant luxury and leisure consumption: eating in *comedores,* taking frequent trips to Huehuetenango, buying new clothing, drinking beer and whiskey and inviting friends to drink, and similar behaviors. Of course, like the *capacitados*, nearly all *superados* sent their children to high school and, when possible, to college. *Superados* often helped finance political campaigns, which required significant personal investments, and some ran for office themselves. *Capacitados* and many non-*capacitados* also threw extravagant parties on special occasions, like a funeral or wedding, sometimes cooking upwards of fifty pounds of chicken or beef for hundreds of guests: a huge expense, a practice rooted in the *cofradía* (Catholic religious brotherhood) system.[15]

Profesionales

In the most basic sense, to be a professional means to have earned at least a high-school diploma. *Profesionales* are that subset of *capacidad* who perform mental labor and are recognized as experts. It denotes someone who is qualified, even if temporarily unemployed, to have a job with a salary and not work as a farmer. The most common baseline example is an elementary school teacher. At the pinnacle of this category are the *licenciados*—individuals with an advanced college degree. The term *licenciado* commands great respect. The vast majority of the professionals among Mayas—from the villages especially but also in the town—are young, below the age of thirty-five in 2004. Although few in number, they are influential. Professionals hail disproportionately from the town center, where a politically decisive group arose in the late 1960s. This was the first generation of children whose parents were able to afford to send them all the way through school, and in a few cases to college. By 2014, there was only one indigenous attorney in San Pedro and only one doctor, but several more were studying for these careers.

Not working as a farmer was the mark of distinction shared by the professionals and the *superados,* and peasant farmers regularly complained that their high-school-educated children were "no longer accustomed" to agricultural work and felt like they were too good for it, preferring *trabajo suave* (soft work). Nevertheless, many parents of professionals recounted working hard to ensure their children's education precisely so that they would not be farmers, which was synonymous with being poor and stuck. Consumption practices among this group varied, depending on an individual's success. Elementary and high school teachers earned a monthly salary of about Q1,000–Q1,500 in 2004, much more than most farmers, but not enough to buy a car. But first- and second-year teachers regularly built homes and bought motorcycles and nicer clothing. Healthy, clean teeth were the norm, as were dress shirts and polished leather shoes. But the promise of *superación* through professionalization had encountered a blockade. A growing problem for young high school graduates trained as teachers was that there were now too many teachers for the positions available. Those who worked as teachers complained of having to live in remote villages to get a contract. Contract employment for one year or one semester was becoming more prevalent, leading to a rise in economic insecurity among this group. A growing number of unemployed professionals had no way to use their skills.

Restless, many opted to migrate to the United States. The dangers of the desert; the high cost of immigration (upwards of $7,000 by 2014, a small fortune); reports of declining work opportunities and discrimination in the United States; well-founded rumors of kidnappings, rape, and extortion during the border crossing; and news of increased deportations and immigrant detention were rarely sufficient to dissuade them. I knew several mothers who made the perilous journey with young children in tow, eager to reunite with distant husbands who were living strange and separate lives. Ironically, professionals typically performed manual labor in the United States, using their education to master the skills required to migrate and to navigate a strange and hostile landscape with minimal resources and without legal permission or protection. Those who had returned successfully lived in homes they had had built in their absence and were considered to have attained a special level of *capacidad* based on their familiarity with an advanced and deeply contradictory society, especially if they had learned English. People with experience in the United States always looked at me differently: knowingly, with more familiarity and less deference, and even complete strangers often stopped me to let me know they had been there.

No Quieren Desarrollar

I became acquainted with another, much-more-distressing form of categorization with origins in discourses of development during my first week in Los Altenses: a subset of people about whom it was said that they *do not wish to develop*. I was first made aware of the existence of this category while interviewing a couple in their late sixties who lived among the Ruíz family. Although the husband, Paulo, was himself a Ruíz, he exasperatedly began to decry the way that the rest of the people in his zone lived:

> The Ruíz family is just barely holding on. They live really fucked. They don't have land. They're just stealing. They cut firewood on other people's land. They are not smart, and they don't have any money. They don't know anything or how to make money. They don't know how to manage money. Other people have a good life (*vida buena*). They already bought land and planted coffee. . . . They drink. They don't live well in with their family and with their women. They look for other women. Where do they get their corn? They're barely buying it. They go work a little with the people here, as *jornaleros* (day laborers). They are working, but they are very backwards.

I encountered similar expressions of moral outrage directed at families and individuals on many other occasions. Paulo's tirade was ironic. A fallen evangelical and a serious alcoholic, he kept his family finances afloat only with money sent by children who had migrated to the United States. This man was describing a large, extended family living in extreme poverty without land, food, income, a cash crop, education, or much hope, and he blamed their squalid condition on backwardness, a lack of intelligence, and alcohol. Although he did not say it, the word associated with these negative characteristics was *Indio.* Even if the word was out of use, the space it occupied was still part of the imaginary, sometimes used in anger, and incessantly conjured up as the inferior opposite of *capacidad.* Paolo never mentioned the history of dispossession, racism, exploitation, violence, and abandonment: a toxic combination that makes these outcomes inevitable for the vast majority of indigenous campesinos in Guatemala, regardless of how hard they try to escape. *Capacidad* legitimated discrimination among Mayas and recast racist rationalizations for social exclusion in race-neutral terms.

One person who appeared to reject *capacidad* and invite these criticisms was Felipe Ruíz. He lived on the edge of the village farthest up the mountainside in a one-room house made of sticks and plastic. He unapologetically claimed these traits when we met:

> There is no money. After the coffee harvest, then there's money. We are barely eating. *Yo se chupar.* (I know how to drink.) I can drink 15 beers. When I've got money, I won't come back home to the house on Sunday, not until Monday. I'll sleep on the floor of the cantina. Sometimes I spend Q200 on beer. That's why there isn't any money.

Another way that Felipe "fit" this type was his behavior toward other people's property. Felipe had been promised an electric light connection by the newly elected FRG *alcalde,* who had offered to pay for the post and cement if Felipe dug the hole and supplied the sand and gravel to stretch and strengthen the cement. On our second meeting, he enlisted me in gathering gravel and handed me a large *costal* (a nylon sack used for 100 pounds of dried maize or coffee) and a *mecapal* (tump line). Grabbing a small pick, he led me down the steep, slippery slope to the *peña* (rock outcropping) on a neighbor's land. While filling the bag with rock that he chipped off the *peña,* he told me that he did not have permission to gather gravel; we were stealing it! With the veins in my neck popping out as I strained against the weight of the *mecapal,* my boots slipping on the thin footholds in the steep muddy trail, I pondered not only the difficulties of everyday peasant labor but also the humor that would be expressed if I were to die by having my face smashed into the rock by the eighty-pound bag of stolen gravel that teetered precariously on my back. Eager to live down stereotypes about work-averse gringos, I trudged on out of embarrassment for how much more difficult the task was for me at 160 pounds (at the time) than for Felipe, who weighed at least 30 pounds less.

Felipe was not an active participant in development or in community social life in general. He had never served on a village committee, nor did he care to. However, on occasions he helped with community work projects, such as cleaning the road with machetes, and even showed up to help build the foundation for the new Catholic church in the village. When I asked him why he had decided to help out, he replied: "I don't have a religion. I only went to help with the church in case one of my children wants to hear the word of God. I believe in God, yes, but I don't go to church." Felipe's seeming lack of care for his soul and uninterest in personal development did not resemble a rejection of his neighbors' normalizing value judgment, but ownership of it. Felipe was not resisting development in the name of a counter-ideal; he was uninterested in working to make his life resemble the norm of proper behavior. There were many people like Felipe who, in some sense, seemed to like to break the rules, publicly and audaciously. Most often this happened when they were drunk, drunkenness being the quintessential habit of someone who rejected development (even though men with *capacidad* drank frequently). Being drunk was like a crime against *capacidad*. It undid it, prevented it, or put it on hold. A decidedly masculine performance in San Pedro, drunkenness was a publicly recognized abandonment of responsibility and was often self-destructive. One of the great appeals of evangelical religion was its renunciation of alcohol, to end drunkenness and the mind-set that accompanied it. Felipe was consciously enacting an anti-norm, staging what seemed to be small, ultimately futile inversions of his neighbors', and perhaps his own, notions of acceptable, healthy behavior or anything resembling becoming "developed."

Felipe lived in a village subsector occupied exclusively by his extended family, almost all of whom had voted for the FRG. When I asked him why he voted for the FRG, Felipe responded with brazenly disengaged fatalism:

NC: Why do you vote for the FRG? Many people say that Ríos Montt killed a lot of people. What do you think?

Felipe: Yes, he is an *asesino* (murderer). I only went to vote for Mariano Díaz (the FRG candidate for *alcalde*). I don't participate in politics. I just mark an "X" and go back home. I voted for the FRG because they said they would pay the patrollers and they also gave me a job. But the job is over already. I don't have a political party; there isn't one of them in favor of the people.

At first I thought of this cavalier attitude as another in a string of crimes against the norms of *capacidad* and good citizenship, but I later came to understand it as part of a more widely shared set of understandings about the futility of politics, a theme to which I return in chapter 4.

Capacidad and Gender

As the ethnographic vignettes at the beginning of the chapter make clear, *capacidad* is intertwined with dominant notions of masculinity. This reinforced the tendency in rural Guatemala for parents to favor the education of their boys over that of their girls, even as girls' education had risen significantly since the 1970s. Despite it being less available to women, *capacidad* was a route to a certain level of gender equality. Being *capacitada* allowed woman to speak and act with more authority in spaces and on matters historically reserved for men, but it remained difficult for women to speak among men and be taken seriously. Although professional women had a higher social status than un-capacitated men, the *capacidad* of moderately capacitated women was rarely considered equal to that of somewhat less capacitated men.

Concepción Bravo was a woman who was considered highly capacitated. In 2004 she was single and in her early forties. She had no children of her own but had raised one of her brothers' daughters with her sister and later adopted a son. Concepción lived with her sister, who was also single and had two children, each from different fathers. Concepción and her sister shared the responsibility of caring for their aging parents. Concepción had a sixth-grade education and said she never wanted more. Most important to her identity as a capacitated person was her employment as the local representative for DIGESA's women's programs in the 1980s and 1990s. Both she and her sister worked closely with a Peace

Corps volunteer when he was in the village, and they still remembered him fondly. She explained that she was chosen to be the local coordinator for the DIGESA's women's programs because she could speak Spanish and was not afraid of strangers or foreigners.

Concepción participated in almost every form of local development. There were very few women like Concepción from her generation in Los Altenses. She associated with a fairly close-knit group of women leaders in the village, the majority of who are also from the Bravo family. They, like their husbands, are considered the most *capacitada* in the village. One day I met a young woman while walking home from the town. She was a recent high school graduate who stood out as brave enough to strike up a conversation with an outsider, especially a gringo. I later found out that she was a leader among her peers (men and women) and one of the best athletes and academics of the young women in the entire town (Mayan or Ladino). When she found out that I lived near the Bravo family, she remarked about how much she admired Concepción, describing her as *muy creativa* (very creative) and as a role model.

After DIGESA was closed along with the rest of the Public Agrarian Sector in 1996, Concepción stayed active as one of the two women on the new Consejo Comunitario de Desarrollo (COCODE), headed up by Arturo Bravo. The other was an elderly evangelical woman. Whenever there was an announcement from some institution or another about a project for women in the village, Concepción would sign up and tell others. She attended a number of meetings that were not for projects but for *capacitaciónes,* sometimes walking to the town center or taking a bus to Huehuetenango. She was active in the Huehuetecan Women's Forum, a government-sponsored women's organization, and also went to talks given by the *Defensoria Maya,* by *Asociación* Ceiba, and at least once by the National Coordinator for Guatemalan Widows (CONAVIGUA). Often, she translated between development organizations and village women who only spoke Mam. Concepción was a devout Catholic, active in church organizations, such as the Catholic *Maria Auxiliadora* (Mary Help of Christians). Remembering DIGESA's programs, Concepción mentioned learning how to bake a cake on a *comal* (iron stove top), saying it had been years since she tried it. It reminded me of my mother learning to make macramé plant hangers in the 1970s: a supposedly useful skill acquired but never used.

Economically, Concepción was fairly comfortable relative to her neighbors. She had already inherited from her aged parents some productive coffee land. She had a modest cash income, which was mostly spent on health emergencies. Her decision to adopt an abandoned child, in addition to being unusual, was an expensive choice born out of compassion and perhaps regret at not having children of her own.[16] Because she could not breastfeed, she paid nearly Q50 a week for formula. Like most women in the village, Concepción spent many of her days weaving, mostly *huipiles* (blouses), *cortes* (skirts), *or morrales* (handbags). She would sell some and make others for her nieces, for whom Concepción and her sister were parental figures. This did not make her much money, but Concepción enjoyed it. She was talented and proud of her work. Concepción once started a small weaving cooperative with local women, buying bulk thread with the help of a Peace Corps volunteer, but it did not work out. She complained that local women mistrusted group leaders who hold money and that she had once been accused of theft, making it not worth the trouble.

I first met Concepción at the meeting with the COCODE before asking the village permission to conduct research. At Arturo's suggestion, when I started collecting oral histories, I offered her a job as a translator. She spoke Spanish well and had worked for outside organizations before, and I was eager to learn more about her experience with DIGESA. *"Ella no tiene miedo."* ("She is not afraid.") That would not be the last time I heard that said about her. Beyond those qualifications, she was available and needed the work. Although she did not appear particularly interested in the interviews themselves or overly curious about my research, she quickly grasped the kind of information I wanted and was a quick translator. Lack of interest aside, she was intelligent and insightful, was a good source of news, and had a somewhat irreverent sense of humor.

I got to know her much better after she found out that I was looking for a residence in the village. She offered to fix up an abandoned home in the cluster of houses where her family lived. The house belonged to her brother-in-law, who had since moved to another village. Having hoped for a room in a house at best, I was very happy to have a larger space that would afford me the privacy that I had never quite grown accustomed to losing during fieldwork. I offered a mildly inflated sum for rent and moved in at the end of the week. Over time, I became close with all of the Bravo family and one unrelated neighbor family, a young couple with two young children who lived next door. As fieldwork became more time consuming, I accepted more invitations to eat with the Bravos. I made a point to pitch in on food purchases and, whenever I could, to cook and clean, although my efforts at making tortillas produced more laughter than tortillas. I spent many evenings with the family around the stove processing the day's events. Luckily for me, Concepción was a willing translator of Mam on most evenings.

It struck me as odd that someone as well off, fun, and *capacitada* as Concepción had never married. It was not for lack of opportunities; she had had several boyfriends. She told me that she was once thinking about getting married but that the relationship ended when her boyfriend went to the United States. She had also turned down proposals from two prominent men in her village. One came while she was working for DIGESA, and she told him to wait until that was over, but she never responded to him. The man, a widower, got angry and stopped talking to her. It occurred to me that it would take a special man not to be intimidated by Concepción's level of *capacidad* and her reputation as intelligent and independent. It was also possible she never married because she recognized the freedom she would lose as a wife, who would be expected to stay home, cook, clean, and bear and care for children. She laughed when I asked if this were the case but said it was probably correct. I noticed that many highly capacitated women of her generation, among whom it was less common, were single.

Concepción paid a price for her relative freedom. An incessant joke that circulated soon after I moved into the house near Concepción was that we were bathing together in the *chuj* (steam bath; *temascal* in Spanish). Some claimed to have seen pictures of this fictitious event. I felt bad and hoped these jokes would end, but they never seemed to get old for both men and women, who would still ask and giggle years after I had left the village. These were not the first rumors about her sexuality, which were fueled by her tendency to move independently outside of domestic spaces. It is quite possible that she exercised some sexual freedom, but men's sex lives were rarely similarly criticized. Being *capacitada* was double-edged because to the extent that it expanded a woman's freedom, it exposed her to gendered criticism.

Comparing Concepción's role and status in the community to Juan and Arturo's further elucidated how notions of *capacidad* were gendered.

Women like Concepción could speak in public meetings because of her recognized level of understanding. Men in general, regardless of their *capacidad*, have the presumed right to speak, although men with more *capacidad*—as demonstrated by the male-male conflicts fought in the idiom of *capacidad*—claim more. Concepción, because of her work with DIGESA, was recognized as possessing certain expertise and was seen as a trustworthy conveyor of information.

Yet the *capacidad* of women was only rarely considered equal to that of equally capacitated men. If present at a community meeting, a capacitated man would always assume a leadership role over a woman. Concepción and other women might speak to address a particular point but would cede the floor to the male leader. Even in cases where a woman was seen to be more *capacitada* than many men, her leadership domain was limited to other women in the village. Only men, it seemed, commanded the authority to lead the entire community. These limits were apparent when Jose Antulio Morales included Petrona Lázaro, a Mayan *licenciada* from the town center, on his political team as second *consejal* (councilor). Other men in the organization were furious that they had been passed over and insisted that it would hurt the party to include a woman, whom many did not take seriously. Despite the limitations on *capacidad* imposed by gendered structures of power, it challenged prevailing gender roles and opened new spaces for women's agency in their family and in the community. This promise of freedom and empowerment through increased practical knowledge and skill—in addition to whatever immediate material benefits—no doubt motivated some women's attraction to *capacitación*. Most men remained skeptical of women's new freedoms, although men with *capacidad* were generally more open to women's advancement. *Capacidad* opened some space for individual women within a highly asymmetrical gendered order but left those structures largely intact, especially as men had more access to the means to self-improvement.

Capacidad and Indigeneity

Although attaining *capacidad* was first motivated by a desire not to be treated "like Indians," Sampedranos did not equate development with assimilation or becoming Ladino: an implicit and sometimes explicit goal of state development programs. Modernizers continued to speak indigenous languages, live (mostly) in villages, marry endogamously, and maintain a separate ethnic identity. Even the most capacitated Sampedranos continued to speak Mam, professional Mayan women continued to wear traditional dress, and many *capacitados* continued to live in villages. Intermarriage between Mayas and Ladinos was frowned upon by members of both communities, and somewhat rare. However, this new space for "non-Indian" identity was not at first overtly understood as "indigenous" or "Mayan"; those concepts were not prevalent in rural communities in Huehuetenango and much of the western highlands until later.[17] Native peasant populations had been classified as Indian since colonial times, and Sampedranos previously understood themselves as *Mames* (Mam-speaking) or *naturales* and engaged in a range of behaviors that marked them outwardly as such, such as eating herbs, bathing in *temascales,* and living in villages. Moreover, indigenous villagers shared a language and a wide body of knowledge and practices that most recognized as theirs, usually referred to as *costumbre;* examples include prayer to Mother Earth, purification rituals, participation in village hierarchies, beliefs about saints, and conceptions of community and kinship, medicine, shamanism, and more.[18] Catholic Action's campaign against *costumbre* in the 1970s was effective but never complete.

Sampedranos adopted Mayan-indigenous identities in the flow of struggles against discrimination and efforts for individual and collective advancement, a process aided by a range of institutions and programs espousing conceptions of indigenous rights, culture, and tradition. Among the most influential of these institutions in San Pedro was the Academia de Lenguas Mayas de Guatemala (ALMG), a semiautonomous, state-funded program founded in 1990; guided by a positive conception of indigeneity, its aim was to recover and catalogue local traditions (Fischer 1996, 66–67). In a similar manner to long-standing conceptions of Indianness, new discourses of indigeneity highlighted a distinct identity and cultural traditions, with the key differences being that they assigned a positive value to tradition and recognized indigenous people as subjects of a unique kind of rights rather than as inherently and irrevocably inferior. Some modernizing villagers found jobs running ALMG investigations, interviewing elders about tradition and language, transcribing them for the organization, and leading workshops in indigenous culture and indigenous rights. The ALMG's efforts were soon supplemented by a range of programs and institutions of national and international origin with the explicit mission of promoting indigenous rights.[19] These notions infused grassroots political organizations in San Pedro, whose leaders easily saw their long-standing struggle against Ladino authority, discrimination, and the state through the frame of racism. Ironically, those villagers with the highest levels of *capacidad*, who were the most exposed to national-level politics were the first and most likely to identify explicitly as "indigenous" and "Mayan" and pursue politics under that sign. This is similar to what Kay Warren (1989) found in San Andrés Semetabaj in the 1970s.[20] Some were bilingual instructors or had worked in Maya-centered organizations or in various other NGOs and government programs that promoted Mayan culture. Indeed, Mayan culture was frequently discussed as something that a person could become capacitated in, rather than knowledge that indigenous people inherently possessed.

Although Indian identity dates back to the conquest and a colonial culture that, at various points and in contradictory ways, codified native tradition alongside a process of dispossession and exploitation, "Mayan" identity was a more recent "articulation" (Li 2000) in San Pedro. It emerged at the historical conjuncture of the defeat of the guerrilla movement; genocidal violence and militarization targeting indigenous communities; official recognition of indigenous culture; the long-standing cultural activism of indigenous intellectuals, particularly around the 1992 campaign against celebrations of the 500th anniversary of Columbus's voyage; international discourses of indigenous rights; and other factors.[21] The adoption of discourses and practices of capacity development, rather than provoking "culture loss," furthered this ethnic identification. These events reinforce a view of Mayan identity as a fluid, relational, and heterogeneous process that cannot be understood through the binaries that have historically framed these questions (modern/primitive, urban/rural, indigenous/Ladino).[22]

I observed numerous manifestations of Mayan identity in San Pedro. Of course, indigenous villagers spoke Mam and listened to marimba as they had before the arrival of indigenous rights, but now there were development organizations with Mayan names, and a *Casa de Cultura* was under construction on the edge of town. Some young couples gave their children Mayan names: Ixchel (the Mayan goddess of midwifery and medicine) and Ixmucane (the Mayan goddess of creation) were common choices for girls. I met fewer boys with Mayan names but knew at least one Balam (Jaguar). Some high school students I met had been assigned passages from the *Popul Vuh*, the K'iche' book of life. I found that a vast majority of Maya Sampedranos supported the idea that they had a distinctive culture that merited special rights and protections from the government. And many individuals were investigating and experimenting with indigenous spirituality. One notable case was a retired Ladina teacher and widow who over the course of a relationship with a Mayan teacher from a neighboring town—kind of a public secret—began wearing indigenous *traje* in certain contexts.[23] I once saw her participate in a Mayan solstice ceremony in Zacaleu, an archeological site located near the department capital.

Although such expressions were limited and mostly reflected the proclivities of relatively well-educated and younger residents, indigenous rights were highly salient in party politics given the long-standing Ladino dominance of the town. However, traditional political structures such as the *alcaldes auxiliares,* a body composed of male representatives named in each village, had little authority relative to political parties, their sovereignty limited to improving communication between the village and town and resolving disputes between villagers. Such responsibilities are not insignificant but have little influence over resources or other roles commonly associated with sovereignty. Elected officials hold considerably more sway, and many villagers opt to use the state-linked justice of the peace over communal justice systems. This is distinct from other regions in the highlands, where indigenous identity is more pronounced and where traditional structures of power separate from the state are more firmly grounded and have gained strength since being recognized by the peace accords, bolstering earlier protections in the 1985 constitution.[24]

Although discourses and practices of *capacidad* were hegemonic, very few villagers had completely assimilated to its norms. Beyond lack of access and the way that *capacidad* is an ever-receding horizon, was there something irreducible or antithetical to discourses of *capacidad* that could be seen as an "indigenous" sense of self? Even Felipe Ruíz still constructed his "self" in terms of discourses of development and *capacidad*, if only to invert them. Thinking about this question also leads me back to Pedro Bravo, the person who was seen by his family as "undeveloped," whose unassuming manner was coded as simple backwardness. What Pedro did not do, and what made his difference stand apart from the norm of *capacidad,* was that he did not conceptualize his self as an object he was trying actively to fashion and improve throughout his life span. He did not treat his self as a "work in progress" that he was shaping and cultivating for public circulation and display, like Juan Jiménez or Arturo Bravo. He took pride in his accomplishments as a father and farmer but did not brag like his younger brother. Pedro worked hard to provide for his family and participated in village life, but being a good person for him did not require institutional training. Although he attributed status to highly capacitated people, he rejected the market-oriented individualism characteristic of neoliberal life.

Thinking about Pedro reminded me of something I was told by Gabriel Martínez, a man in his early fifties who was a former catechist, a DIGESA community representative, and a careful thinker who was considered quite *capacitado.* While conversant and confident in the Ladino world, Gabriel described a recoiling from development that he likened to aversion to other sovereign forces that impose their wills on villagers:

> The people here have a way of speaking, very humble, slow, with great respect. Now, the information or news always comes from outside; it comes very hard, from above. It's obligatory. Sometimes the people run away. We feel commanded. This is how the church speaks today, also the political parties. You have to do this and this; you have to do that.

Discourses of *capacidad* encountered alternative ways of conceptualizing the self and social world that limited its adoption. Although Gabriel believed that Mayas should develop and become *capacitados,* he was critical of the violent and absolutist form in which the process was usually presented. He also valued humility and respect as meaningful differences that were being disrespected and pushed aside.

Reflections on *Capacidad*

These examples clarify how *capacidad* had become an important conceptual framework to think about oneself and distinguish among types of persons in rural villages. The common statement: "Before there was no development, but now that is changing" was evidence of this reconfiguration, which was almost universally understood as a hard-won achievement for indigenous people. These categories and implicit narratives of teleological progress became embedded not through blind faith in development but as a result of the changes that these new forms of thought, practices, and technologies made possible. The naturalness and validity of competitive, market-oriented individualism were reinforced through the ways they became useful to people faced with the everyday challenge of navigating economic and social exclusion. The rise of *capacitación* was almost universally invoked by Sampedranos as a path out of racial subordination and economic destitution and toward personal advancement and freedom; the terrain on which this struggle took place was generally taken for granted.

Being *capacitado* meant to be important, knowledgeable, powerful, and unafraid. It connoted one's seriousness as a person; it gave one the right to speak; it was the knowledge that was worth suffering to attain and important to share. Becoming *capacitado,* at least in theory, allowed *indígenas* to be considered equal to Ladinos; it charted a path for collective racial dignity through individual improvement. More training, more certificates, and more money were proof of fundamental equality between the races. Quite practically, it protected Mayas from deception and opened new possibilities for economic and political advancement. It was no longer necessary to humiliate themselves to Ladinos or to fear them. However, as individuals advanced, people with *capacidad* outpaced their neighbors economically and edged them out as leaders; the collective was left behind. General levels of poverty remained unchanged, and social bonds grew weaker as *capacidad* aroused envy and mistrust and significantly increased accusations of dishonesty, egotism, and self-interest.

Capacidad held out the promise of equality while providing a new justification for inequality. Not everyone wanted to become *capacitado* or had the means available to do so, yet this was framed as a universal standard and an individual choice. *Capacidad*'s conflation of intelligence and schooling was a tacit devaluation of knowledge that did not come from institutions—including most "indigenous" forms of knowledge—as well as of individuals who had not been shaped by them: a hostility to ways of being human that were less individualistic and less enterprising. *Capacidad* was also gendered, not only in that it was associated with masculinity and that the means to achieve it were more available to men, but also in that the women who attained it remained subordinate to men of equal or lesser *capacidad*. Everyone was encouraged to evaluate themselves and each other—literally "their selves"—on an individual basis according to this new standard, even though it judged most of them harshly. Ironically, despite its hostility to indigenous ways of being and knowing, *capacidad* played a role in the positive reconceptualization of Mayan identity.

3

The Capacity for Democracy

Transforming Democratic Imaginaries

The Government can respond to the needs of its constituents
only if it is made aware of these needs. Two elements of the
program—expansion of the cooperative movement and group
training activities—will open a way for these needs to be proclaimed
by the alienated and under privileged rural majority. New interest
groups will be able to make demands (more credit, services, better
marketing system, favorable prices, etc.). Politicians seeking rural
support may well link themselves to these rising interest groups
and identify themselves with their demands. The political balance
between urban and rural may well change and be reflected in
changes in political parties and legislatures tending in the direction of
functional democracy.

USAID, CAPITAL ASSISTANCE PAPER, 1970

Remember that in our countries we have lacked political leaders
and if we want to have a real democracy we also need to educate
the youth for the future so that they themselves can make political
decisions that benefit those countries. And the problem is that
farmers [also] need leaders in the local sphere where they can
consider if there is some productive project that they are able to
make that intervention to achieve those processes. Those processes
were the *capacitaciones* of DIGESA.

FORMER DEPARTMENTAL DIRECTOR OF DIGESA (INTERVIEW, 2015)

In 2003 associates of José Antulio Morales, San Pedro's *alcalde* from
1996 to 2003 and the most influential Mayan politician since the extreme
violence of the early 1980s, described themselves as *técnicos políticos*

(political technicians), referring to their ability to run political campaigns. Antulio Morales' coalition was backed by modernizing leaders in each village: men with experience on development committees and on the civil patrols, evangelicals and Catholics, former guerrilla sympathizers and detractors. These individuals understood their democratic expertise in terms of *capacidad,* an elusive and context-specific term that referred broadly to technical ability learned through institutions. *Capacidad* was a manifestation of a "will to improve" (Li 2007b), Amartya Sen's (1999) concept of capability, and a key aim of neoliberal development (Philips and Ilcan 2004). It was also the defining attribute of ideal democratic subjects in San Pedro. *Capacidad* was promoted alongside democratization, and the two were treated as naturally coexistent and mutually reinforcing.

Being a *técnico politico* meant *gestionando* projects and turning them into political support by promising them to various villages in exchange for votes. *Gestionar* means to "manage" or "negotiate," which in this context referred to planning and soliciting projects from state and nonstate institutions. These self-described *técnicos* remained proud of their skills despite having just suffered a catastrophic and unexpected defeat by a rival organization whose leaders, they thought, "lacked *capacidad*" and were affiliated with the FRG. When I asked how this happened, one replied, "*Eso es lo que no entendemos.*" ("This is what we don't understand.") Not only could they not fathom how their neighbors could have voted for Ríos Montt—a notorious mass murderer—they also could not understand how *they* lost to the local FRG candidate, Mariano Díaz, someone they saw as inexperienced and foolish.

How had these individuals become *técnicos* when most of their neighbors had not? In what sense does democratic citizenship require specialized knowledge and technical training? Why in this case had their *capacidad* failed them so miserably? What does this reveal about the effects of neoliberal development on rural grassroots politics and the conditions surrounding Mayan support for the far right?

Chapter 2 explored how discourses of *capacidad* promoted an improvement-oriented, market-savvy individualism in San Pedro. This chapter examines how *capacidad* both articulated and transformed grassroots desires for democracy. Discourses and practices of *capacidad* were introduced as part of a vision of political development and were adopted by certain villagers whose political imaginaries and organizational strategies were shaped as a result. Mayan reappropriation of *capacidad* opened new horizons for indigenous advancement but produced a regulated form of democratic politics predicated on self-discipline, training, and social differentiation. *Capacidad* supplied the human infrastructure for democracy in San Pedro and reorganized the political field during the neoliberal democratic transition in subtle yet consequential ways that undermined historical struggles and thus had troubling continuities with counterinsurgency objectives.

Capacidad challenged racial ideologies, enabled limited individual economic autonomy, empowered indigenous political organizing, and legitimated an indigenous right to govern. It aided in the election of the first indigenous mayor since the 1960s, improving the access to development resources in rural villages. *Capacidad* became the foundational creed for a path to indigenous rights and inclusion through market advancement and municipal politics but steadily chipped away at radical imaginaries by reframing poverty as a result of individual choices, not structures; legitimating interpersonal discrimination; and recasting democracy as private economic advancement and electoral participation *within* a political and economic order built on indigenous dispossession.

Development and Indigenous Politics

An influential strain of post-structuralist anthropology condemns development as a central apparatus of postcolonial governance, a hegemonic discourse and set of institutions and practices based on a primitive/modern binary that extends market rationality, bureaucracy, and state power while eradicating traditional lifeways (Ferguson 1994, Escobar 1995). Ferguson argues that, rather than resolving poverty, development depoliticizes it by erasing the historical power relations that produced it, rendering it as a problem for technical management. Critical anthropologists have further shown that even seemingly progressive development projects often uncritically disseminate discourses and practices of self-help, empowerment, and individual responsibility that foster market-oriented subjects adapted to survive in harsh market conditions without state support.[1] Post-structuralist critics focus on indigenous and subaltern resistance to development and antidevelopmentalist alternatives. Development contains many hidden dangers but can also provide critical resources and strategic advantages for marginalized populations. Antidevelopment critics tend to disregard its diverse forms, its contested and uneven implementation, and the ways that subaltern groups often actively pursue development and adapt it for their own ends.[2] In San Pedro, discourses and programs of *capacidad* enabled modernizing indigenous political organizations to pursue their social and political objectives through market advancement, municipal electoral politics, and village development.

Guatemala's military government and the US Agency for International Development (USAID) promoted development in rural indigenous communities as part of a cold-war counterinsurgency strategy to combat regional instability understood to derive from inequality. In 1970 they launched the Public Agrarian Sector and two five-year national development plans, the stated aim of which was to include "Indian" peasants into national life. Agrarian modernizers disseminated green revolution technologies, new organizational forms, and skills associated with individual market advancement: an assimilationist alternative to revolution. Planners hoped that new seeds, fertilizers, pesticides, and credit would render agrarian reform—the popular objective of revolutionary nationalist movements across the continent—obsolete (Copeland 2012).

USAID wanted "apolitical" cooperatives to aid "nonconfrontational" dialogue between rural indigenous communities and the state as a pressure valve to reduce tensions created by unmet demands.[3] USAID cooperatives were imagined as displacing autonomous, politicized co-ops in remote rural areas. The Rural Cooperative Development Project (RCDP) would extend state authority into highland villages and resolve the "Indian problem" with only minimal modifications to the social order. Rather than "bracketing political economy" (Li 2007b), the RCDP and DIGESA promoted an incremental plan to ameliorate poverty and inequality in Indian communities through hard work and market-oriented advancement.[4]

Program officers for DIGESA, the main institutional manifestation of the RCDP, trained community members to be market subjects. They were encouraged to take loans, to save money, to reinvest, and to calculate the future in terms of risk and reward: habits and dispositions assumed to be lacking yet transmittable through targeted governmental intervention. These programs resembled Catholic development initiatives and existing cooperatives, but they were better organized, with more expert personnel;

a disciplinary pedagogy; funding to support credit, training, extension, and input subsidies; and even modest salaries for village representatives.

DIGESA arrived in San Pedro in 1978, too late to prevent many of the residents from joining the guerrillas, and closed during the extreme violence of the early 1980s, during which time the army viewed *any* rural indigenous organization as a threat.[5] DIGESA reopened after the violence abated and began preparing the ground for a democratic transition that army and economic elites now viewed as inevitable and intended to control through party-led development under continuous militarization.[6] DIGESA was a major purveyor of discourses and practices of *capacidad* focused on scientific and market-oriented agriculture. Local and regional development agents pushed market rationality, new technology, credit, and new seeds and fertilizers. They also disparaged subsistence agriculture and Indian culture while treating historical structural inequalities as inevitable and ignoring the more radical political demands within indigenous communities. Training was administered by local Ladinos who were wholly unaware of the strategic implications of their labors, which were riddled with overtly and implicitly racist and essentialist assumptions, with assimilation to Ladino and North American culture being the unquestioned goal.

As an additional component of these programs, training was provided to villagers who learned how to organize, navigate state institutions, and manage development projects, knowledge that individual leaders applied to planning and executing electoral campaigns. This was in fact a central goal of USAID and DIGESA's directors, whose intention to use agricultural modernization to build rural political leadership in order to strengthen the incremental inclusion of rural communities in the political process is evident in this chapter's epigraphs. This plan required indigenous participation in forms of training that provided a narrow pathway for addressing economic and political exclusion.

Rather than reject development, Sampedranos viewed discourses and practices of individual capacity development and market rationality as extensions of, if not explicit concessions to, their economic and political struggles. Their engagement was similar to David Gow's (2008) conception of "counterdevelopment," by which he means both of a form of "resistance to the state" and a pragmatic, critical reworking of development to strengthen community "demand[s] to be recognized as indigenous and treated as citizens, to become a vital part of the nation" (3). Events in San Pedro reveal the perils of counterdevelopment and counterdemocracy, which constituted central elements in postwar regimes of power.

Many Sampedranos eagerly embraced new technologies, market-oriented pedagogies, and conceptions of *capacidad,* and underwent difficult processes of self-discipline, often taking great personal risks because they viewed development as a way out of economic marginalization and discrimination. Indigenous leaders saw in *capacidad* an alternative to annual migrations to coastal plantations and wage labor for local Ladino bosses, both of which were highly exploitative (Copeland 2015b). Where many Ladinos feared and resisted what they viewed as a threat to the natural order and to a cheap labor supply they took as their right, indigenous leaders saw a path to dignity and equality through hard work and personal transformation. Modernizing villagers embraced *capacidad* and market rationality as a way to "stop being Indians," to escape a devalued identity category, a path that remained open after the violent repression of more-radical alternatives.

By the 1990s, indigenous individuals with *capacidad* ran village development committees, worked for development agencies, and ran for office, and there were a growing number of indigenous professionals, teachers, and successful small business owners. Most but not all of these individuals lived in the town center or in nearby villages. In the villages, many individuals had gotten ahead through commercial agriculture (mainly coffee) and through business, although even more had not. In the process, villagers resignified *capacidad* and applied it to their own ends, but rather than subvert development planners' designs from within, Sampedrano appropriations of *capacidad* completed them, at least in part. Through the successful adoption of development, *capacidad* exacerbated socioeconomic differentiation, reoriented revolutionary imaginaries, and limited the horizons of Mayan advancement to individual *superación* and local political power within a neocolonial political and economic order.

Democratic Organizing after *La Violencia*

After 1983, as the most horrific chapter of the war was drawing to a close, a group of indigenous leaders from villages near the town center formed a new organization in order to acquire development projects and to elect an indigenous *alcalde*. Antulio Morales' organization was led by development-minded villager headmen, both guerrilla opponents and sympathizers who had set aside differences under the civil patrols and had the trust of the majority of villagers. Despite this mixed composition, Antulio Morales told me that "the idea to have a campaign for mayor came from the guerrillas—to end the discrimination." The organization focused primarily on rampant discrimination in the distribution of municipal development resources. In the 1970s, villages had formed development committees in hopes of getting potable water, schools, and roads but found little support. In the aftermath of the extreme violence, the army put forth security and development initiatives, focusing on food assistance, road building, and sometimes village school building, but these efforts were sporadic and short term.[7]

In 1985 the government instituted the 8 percent municipal tax, the funds from which were to be used to finance public works projects. These funds were monopolized by Ladino *alcaldes* and directed to the Ladino-dominated urban center. The new indigenous political organization eyed these funds as a way to raise the standard of living in rural villages where the need was more urgent. An opportunity arose when representatives of the conservative National Advancement Party (PAN) approached the organization in 1988, offering to finance a mayoral campaign and promising projects for the indigenous communities. However, one of Antulio Morales' lieutenants explained that there was always a condition:

> When we entered into PAN, they gave us opportunities for projects; the only thing was that they told us that we couldn't participate in or help social movements, like the URNG or CUC. They made this very clear. If we were going to help groups like the URNG, there would be no projects. We were taking advantage of them, but they were also taking advantage of us.

Convinced of the ineffectiveness of popular movements, and eager to win elections and begin development, they accepted these terms. However, the leaders of the organization, including Antulio Morales, were afraid to run.

Pedro Ramírez was a large and gregarious villager who become the first indigenous candidate for *alcalde* after the extreme violence. After initial support, Ladinos began a smear campaign, calling Ramírez and his allies guerrillas. Ramírez lost to a Ladino who had been the first head of the civil patrollers in San Pedro. Frustrated but determined, the group continued in the next round, in 1993; this time their candidate was Natanael Aguilar, a teacher from the village of Canoguitas, still the only indigenous contender and also with the PAN. By then, there was a ceasefire and preliminary peace agreements were being negotiated, making it harder to mount a credible scare campaign against Aguilar, who, in a shock to town Ladinos, won by a landslide. By then the organization had mushroomed into a broad base of indigenous leaders in various communities near the town center. With José Antulio Morales as his first councilor on an all-indigenous team, Aguilar began to work. As promised, he sent numerous projects to communities that had supported him and was reelected after a two-year term, this time with the center-right Democratic Union.

According to Antulio Morales and many others, Aguilar's decision to seek a third term as *alcalde* created a rift, violating the agreement of the group to serve only two terms each. Aguilar argued that the first term was only two years and that the *alcaldía* term had been extended to four years only for his second period, justifying a third term. Nonetheless, Morales, who had spent more time in the municipal building than Aguilar, who resided in Huehuetenango, split off and became the recognized leader of the growing organization. Morales defeated Aguilar in the next election.

Morales had the good fortune of being *alcalde* at a time when international development funds earmarked for postwar reconstruction in war-torn indigenous communities poured into Guatemala. The government had established the Social Investment Fund (FIS), the Indigenous Development Fund of Guatemala (FODIGUA), and the Secretary General of National Planning (SEGEPLAN), among other national groups involved in infrastructural development. Internationally administered funds came in from Community Development for Peace (DECOPAZ) and the National Peace Fund (FONAPAZ) and various other groups. These programs supplemented the funds the *alcalde* had at his disposal from the municipal tax, which by then had risen to 10 percent.

Antulio Morales won the 1998 elections, this time against six other indigenous candidates and more than ten parties. Several Ladinos had joined Morales' team, including some town civil patrol leaders. By the time his second term ended, Morales had transformed the physical landscape: in eight years he had helped with more than seventy infrastructural projects, many of them large, at least one in each *aldea* and several in the town center, most notably a new municipal building. These accomplishments represented a dramatic change in the distribution of municipal resources and the balance of power between the mostly indigenous rural villagers and primarily Ladino townspeople.

In the 2003 campaign, Morales, keeping with the two-term agreement, left the mayoral race and joined the Center for Social Action (CASA), an indigenous political party headed up by Rigoberto Quemé Chay, the then-*alcalde* of Quetzaltenango, Guatemala's second-largest city and the indigenous capital. Morales wanted to be a *diputado* (congressman), and CASA gave him the chance. He also liked CASA because it was fielding an indigenous candidate for president. When Queme Chay left CASA over internal divisions, the party collapsed, and Morales and his followers—he had helped pick his replacement mayoral candidate—joined the progressive New Nation Alternative (ANN), which Morales described as the "sister party" to CASA, and which had offered him a spot as a *diputado*. The election went badly for Morales. The FRG won locally, and he lost his bid for *diputado*.[8] In October 2004 he died in a accident on the Inter-American Highway during my fieldwork, prompting wide-ranging reflection on his political career and its legacy.

With the rural development plans, USAID collaborated with the Guatemalan government to empower a modernizing indigenous leadership with the skills, confidence, and encouragement to navigate state institutions for development projects and to run political campaigns, and whose conception of advancement and well-being was more consistent with neocolonial inequality and free markets.[9] In the late 1990s in San Pedro, it seemed that the dream of USAID planners had finally materialized. Had it really? What political vision were these Mayas putting into practice? And why did it fall apart?

Capacidad, Leadership, and Electoral Politics

Opposition to DIGESA from the army, from some Ladinos, and even from villagers worried about army reprisals initially limited participation in the program. However, many early opponents of the program changed their tune when DIGESA reopened in 1984, by which time the army was less hostile toward development because the guerrillas had been largely defeated and villagers were organized into civil patrols. Despite heightened interest, access was extremely limited as state investments in subsidies, credit, and extension remained quite modest.[10] Even decades later, only a small percentage of villagers, mostly but not exclusively men, were recognized as having attained *capacidad*. Despite uneven access, by the late 1980s, developmentalist leaders had converged with the civil patrols, and *capacidad* had become a necessary qualification for community leadership.

Under the *cofradía* system, men in the village occupied leadership positions for a year term, and almost everyone interested served at least once. Elders had a higher status than younger men, and a council of elders made decisions that applied to the entire village. Since the disruption of *cofradía* authority and ancestor worship by the actions of the Catholic Church, village leadership positions "depended neither on age nor on service in the village hierarchies" (Brintnall 1979, 147). Younger male villagers emerged as leaders. Writing about Aguacatán, Brintnall was unclear what was to replace the vacuum created by the fall of the hierarchies.[11] He focuses on schools, agricultural cooperatives, political parties, and peasant leagues as new sources of community authority, each with their local correlative affiliate: the bilingual educator, the catechist, the labor organizer, and the party representative. Village authority was linked to these outside groups and institutions. The war soon shut down many of these spaces in San Pedro, targeting bilingual educators, catechists, labor organizers, and politically active Mayas. All that remained were the leaders of new development committees, the civil patrol, and, after 1985, party leaders—who were frequently the same men.

The reorganization of village authority into development and the civil patrol system provided a framework for participating villagers to establish a set of seemingly neutral standards for community leadership organized around *capacidad*. The PAC imbued these new norms with a compulsory tenor. When I asked what he thought about the civil patrol system, Arturo Bravo explained:

> For a part, it was always necessary. There were always people who took advantage [of the situation] in that time. Many people don't want to help

the community. But when the patrollers were there, that's when all of the people got together. Whoever did not show up, commits a crime or gets punished. All of the people got more organized. There was more respect in the entire community. Whatever happens, the people are there united. But there was a bad side to the patrols too. We always lost a lot of time. Always, even to our crops. All work was left abandoned.[12]

The primary reason for the ascendance of *capacidad* as a norm for leadership was because DIGESA program leaders received a form of training that would prove incredibly important in terms of access to resources in the early post-violence years. Bravo explained that "DIGESA didn't have [infrastructural projects], but they always oriented us in other meetings, how to get them. [They would tell us] 'This institution helps with such and such.' We learned how to gain projects." Creating political leaders was a central program objective. Negotiating development projects with the state, although slow and frustrating, gave villagers faith in the postrevolutionary generation of leaders, whose claim to political authority consisted primarily in their role as development brokers. Certain individuals gained reputations for their ability to successfully navigate institutions and bring projects to the villages. The few leaders trained by DIGESA since the late 1970s gained a particular advantage in this regard. As state resources became available, *capacidad* and leadership were synonymous.

For several decades, Sampedranos had imagined municipal politics as an interethnic competition for control of town resources and institutions. As new decentralization laws investing *alcaldes* with authority over the distribution of the 8 percent municipal tax raised the stakes, *capacidad* became a central weapon in the efforts to elect an indigenous mayor. Beyond training individuals to find projects, *capacidad*'s insistence on a neutral scale of evaluation gave moral force to Mayan desires to govern, provided that candidates had adequate preparation. Rigoberto, a high-school-educated Maya, a professional, and a high-ranking member of Antulio Morales' political coalition who had also run for office, explained:

Before there wasn't a lot of *capacitación*. Before, indigenous people were more discriminated against. Before in San Pedro, there were only Ladinos. Natanael was the first indigenous person. Afterwards José Antulio, then Mariano, so the people are preparing themselves. Now, the majority of indigenous people have studied. There are doctors. There are more educated people. Year after year there are more people who have studied. I have analyzed this. Ladinos have another form, another culture to live. Ladinos, they are, well, now not so much, but it still exists . . . they think that they are more able . . . that they are the ones that . . . but it's not that way. They always think they are better than the rest. But it's not true.

Rigoberto imagined *capacidad* as steadily eroding the ability gap between indigenous and Ladino. After the defeat of the guerrillas, Mayas used this discourse, which was previously used to justify their marginalization, and expanded it into a moral argument against continued exclusive Ladino control. The idea shared among Maya Sampedranos was that Mayas who were educated deserved the right to govern, the same as Ladinos, especially given that Ladinos had almost always controlled town politics, even when indigenous men had won the elections.[13] *Capacidad* allowed them to "be recognized as indigenous, and be treated as citizens" (Gow 2008, 3).

The idea of equality through *capacidad* resonated with prevalent religious discourses—evangelical as well as Catholic—that insisted on universal brotherhood. It could not simply be any indigenous person, however, because not everyone possessed *capacidad*; a qualified candidate, regardless of race, had to have the technical capacity to govern. *Capacidad* provided a color-blind method of assessing legitimate authority. The more *capacidad* they received, the more Mayan leaders were emboldened. For most, however, this discourse of equality applied exclusively to men; a woman (Maya or Ladina) has never run for *alcalde,* and town politics remains a hostile terrain for women. However, Antulio Morales used the logic of *capacidad* to justify women's participation in town politics, despite criticisms from his own followers.

In 2003 Pedro Ramírez, the former mayoral candidate, worked as a municipal policeman, a position he had held since his friend Antulio Morales was *alcalde*. When I asked him why he decided to run for office, he began by describing his involvement in DIGESA's youth-oriented 4-S program (like 4-H in the United States) when he was fifteen. Later on, he established leadership credentials by helping locate funds for a road project. When political parties began looking for indigenous candidates, they looked for organized groups. Pedro explained that he did not initially want to run because he felt he lacked experience, and the group searched for an indigenous candidate with sufficient *capacidad*. José Antulio Morales and Natanael Aguilar, while more trained, were afraid they would be denounced as guerrillas. So Pedro Ramírez volunteered. It seems clear that the increased level of *capacidad* among the organization's members was helping to reduce their fear. After Ramírez lost, the group chose Aguilar as the next candidate because he was an elementary school teacher; they hoped the villagers would trust an indigenous professional.

José Antulio Morales—the most prominent Sampedrano politician of the 1980s and 1990s—provides an excellent illustration of the political significance of *capacidad*. Antulio Morales was a skilled orator and political operator who had earned a high school degree, socialized with party elites, maintained investments, and owned residences in San Pedro and the department capital. Before he entered politics, Antulio Morales was considered without question the most *capacitado* individual in his village. He had participated in DIGESA's 4-S program and had a sixth-grade education—a rare accomplishment for his generation—and later finished high school while working in the *municipio* with Aguilar. In his mid-twenties, at the prompting of Arturo Ramírez, an indigenous leader from the 1960s and 1970s, he trained as a *promotor sociale* (social promoter) at Rafael Landívar University in Huehuetenango.

Politics was José Antulio Morales' talent and passion, and friends and foes alike remember how he astutely tailored appeals to woo prominent and influential supporters. A venerable war widow told me that Antulio Morales promised to build a statue of her deceased husband in the park. She was delighted that he would finally get the public recognition she thought he deserved, and she also felt used when Antulio Morales never delivered.[14] He told Juan Jiménez, the aspiring papaya farmer, to "forget about coffee. Get coffee out of your head," promising that if he won he would send an agronomist to the village to figure out what exotic nontraditional export crops would flourish at Juan's precise elevation and soil type. Juan joined the campaign, but the agronomist never materialized, a fact that still perturbed him months later.

Although official definitions of *capacidad* were assimilationist, members of Antulio Morales' coalition redefined the term to include specific indigenous concerns. Another coalition member, a middle-aged Mayan man named Geraldo, a former guerrilla sympathizer turned civil patrol leader, explained an interesting difference between the way that Mayan activists and

Ladinos defined *capacidad*: "For me it is important, because he dominates two languages. They give their speeches in Spanish and then in Mam. The people understand. Indigenous people are simpler, they are more humble. More . . . how can I say it? They have more patience to work with the people." Geraldo redefined political *capacidad* as including the ability to speak a Mayan language and possession of an interethnic sensitivity. The *alcalde* has to be able to speak to and serve two cultures on their own terms, which requires a special understanding and patience to understand a difference that Geraldo was at a loss to put into words. One must also know how to deal with Ladinos, who are assumed to be more clever and arrogant.

Valuing this type of sensibility in a public official exemplifies a Maya redefinition not only of *capacidad* but also of what constitutes legitimate government. Geraldo was not saying that only indigenous people should hold office; Ladinos could also conceivably possess these abilities. Geraldo was pointing to the reality that no Ladino in local politics met this standard. This revised norm recognized and satisfied demands for equality—anyone can be *alcalde*—and difference—an *alcalde* has to recognize the needs of citizens whose differences are meaningful.

Poststructuralist development critics argue that discourses like *capacidad* posit a gap between "developed" and "underdeveloped" that can never be surpassed; the subaltern will eternally be "underdeveloped," always needing to "catch up."[15] Li sees a fundamental contradiction in that "programs of development designed to reduce the distance between trustees and deficient subjects reinscribe the boundary that places them on opposite sides of an unbridgeable divide" (2007b, 31). Nevertheless, this gap was bridged at least momentarily in practice in San Pedro when indigenous leaders seized on the notion of *capacidad* using their own "moral imagination" (Gow 2008) to advance their collective struggles for political and cultural equality with Ladinos and to pursue economic advancement. But *capacidad* reorganized local conceptions of advancement and had unintended effects on political imaginaries and organizational forms.

The Privatization of Well-Being

One of the most significant effects of the rising salience of discourses of *capacitación* and *superación* involved how villagers conceptualized

well-being and its attainment. Romanticized images of historically har-
moniously and unchanging Mayan villages overlook heterogeneity and long
histories of conflict and change. But it remains true that communal land
tenure and the *cofradía* system, combined with the general absence of
opportunity, held socioeconomic differentiation in indigenous communities to a minimum. Life was more mutual, egalitarian, and interdependent,
and well-being was understood in terms of maintaining reciprocity, balance, respect, and protection from external forces, not individual improvement or advancement. Politics in the mid-twentieth century reflected a
rise of individualism balanced with emphasis on collective well-being and
focused on redistributive justice and social democracy. State terror aimed
to destroy redistributive movements and reduce freedom to market spaces
(Grandin and Klein 2011).

Individual capacity development was central to habituating rural indigenous political subjects to this restricted model of cold-war freedom. It
trained villagers engaged or invested in collective struggles for well-being
to redirect their struggles for advancement through the terms of individual
market activity and party politics. A small but visible number of villagers
took DIGESA's (and subsequent groups') training to heart; they began to
understand themselves and their well-being in new ways. They took loans,
diversified production, bought more land, grew cash crops, and reinvested
profits. Arturo Bravo explained that "no one got rich, but there were your
centavitos, little by little." Some failed, but many found success, not out
of poverty all at once or at all, but as a buffer from indifferent market
forces. Rising coffee prices and the relatively inexpensive cost of land and
chemical inputs further aided upward mobility. A growing number of
indigenous youths graduated from high school and became teachers with
modest salaries.

An important aspect of the shift to reconceptualize economic well-being
as a private responsibility of individuals and families through market activity was the manner in which Sampedranos came to talk about the causes
of and the solutions to poverty and social stratification. In the 1970s, discourses of development in the autonomous cooperatives and in the guerrilla movement emphasized individual hard work, new technology, and
education but also treated material redistribution—especially land and
state services—as a prerequisite for economic well-being. Individuals *and*
collectives were subjects of development. DIGESA's programs and those

of subsequent organizations taught villagers that well-being was achieved by individual farmers using chemical inputs and training, calculating the optimal combination of inputs and crops to maximize yield on their parcel. In San Pedro the primary mechanisms for wealth redistribution and risk sharing were private generosity among extended family at weddings and funerals or during medical and economic catastrophe.[16] Farmers were encouraged to critically assess their individual and family choices and their outcomes. NGOs that received public funding for service provision after state privatization were prohibited from discussing politics, such as the historical causes of poverty, or criticizing the government.

This framework shaped Sampedranos' attitudes toward one another, their attitudes about inequality, and their actual agricultural practices. Mayas used notions of development, and especially *capacidad*, in numerous ways to blame other individuals and themselves for their own poverty: failing to diversify their crops; planting corn, not coffee; failing to save, or spending unwisely, especially on alcohol; having too many children; failing to send their children to school; not wanting to take loans and investment; failing to take advantage of development programs; burning their *milpa* (as a fertilization technique); not wanting to apply chemical inputs; being lazy; "not wanting to develop"; failing to plan. These faults were frequently attributed to adherence to backward cultural practices rather than as being seen as structurally inevitable in situations where more than a third of residents lived in extreme poverty. Moreover, discussions of shared economic struggle were nonexistent; people developed for themselves and their families.

The extent to which this kind of thinking penetrated everyday relationships between villagers—which were increasingly marked by class domination and subordination—became clear on an afternoon I spent with a young married couple, Santos Bravo and Elvira Mendez. Santos was handsome and was well off by community standards; he owned one of only four trucks in his village and earned decent money running *fletes* (freight runs) for other villagers. He played in the band for the Catholic church and was director of the potable water committee. Although Santos mostly kept out of party politics, his eldest brother was a high-ranking member of Antulio Morales' coalition. Elvira was a bright, attractive woman from the same village and an excellent weaver who hailed from a large family of moderate means.

In response to my request for an interview, they invited me to visit their coffee field in a nearby *aldea*. After walking for about an hour, down the valley and up the other side, we arrived. Santos proudly showed me their coffee plants, saying that he had nearly thirteen *cuerdas*. Many villagers had only one or two, some had none, and a few had dozens. It was all chemical coffee, not organic, he said, and he explained that he was able to get between two and three *quintales per cuerda* annually, much better than average. "This is good land," he assured me. Then, somewhat suddenly as we were admiring their plants, Santos seemed angry or annoyed, and he walked to the door of a small, dilapidated adobe house fifteen meters away. Upon entering, a smoldering fire signaled that whoever was staying there had been around recently. He became upset and spoke in an annoyed tone to Elvira in Mam, apparently not wanting to involve me in the matter. We then left the house and began to pick fruit, which instead of the interview was the point of the trip for Santos and Elvira. We gathered nearly 20 pounds of *limones mandarinas* (mandarin limes), knocking the pale-yellow fruit out of the tree with a long stick.

As we were finishing, a stern, deep voice bellowed from behind some nearby trees in Spanish, "Who gave the order to pick fruit?" Santos jumped out of the tree and identified himself as the owner of the land. The voice was Esteban's, trying to sound intimidating. Santos had hired Esteban to live in the house, protect his land, and to work as his *mozo* (peon). Esteban was defending Santos's fruit. Esteban was about forty years old and very poor. He had several missing teeth, his clothes were tattered and stained, his hair was disheveled and unwashed, and he was very thin. The contrast to the well-kempt and healthy Santos and Elvira was stark. Right away, Santos began to lecture Esteban in Mam. Listening closely, I understood some of what Santos was saying, mostly Spanish words: *"No me gusta"* ("I don't like it") and, in Mam, *"At puac"* ("There is money"). Esteban did not concede it easily. He repeated the phrase *"Min ti puac"* ("There is no money") several times and, in Spanish, *"No me alcanza"* ("It doesn't last me"). This interaction lasted about five minutes. Santos listened for several long moments to Esteban's concerns but never wavered. Esteban finally conceded.

Later that evening, when I asked Santos what had happened, he explained that Esteban was an alcoholic and that they let him live in the house because he was poor and they felt sorry for his wife and child.

However, the expectation was that he would work—not just guard the property—in exchange for the use of the house and a small payment. But he did not do very much. Santos wanted to ask Esteban to leave the house today because work was not getting done. He was also angry that Esteban yelled insulting things to Santos and to his parents when he got drunk and also spread rumors that Santos did not pay him for his work.

Esteban and Santos occupied antagonistic class positions, a reflection of the ways in which capitalist relations had taken hold among indigenous villages, in the sense that some owned land and hired the labor of others who sold their labor for a wage (Li 2014; Copeland 2015a).[17] More than an interpersonal conflict, this situation showcased local frustrations emerging around growing class divisions among indigenous villagers, some who had gotten ahead and some who had not, and had perhaps fallen further behind, as well as the ways that class divisions are normalized. Local perceptions of this situation were likewise bifurcated (at least), although interpretive tendencies did not necessarily follow along class lines. The next week, I asked Esteban his perspective on that event. He explained:

> Santos got angry because I hadn't done all the work. But Santos only pays me Q10 a day, and he wants me to work every day. He only pays ten because I live in his house. But the money is not enough for me. Corn is expensive. Sugar is expensive. There is no food for my family. I don't have any *milpa*. I don't have any other place to live. Santos says that there's money, but there is not. I don't know what to do. There is no work here. And how am I going to work elsewhere when he wants me to work for him every day? It's hard. [long pause]. Is there work in the United States? I'm thinking about going because here there is no *chanca* [opportunity].

Later in the conversation, Esteban asked if it was true that he needed a set of false teeth to fit in in the United States, self-conscious about his snaggle-tooth smile. In Esteban's view, he would still be very poor no matter how hard he worked, knowledge that gave him little incentive to follow Santos' advice. Instead of encouragement, it left him bitter, and he expressed anger when he was drunk. Perspectives like Esteban's, which pessimistically recognized structural limitations to advancement, were generally excluded from serious public discourse, which optimistically championed individual initiative and blamed failure on individual choices.

At the same time that norms for *capacidad* were becoming crucial to village leadership, they were underwriting discrimination against people who were seen as less *capacitados* or as not wanting to develop. Carlos Ruíz was a teacher who worked on a contract basis. He was thirty-three in 2004, married with a young child. We met at his new house, one small room with fresh adobe and white pine. Although it was *"muy humilde"* ("very humble"), he was proud to have built it on his salary. He told me that friends and followers of José Antulio Morales had criticized his father, Rodrigo, the family patriarch, for being poor and uneducated. Carlos talked about life before schools:

> Before there were people whom although they had not gone to school, but still more or less knew a little. Plenty. But now education is a great advantage. . . . I see a lot of illiterate people. If you give them a piece of paper in the hand, they can't read it. This means a cloth is blinding their eyes.

Carlos recognized the importance of education:

> Sometimes there are insults. I realized because of my father. Before, before, he was very poor. He didn't have any possibilities to buy something for the week or to dress us, his children. [They would say] Don Rodrigo is ignorant; he's an Indio. That word already died. Yes, it was used between families. [He] gave this some thought. "My children are not going to be like me." Through the insult, my father began to analyze. [Rodrigo said,] "Thank you for making fun of me. This is going to be an idea for me, an experience."

These stories exemplify how discourses of development recoded individual economic differences and misfortune as an individual failure. I was taken aback when Carlos discussed villagers using the racial slur *"Indio"* to talk about their own neighbors. He explained that the word became prevalent in the 1980s and was discarded after the peace accords.[18] Apparently, the recent emphasis on human rights enshrined in the accords and elsewhere precipitated a rethinking of local discrimination. He continued:

> Let's go for the constitution of the Republic. One person cannot be less than another. Many times there is ridicule or discrimination. But if we go with the law, the person has value. Some people always say, "You don't have *capacidad;* you have no schooling." But for me this is illogical. It's not good to say to a person that [they] don't matter. It's very illogical.

Was the category gone, or did it continue to operate in a disguised way through terms such as *capacidad,* which marked as "Indian" people who lacked or refused *capacidad*? *Capacidad* created a path for Mayas to become equal with Ladinos provided that they adjusted to the norm, while at the same time legitimating discrimination against the majority of indigenous people who did not. Significantly, neither Carlos nor his father disputed the value of *capacidad,* only the extent to which it was used to devalue others. The elimination of "Indio" from the local lexicon did not prevent discrimination against their family; they took discrimination to heart as an incitement to personal and familial improvement.

Eroding Radical Imaginaries

Although many Sampedranos clearly understood that their poverty was related to historical dispossession and ongoing discrimination, capacity development offered a new way of thinking about the origins of poverty and inequality and paths to well-being within existing structures. These individualizing explanations diverged markedly from the direct confrontation with social hierarchies prescribed by the revolutionary narrative. Sometimes this divergence took place in individual minds. Juan Jiménez once said that the people were poor and the country so unequal because "the rich want it that way" but quickly added, "They [poor people] don't know how to work."

In addition to fueling victim blaming, the lens of *capacidad* jaundiced memories of local participation in the guerrilla, which Fernando Bravo, a leader in Antulio Morales's coalition, attributed to

the ignorance of the people. Because the people were not learned. For example, we, in our family, we analyzed it thoroughly. Because it is not simply deciding on a thing. For example, if someone comes right now, I can listen, but I'm going to ask for their identification, where they come from, what institution, what it is that they want.

Likewise, when the guerrillas visit a family and start telling them "Look, *señores,* we're the guerrilla army of the poor. We are going to give you land. We're going to take it away from the rich and give it to you as a gift. Don't you want that? We want you to help us, to give us food, clothes, or a place to stay." It sounds nice, right? It's the same if someone comes who wants to give a *capacitación* to the people. A coffee expert, for example. The people say, "We don't want *capacitación*." But if he says, I come on behalf of a bank, or a company, or a business and there's money for loans, credit, then the people come. Worse if there's no guarantee [of repayment]. The people come quickly. They don't analyze . . . we don't analyze. That's how it happened before. I have analyzed it thoroughly. The people listened to the guerrillas out of ignorance. They offered and offered. It's the same as a candidate. I'm going to give you something, a *lamina* [corrugated tin roofing]. And then nothing comes. The army had a political objective, and so did the guerrillas. They were offering. And for that reason the people went to them. Then when the army came, the situation changed. There was war. So, more for ignorance, they didn't understand how it was, how it is, what results will follow.

It sounds good. A person gets to talking with his wife, between friends: "Hey, let's go with them. They're going to give us land. They're going to take it from the *finqueros*, and they're going to give it to us." This was the main part of the problem. The people aligned with the guerrillas to help, but they didn't know what would happen afterward.

Instead of recognizing revolutionary demands as legitimate or affirming indigenous investments in them, Fernando thinks that they were too good to be true and that Mayas had been duped into believing because they were ignorant, just as they continued to be duped by political parties or development agents. *Capacidad* thus reinforced fatalism about the revolution originally inscribed by state violence by framing the movement as immature and unsophisticated. Unlike revolutionary fantasies, development produced something concrete, but it involved hard work, which "ignorant" people avoided, or so it was said.

Discourses and practices of *capacidad* and the narratives of *superación* they support permeated thinking about political alternatives for the post-1983 generation of Mayan leaders. When José Antulio Morales died, the entire village, even some of his most bitter political enemies, mourned: "There was no one else like Chepe." On the day before the funeral, I met with Mateo, one of his closest friends, who was just back from two years in the United States, where he had saved a reasonable sum working landscape and construction. Our conversation that evening ranged from his thoughts about work in the United States, to the limits to Maya-Ladino relationships, to Chepe's political dream:

> Chepe worried a lot about education. [Pretending to be Antulio:] "Let there be more Mayan professionals!" That was his goal. He would speak of the

year 2010, when there would be more professionals than now. His people were, for the majority, *gente campesina* (peasant people), but with experience, with preparation—the entire group was *superado!*—and they also had professionals participating. . . . His goal was that there was *superación* in San Pedro Necta and in all of Huehuetenango.

This was not idle political rhetoric; Chepe preached education and individual capacity building as the ideal route to Mayan advancement. He believed in *superación*, which he himself had accomplished. For Chepe, as for many other Mayan professionals of his generation, personal development and *superación* overshadowed prior interest in revolutionary politics, especially in the wake of extreme state violence.

Discourses of *capacidad* influenced indigenous leaders' perceptions of leftist organizations long after the latter became legal. Antulio Morales criticized the URNG because it did not offer him a post as a mayoral candidate, or later as a *diputado*. He complained that the URNG favored ex-combatants and neither recognized nor appreciated the *capacidad* he had accrued over many years in the *alcaldía*. On a deeper level, however, for some of San Pedro's most influential and successful indigenous leaders, development made revolutionary politics seem unnecessary. Revolution was antithetical to *capacidad* and redundant. What is more, they believed that revolution was impossible and that development could produce tangible results in people's lives. I met more than a few prosperous farmers who saw genuine opportunity in free trade agreements for nontraditional crops.[19]

In addition to the other ways that notions of *capacidad* shifted political reflection away from structural reform, the concept was deployed to explain and present a technical solution to problematic voting patterns. Reflecting on his recent defeat by the FRG, but speaking more generally, the well-educated Fernando attributed the deficiencies of democratic politics to a lack of *capacidad*:

If the people think it through. If the government were to worry about the people, and trained them about what it means to vote. Perhaps things could be fixed. It would be great if the government came in to explain what voting is. If the Tribuno Supremo Electoral put more people to work, then yes. But what happens? They send a few in the months just before the elections. Only in the closest areas. And so the people always vote for personal interest.

Fernando suggested that people should be trained to vote for candidates with plans and *capacidad* rather than for personal interest. He depicted Mayas as democratic novices who do not understand voting, much less have the ability to distinguish between candidates and political platforms; they need training. When a candidate dropped out because he was tired of lying about projects, he ceded his slot to Fernando, who made many false promises but lost anyway. Now he longed for a campaign that focused on *capacidad,* which would give him an edge.

This is the same point of view shared by many international NGOs and the Guatemalan left, whose organizations give *capacitaciones* and *talleres* (workshops) on *el voto consciente* (informed voting), which villagers might find helpful but are tainted by images of gullible villagers believing in lies and mindlessly stuffing ballots into boxes.[20] This perspective on voting, as much as voting behaviors themselves, is an element of emerging democratic sensibilities in a society where free and open elections were recent innovations, among a people who have historically been excluded from citizenship and for whom electoral politics and procedures were still relatively alien.[21] The problem with attributing party alignments to ignorance is that it obscures the myriad constraints on indigenous agency in electoral politics that make such training irrelevant and confound any easy external determination of supposedly objective political interests.

Limits of *Capacidad*

Capacidad did not deliver collective advancement in the way that many Mayan Sampedranos had hoped; its effects were simply overwhelmed by structural forces. The vast majority of people remained untrained, market access and economic success were unevenly distributed, and unemployment was rampant. The global decline in coffee prices that started in 1989 persisted for most of two decades, pushed many farmers into bankruptcy, and forced others to sell land to pay back loans. Families lost meager savings for medical emergencies or for natural disasters that destroyed homes and crops. Furthermore, subsistence farming was threatened by a lack of fertile land, rising costs and decreased effectiveness of chemical inputs, the closure of state extension programs, and declining fertilizer subsidies. Although some Guatemalans successfully adopted nontraditional agricultural export (NTX) crops or found work in *maquilas* or in tourism, many were economically the same or worse off than before.[22] I heard more than a handful of stories of farmers, who, overcome with debt and desperation, had attempted suicide by drinking Gramoxone, a Paraquat-based herbicide. Even relatively successful small producers had trouble breaking into monopolized markets, particularly after the privatization of public-sector agrarian programs. What seemed like an entire generation of young professionals and wage laborers migrated north to look for work in the 2000s. Some sent remittances to their families, but many did not.[23] Cuts in state services and subsidies—already bare bones—raised prices for basic goods, especially electricity. Nevertheless, as economic inequalities widened alongside the implementation of neoliberal reforms in the 1990s and 2000s, they came to be understood less as an inevitable feature of a political order founded on indigenous dispossession and exploitation and more as an index of individual effort and *capacidad* against a market reality whose existence and pressures were taken for granted.

Not surprisingly, there was significant overlap between economic success and political power; *capacidad* fostered a local indigenous leadership stratum. *Capacidad* did more than train individuals to become agents of their own self-improvement; it also created a new hierarchy of value used to discriminate between types of subjects, and it enshrined the individual as the privileged site of agency in economic and political life. As O'Neill (2010) argues about evangelical Christianity in Guatemala City, it presented private, individual transformations as the mechanism to change society. It departed from revolutionary conceptions that viewed the dissolution of the feudal plantation economy and imperialism as preconditions for democracy. On the contrary, *capacidad* was introduced to safeguard the existing order, to deepen its cultural roots by opening a path to access material benefits of citizenship through the diffusion of disciplinary market norms and outlooks. *Capacidad* reinforced the privatization of social life and politics and rationalized structures of extreme racial inequality, even as it stimulated interest in indigenous rights.

Benson, Fischer, and Thomas (2008) argue that discourses about crime which blame individuals rather than social causes and prescribe a hard-line response reveal the extent to which Guatemala's violent unequal social order has become normalized. In San Pedro, counterinsurgency, religious conversion, and discourses of *capacidad* had not entirely displaced the radical political imaginaries of the 1970s, turning Sampedrano leaders into *indios permitidos* who normalized structural violence. After the defeat of the guerrillas, the path of *capacidad* provided modernizing indigenous leaders with what they understood as a safer, smarter mechanism to achieve at least some of what the revolution had promised but failed to deliver: development, empowerment, and an end to discrimination. But the partial inclusion of select individuals relegated Mayas in the collective to the status of permanent second-class citizens, multicultural rhetoric notwithstanding.

4

Radical Pessimism

Neoliberal Democratic Atmosphere

An atmosphere is not an inert context but a force field in which people find themselves. It is not an effect of other forces but a lived affect—a capacity to affect and be affected that pushes the present into a composition, an expressivity, the sense of potentiality and event. It is an attunement of sense, of labors, and imaginaries to potential ways of living and living through things.

Kathleen Stewart, "Atmospheric Attunements"

A very difficult air is breathed . . . that makes the "organization of pessimism" the call of the hour.

Walter Benjamin, "The Last Snapshot of the European Intelligencia"

When I arrived in San Pedro just after the 2003 elections, my previous research in Colotenango led me to expect to encounter villagers divided into four main political tendencies largely rooted in wartime divisions:[1] some who feared the FRG, a small number of them nurturing hidden loyalty to leftist politics; a second, more conservative group comprised of Mayas and Ladinos who embraced the FRG as an extension of their support for the army; a third category of villagers who were neutral or sympathetic to the revolution during the armed conflict but generally saw Ríos Montt and the FRG as allied with the poor; and a fourth group of evangelicals who saw him as an avatar of a new moral order.[2] Because the guerrillas were concentrated in nearby Colotenango and Ixtahuacán, and because I had followed the debates on public memory after the violence,[3] I did not expect to find many outward expressions of support for the defeated revolution. However, given the new democratic opening, I thought I might find muted signs of progressive excitement and fledgling organizations bubbling under the surface.[4] Furthermore, unconvinced that a "culture of terror" persisted in rural villages so long after the peace accords, I wondered if development had come to replace violence as a determining force in postwar politics.[5]

Bracketing these preconceptions was the first step in paying close attention to local historical specificity and the actual nature of political alliances in the present, both of which turned out to be far more complicated than I had imagined, with violence playing a far greater role. As weeks passed into months—and I became more aware of practices outside party politics, gaps between public expressions and private feelings, and meanings embedded in everyday talk and rumor—it became increasingly clear that party alliance was a deceptive indicator of political ideology and the nuances of local common sense. Although I met numerous supporters of Ríos Montt and the FRG, I found few who expressed unambivalent ideological support for them, or for most parties. Ethnographic attention revealed a great deal about the narrative frames, affective intensities, and habitual modes of action through which democracy was lived by rural villagers in the long wake of counterinsurgency, a peace process, ethnic resurgence, and post-peace economic and political realities. The terror of the early 1980s had subsided, but villagers felt far from free.

As my investigations into town history revealed widespread spontaneous support for revolutionary demands before the onset of extreme violence, and as my observations revealed clues into the continued salience of violence in political imaginaries, my questions sharpened: What combination of forces had come to bear on the political imaginary and the self-society relations widely shared among Mayan Sampedranos in the late 1970s? What were the lingering, if invisible, effects of extreme violence on political agency in the present? How was counterinsurgent violence different from and similar to violence enacted in defense of the democratic rule of law, both in its targeting and its effects? What kinds of political thought and behavior became normalized under these conditions?

If ethnographic methods are particularly suited at revealing gaps between what people say and what they actually do, studying political violence challenges the ethnographer to ask what people might otherwise have done under different circumstances but did not, and what they may think but leave unsaid. It demands that we look for meanings hidden in silences, constraints on agency, and frustrated desire beneath outward conformity. Violence underscores how ethnographic writing must move beyond documentation to "put into words" things that remain silent in social life (Hirschauer, 2006, 414). Counterinsurgency slaughtered individuals and communities, destroyed the guerrilla movement, engendered silence, and shut down rural society. But democracy is characterized by power, not pure repression. Biopower aims to shape conduct, not prevent it, and to open spaces for life and freedom,[6] whereas spectacles of sovereign violence deployed in the unmaking of bodies close down spaces and render certain kinds of conduct impossible. Power in the democratic period enjoined villagers to participate in civil defense patrols, to learn how to grow new kinds of crops and calculate private futures, and to venture into party politics. Power acts directly on bodies, their capacities and desires. But political violence never went away in the democratic period; it changed form and narrative frame and shifted targets. Violence and its threat infused responses to neoliberal democratic efforts to shape conduct. Violence is not separate from neoliberal democracy or development; it is constitutive of both.

Central to understanding the effects of violence on neoliberal democratic politics was coming to grips with the way that the state is produced in rural communities and how it is perceived and experienced in everyday life.[7] Theorists of the state after Guatemala's armed conflict describe paradigmatic shifts in this regard. The counterinsurgent state was defined primarily by violence against not only suspected guerrillas but also teachers, catechists, community leaders, and any autonomous forms of authority and organizing. By contrast, the "postwar" state is a source of life and protection and a partner in Mayan cultural revitalization.[8] Instead of fear and avoidance, it incites forms of engagement that many scholars see as strategic.[9] But neither ambivalence nor strategic engagement captured the tormented and tragic—although not terrified—entanglements with the state and adjacent sovereigns that I found in San Pedro.

My investigation into state imaginaries was informed by theories of affect, which insist that consciousness is always embodied, situated, and shot through with desire. By centering on the body, on visceral drives, sensations, and intensities, theories of affect go beyond meaning-centered analysis to provide a richer understanding of how power and violence reverberate through everyday life. "Political affect" examines how bodies are located in political fields, how desire moves them and enables them to move others (Protevi 2009). As violence courses through a body politic, it makes and unmakes bodies, provokes nausea, closing down social spaces and flooding minds with traumatic memories; it incites feelings of helplessness and outrage and acts of submission and resistance. Making a concerted effort to remain open to the messiness of the phenomena I encountered led me to a nuanced understanding of the effects of violence on political consciousness, affect, and agency in the decade and a half after the peace accords.

In this chapter I combine theories of state imaginaries and theories of political affect to describe what I call *radical pessimism:* a neoliberal democratic political imaginary and affective formation in San Pedro and elsewhere that meshes radical desire with a lack of faith in collective agency and the belief that meaningful change is impossible. Central to this affective imaginary is an apprehension of the state as a remote and uncaring agent that is allied with capital and always willing to destroy indigenous life but that is also a mercurial source of protection and a bestower of rewards in exchange for complicity. Aside from whatever other benefits the state provided, I found that most Sampedranos understood and experienced themselves as entangled in an insurmountable relationship with interlinked sovereigns that maintained their collective subordination. These perceptions were forged by a state that both killed Mayas and allowed them to die but that was also sometimes a source of life. Anthropologist Daniel Jordan Smith (2008) describes how Nigerians are preoccupied by both the corrosive effects of corruption on society and by their own corrupt behaviors. He argues that "corruption and the discourses of complaint it generates are at the core of contemporary events, shaping collective imagination and driving social action" (xii). I describe how a political affect of radical pessimism constituted engagements with hostile sovereigns and normalized a politics of personal interest and practices of "selling out." Sampedranos were viscerally drawn into self-interested politics that they understood as simultaneously normal, inevitable, and a serious problem that they could not overcome.[10] Personal interests overwhelmed collective interest in San Pedro, fueling a pervasive atmosphere of mistrust that was exacerbated by efforts to hide one's true motives, guilt, and a desire to prevent recrimination. Everyone lamented this situation, but almost everyone was complicit.

Radical pessimism was the contradictory remnant of a radical political imaginary that was unable to find coherent expression in official democratic spaces but that found partial and contradictory fulfillment in the FRG (in ways that I describe in chapters 5 and 6). Radical pessimism was an "atmospheric attunement" (Stewart 2011) to a form of democracy defined by the violent disqualification of long-standing grassroots demands from the field of democratic contestation. This attunement was affected and affecting, produced through historical experience and productive of contemporary reality; it revealed the lingering weight of histories of violent state formation on Mayan engagements with neoliberal democracy. Rather than an exception from the proper functioning of democracy, the situation in San Pedro illuminates the everyday forms of violence involved in maintaining a grossly asymmetrical international capitalist order. I also examine what the emergent anti-extractivist movement in "defense of territory" reveals about the persistence of radical political imaginaries in rural communities and some of the ways that these are being transformed. I conclude with a reflection on the potential for redirecting the force of pessimism to expand political horizons.

Radical Pessimism

By living in villages and talking to locals about politics and town history, and hesitating to take overt political discourses and affiliations at face value, I came to understand that radical sentiments—not to be confused with support for the revolution—were widely shared among villagers, with little regard for party, religious affiliation, age, gender, economic status, or even prior feelings about the guerrillas. Although it was seldom expressed in public, I even found support for the revolution itself in unexpected places. Rogelio Martínez, a prominent FRG activist and a former soldier, explained:

> The war was because we were enslaved. The Spanish dominated us. The
> guerrillas were indigenous people who formed a group. They organized to

make the army of the poor. Right now, they're [the guerillas] in Congress. The Mayan language [sic] is registered. . . . It would be awful [now] if there had not been a war. It would be like the time with the Spanish. . . . The EGP did a good thing.

Rogelio described the revolution as a partial victory of indigenous people against neocolonial enslavement, gained through sacrifice. He admired Ríos Montt and denied his role in the violence. Although he voted for the FRG, he thought that it, like all parties, was corrupt. He admitted with little shame that he voted for personal interest.

Many villagers held an equivocal view of the guerrillas. They liked their objectives but criticized their methods and knew that their defeat had been inevitable. The patrols were another "two-faced" enterprise. Many believed the patrols had a positive aspect because villagers were united in pursuit of state development projects, but even patrol leaders were bitter about the suffering that they endured during the armed conflict. Many former patrollers joined the movement for the compensation that began in the early 2000s and became Ríos Montt's signature campaign promise in 2003, less out of ideological affirmation of the paramilitary's antiguerrilla mission—the movement's official stance—than the sense of having earned it and having been promised payment.[11]

Radical leanings were present in everyday talk and in conversations and interviews. Villagers bemoaned that the country was run by *los ricos* (the rich), who kept poor Mayas "under their boots." One village leader, a member of Antulio Morales' coalition, commented that "the people from CACIF [Coordinating Committee for Agricultural, Commercial, Industrial and Financial Associations] are very clever about tricking the people." In addition, I often heard the notion repeated that "the rich get richer, while the poor get poorer." On one occasion, I was drinking a Gallo beer with a few men from a Mayan family who supported the FRG but had once upon a time supported the guerrillas. One of them told me to peel the label off my beer bottle because replacing the labels "gives a job to the poor."

During my stay in San Pedro, I asked dozens of villagers their opinions on a range of political demands associated either with the guerrillas or with progressive movements before and after the peace accords. The vast majority expressed support for the accords, human rights, democracy, truth commissions, indigenous rights, and even land reform. The main exception was that many specifically opposed the aspects of human rights that they felt "let [local] criminals free"—free to violate *their* rights. The use of human rights to prevent army assaults on civilians was widely supported. Most indigenous Sampedranos who knew about free trade agreements opposed them, and Sampedranos condemned mining concessions in a near-unanimous 2007 *consulta*.[12] The majority considered leftist parties and organizations reliable sources of trustworthy news and political critique. Crucial vestiges of a radical imaginary were alive and well in San Pedro, despite decades of repression aimed at stamping it out. Most Ladinos did not share radical leanings; neither did the former Mayan spies and military commissioners I met and some villagers who had achieved considerable economic success. Although younger Mayas frequently shared elements of radical common sense, most were unfamiliar with social movements or their demands, much less guerrilla objectives.

However, some Sampedranos were actively involved in leftist organizations and social movements, including the CUC; the National Coordinator for Guatemalan Widows (CONAVIGUA), a victims' rights organization; and *Asociación* Ceiba, which talked about human rights. Many indigenous teachers joined the Guatemalan Educational Workers' Union (STEG) after teachers won the right to collectively bargain in 2003, and unionists frequently formed alliances with progressive forces such as the anti-mining movement.[13] In contrast to other political parties, the URNG, the newly legal guerrilla party, appeared exempt from accusations of self-interest. URNG members regularly lamented that everyone who supported "parties of the rich" (read "non-URNG") *"se vendieron"* ("sold themselves"). Despite never offering projects, the URNG attained more than 700 votes in 2003, placing third in a hotly contested race with numerous projects at stake.

As in Nigeria, "debating and analyzing popular woes was [also] a national obsession" in San Pedro (Smith 2008, xii). The main concerns were the nature of the government and the designs of powerful interests: the opacity of these entities provided fertile ground for rumors and conspiracy theories.[14] Of all the ways that Mayan Sampedranos claimed to be deceived, many understood a racialized interstate capitalist nexus (my words, their ideas) as the principal axis of their oppression.[15] These interpretations made sense of lived experience by placing it in narrative frames that were well established in local memories and common sense, and generated patterned emotional responses to shared circumstances. But grassroots imaginaries were also messy: they included echoes of radical ideology alongside counterinsurgency truth, development discourse, religious understandings, notions of human rights, and rumors and theories that pushed the boundaries of acceptable proof and assumptions of causality and that defied easy political categorization.

Radical discourses resonated with Sampedranos, but most kept their distance from leftist movements and ignored leftist parties at the voting booth in favor of conservatives and even overt authoritarians. The vast majority of Sampedranos viewed party politics as corrupt, divisive, and driven by self-interest—the opposite of respect (Ekern 2011)—and party leaders were commonly understood as racist Ladino businessmen and mafia types who maintained links to the military and exploited indigenous people and poor peasants. Although these investments bore superficial resemblance to authoritarian populist rhetoric, villagers viewed authoritarians with much the same disdain as they did other parties, and frequently more. These remnants of a radical political imaginary were inextricably embedded with embodied memories of colonial victimization and counterinsurgency violence. Violence and the threat of violence weighed upon collective imaginaries, shutting down capacities for collective action and convincing most Mayan Sampedranos that radical change was impossible.

Instead of confrontation with and victory over these forces, or principled refusal, local imaginaries prescribed avoidance or selective engagement with the state and capital in order to obtain small benefits.[16] Commonplace expressions of anger toward the state were deeply imbricated with profound feelings of powerlessness, frustration, and cynicism regarding the possibilities for urgently needed reform. This radical pessimism was a prominent feature of a shared political imaginary, which was not a survival of a premodern indigenous cosmovision, or a seamless whole of any kind, but an unstable, nonrandom assortment of sometimes-contradictory discourses that had been refined and modified through experience. At one level, radical pessimism discouraged participation in radical parties and social movements even after these were legal, and fostered widespread disengagement from party politics. At another, it helped normalize increasingly self-interested, corrupt, and divisive forms of political participation, including support for authoritarian parties.

Miguel Ramírez was a widely respected community leader who had been very active in José Antulio Morales' coalition. Although once a feared patrol leader, like many in the organization he considered himself a guerrilla sympathizer. When I asked his thoughts about agrarian reform, he said it was a "good idea," quickly adding, "but it can't be done. We tried for years. The *finqueros* are too strong." In his estimation, peace and democracy excluded these important revolutionary goals. Regarding land occupations, he explained, "It's fine if you have a title, but if you don't it will bring consequences. Look at what happened in Nueva Linda." Miguel was referring to the recent (2004) headlines about President Berger's administration's (2004–2008) attacks on peasant activists. For him, land redistribution was a good thing, but breaking the law was too dangerous. The rule of law was not neutral but was infused with violence. He withdrew from party politics after becoming frustrated with Antulio Morales' corruption and greed.

Anastasio Bravo, another high-ranking member of Antulio Morales' organization who was still active in party politics, expressed great frustration with the limits of democracy and development. Bravo was a catechist from a relatively well-off indigenous family. He had enrolled in weekend high school classes during my fieldwork, and one of his teachers had assigned readings summarizing the truth commission findings. He explained his understanding of these in the following way:

> They want to fix Guatemala, but with each attempt, it is sinking deeper. When a child is born, they already owe money to the United States. They are never going to be able to pay it. Have you heard of the Bishop Juan Gerardi? He published a book about the violence. It's called *Nunca Más* [*Never Again*]. What does that mean? It means that Guatemala is never, never, never going to change. The *diputados* [congressmen] want to raise their salaries, and what do they do? They don't do anything. And then they killed Gerardi, for being in favor of the poor. There's never a government that worries about the people. Here there's a hospital, but there isn't any medicine. They prescribe [medicine], but you have to go buy it, and there's no money. And there are many towns where there isn't even a hospital. Only the church helps with the hospital here. That's why the government in Guatemala is backwards.

Bravo was disgusted and hopeless. *Nunca Más* was the Catholic Church's truth commission and was originally intended to be a renunciation of the violence, an unequivocal resolution to never permit genocide to happen again, in Guatemala or anywhere else. I was speechless when I heard a Mayan political leader who had recently taken a course on the subject twist the intended meaning into an affirmation of the inevitability of oppressive government. Several village leaders repeated this interpretation. When I asked Anastasio Bravo what he thought about the peace accords, he said that "peace was just on paper with the signing of the government and the URNG. The armed conflict ended, but true peace . . . it doesn't exist. There's already violence, and other things, massacres after the accords. There's still racism and a lot of gangs."

Bravo was certain that the state cared nothing about justice, especially for the poor. The hospital without medicine was proof of official disregard for local well-being. He also cited the brutal murder of Bishop Juan Gerardi, massacres after the accords, and other unpunished crimes. Although he disavowed the guerrillas for their violence, he agreed with their goals. He relied on the Catholic Church and social movements for unbiased news, but he did not pursue radical politics. He saw no alternative to the status quo. He instead participated in political parties that he loathed in a game that he saw as socially damaging and utterly rigged, hoping to make a small difference locally, but more likely, he admitted, for personal gain. Rather than crime normalizing structural violence (e.g., Benson, Fischer, and Thomas 2008), Miguel Ramírez understood crime as a symptom of larger social problems, but he linked this political reading to pessimism about the possibility of deeper solutions.

Radical pessimism was directly informed by intergenerational struggles for political transformation, including the revolution. Pedro Lázaro was a community leader from Los Altenses and a key FRG backer. A Catholic in his early sixties, with no education, Lázaro had overcome extreme poverty. He and his extended family were proud guerrilla sympathizers in the seventies and eighties, but had publicly—and vehemently—denied it ever since. Lázaro joined the FRG mostly because he was frustrated that his family had been excluded from José Antulio Morales' favoritism network. But it was not only that. Lázaro explained his current politics in light of his experiences and historical understandings. For him, the motivation for war was direct:

Lázaro: Always for rights. Before, when my father was here, an indigenous person couldn't speak, and couldn't organize in a group. They couldn't talk about their rights. For that reason, they were intelligent people who formed a group. The organization came from another country, and little by little the people organized. Many died for that reason. When there is a strong group, it's like a beehive, strong. The guerrillas were almost the entire town and the villages also. That's why it began, and now, not a lot, but there is a little peace. There's peace. The guerrillas won that right. Many died. But the Bible says that there will be victory with blood.

NC: Was there a time when the people were against human rights?

Lázaro: Ah. Yes. But that changed with the peace accords.

NC: Many people don't have any confidence in political parties. Do you think that there are political parties that are in favor of the people?

Lázaro: Yes, the party URNG. That's the guerrilla party.

NC: But you're in a different party.

Lázaro: Look, I have always worked for the parties for the poor. But they never win. Even good guerrilla leaders change parties; it's always for personal interest.

NC: So you were struggling before, but now you want to win?

Lázaro: Look, I'm illiterate. Ever since my childhood I have never known regular pay. I worked from 7 A.M. to 5 P.M. for 40 centavos every day. Really suffering! When I got married, I worked for two months in the coast in a plantation. In two months I barely saved 20 quetzales ($2.50). I was malnourished, my shirt was ripped, and my pants were ruined. That is the life of an "Indio," of a peasant. Now I am saving the money I make helping the party. If God gives me health, I can make money the entire four years.

NC: What changes do you think would be necessary in the government of Guatemala?

Lázaro: When the government was in his campaign, they tell us that Guatemala is going to have change. Only in their campaign. When they get into power, they leave it to one side. That's what I think. There's never going to arrive the change that needs to be made. Why? Well, right now, the day laborers are making 20 quetzales each day. And what's happening right now? The price of fertilizer just went up to Q150 ($20). Right now, the people feel very much like slaves. And because only those rich, well, those businessmen, they don't go stopping every day; every day they're moving up. The poor every day get poorer. Why? Because the prices are rising.

  To change the government? That's difficult. He is in his power. Now there are a lot of organizations. Many go to protest in front of the president's house. But he, what pain does it give him? He is there in his power, just listening. He never makes good.

NC: So, you don't think that changing the government is possible?

Lázaro: It's impossible.

Here is an example of a strong FRG supporter—a municipal-level party leader—who saw the FRG as an anti-poor party, just like the rest. He rehearsed key elements of radical pessimist common sense, blending radical ideas and concepts with local understandings. His use of the racial slur "*Indio*" alongside "peasant" highlights his understanding of the inherence of racial discrimination in class exploitation. Lázaro also valued human rights, framed as material economic improvements for the poor. The motor of this indigenous vision of social democracy was organization, which he described as a beehive, the whole of which was more powerful than any individual part. Their bloody struggle won some peace, and some rights, which the people saw as legitimate. In his imaginary, the left still represented collective indigenous political desire. However, he believed that the changes needed to satisfy that desire would never transpire. He understood collective indigenous and popular agency to be virtually ineffective. Lázaro imagined the state as an agent with clear intentionality: the pure calculated self-interest of a man ("him") sitting in a government building, indifferent to protest and never following through on campaign promises. He stopped supporting leftist parties and movements because they never won and shifted his loyalties for personal interest, joining the FRG because it had the best shot. Lázaro was painfully aware that Ríos Montt was a mass murderer and that voting for him ran counter to peace, justice, and democracy, although Lázaro publicly denied it during the campaign. He knew that Ríos Montt's victory would cement Mayas as second-class citizens, but he saw his participation as insignificant in the broader scheme of things.

Regarding the participation of former leftists in the FRG, Nelson writes that "those who are lashing in to these state-related identities are challenging their own assumptions about the world and power. They are assuming identifications that challenge the old divide of the war years between the good popular movement and the enemy state" (2009, 71). Many see these "old" categories as of limited use in the reconfigured postwar milieu. Engaging the state, she suggests, especially as it opens new spaces for indigenous and human rights, multiplies agency beyond what is usually possible through collective agency. But in San Pedro, most alliances with authoritarian parties, and especially the FRG, were characterized by pessimism and *interes,* not an uncritical acceptance of populist rhetoric or a calculated "struggle from within." Bleak options motivated others to distance themselves from politics entirely.

Mayan Sampedranos were not *afraid* to vote for radical parties, although many feared what might happen if they joined political protests. But most did not see the point. In their perspective, the left still had nice ideas but was unlikely to win elections or change the country. For many Sampedranos, this point was so obvious it was hardly worth discussing: organizing and protest that challenged the existing powers were ineffective and could bring violence. The turning point in this imaginary was the violence of 1982, when collective political struggle hit a wall. McAllister (2003) argues that counterinsurgency violence interrupted Chupolenses' sense of how to continue to be "good people" who would fight for their rights and forced them to focus on local ethnic politics. In San Pedro indigenous leaders opted to abandon national reform and class politics and to focus on ethnic advancement through party politics and individual *superación,* and in the process altered their conception of what good people should be. Guarded optimism in the immediate postwar moment faded as the limits to democracy became more apparent.

Imagining the Guatemalan State

Nelson (2009) contends that "if the state represents the interests of the elites, it looks strong. . . . But in the postwar it also claims to represent the people . . . and there it looks pretty pathetic" (218). Most Mayan Sampedranos imagine the state as a tool for the wealthy, willing and able to transgress the law to violently crush political reform. They view it as an all-encompassing and insuperable force. Against this imaginary backdrop, "new" violence in defense of neoliberal democratic order was continuous with counterinsurgency terror, marking similar limits on political agency. This imaginary replaces the angry and empowered dissident subject position with that of the abused victim, who is also enraged but frustrated in relation to the state. Within this imaginary, most Mayan Sampedranos did not see the vote as a mechanism for meaningful political change, especially not at the national level. Restless energies were invested elsewhere, such as trying to migrate, lining up projects, criminal activity, or seeking salvation in evangelical *cultos.*

Campaign rhetoric aside, almost no one I spoke with—including party higher-ups—explained their support for authoritarian parties in terms of agreement with their party's plans for government or ideology. Indeed, I met no one who voted for Ríos Montt primarily because of his evangelism. In fact, many FRG supporters, even evangelicals, were very critical of Ríos Montt's past, and many doubted his Christianity. Furthermore, no one I spoke with saw the FRG as more "Mayan" than any other party. Instead, almost everyone cited concrete, immediate, community, or personal benefits: usually development projects. Most voted for the candidate who promised them the most and who seemed most likely to win; some individuals joined for leadership positions. Only URNG members expressed ideological loyalty. Mariano Díaz, who identified as a conservative when we spoke in 2004, joined the center-leftist UNE in 2007 in a failed attempt to win another term. When I asked him why, he told me that after the war ideology no longer mattered.

Although grassroots faith in the revolution was obliterated by the counterinsurgency, the modernizing indigenous leadership retained elements of a radical political imaginary. In an interview in 2009, then-*alcalde* Julio Ambrocio, who had become a regional leader of the anti-mining movement, eloquently expressed a widely held sentiment:

> But I have seen, I have known and I have studied the impact of the political processes that have happened. The pattern is that in all of them, the state has become the worst enemy of all of the people. . . . Because the state is a monster for all of us. . . . The people that occupy those spaces approach with very personal interests. . . . It is the children of the same twenty-two families that generate the government of this country . . . who . . . haven't even known poverty. They are people who sit at a desk and resolve everything technically because in the end it does not matter to them. Because here we have never heard of a government minister or functionary who actually evaluates the needs of a community. . . . There is no direct contact with the people. It is a complete monster that cannot be removed. Look, when the people rise up and protest . . . they want to protest against many things, for example, the case of mining. They put up a wall of soldiers, a wall of police, and a wall of everything. . . . This creates *malestar* [unrest] in the society because it does not get where it needs to go. There is no table for dialogue. There are no direct compromises with the government. The offerings come during the campaign, of course, but those are for problems that the people are going to always have. How are we going to break this? This is why I say the state is a monster.

Ambrocio thinks that the state behaves like a monster because it violently blocks reforms and rules from a distance in an uncaring manner ("People's safety does not matter to the agents of the state").[17] Repeated performances of violence, such as the intensification of attacks on peasant land-rights activists and assassinations and arbitrary incarceration of political leaders and unionists, clarified for Sampedranos the low value of indigenous life in state and corporate calculations and reinforced the foundational violence of the state, the root of popular discontent, by fostering resignation. But more than resignation, a mix of radicalism and pessimism best defines local conceptions of their shared democratic predicament ("the state is the enemy of the people" . . . "how are we going to break this?"). Sampedranos reluctantly accepted that democracy was limited to ameliorating "problems the people are always going to have" to the exclusion of fundamental reforms, and the even lesser goal of implementing the peace accords, which were commonly viewed as more radical than they really were.

Many Sampedranos experienced neoliberal democracy as a continuation of historical oppression, not liberation from it. Guatemala's violent history is the main reason that Mayas have not elected a leftist president and that many avoid radical movements. Frustration and disempowerment are hardly unique to Guatemala, but arguably more pronounced there: violence constitutes the conditions of emergence and operation of neoliberal democracy in most of the world, and electoral options are limited even in Western nation-states. Although indigenous Sampedranos were less organized with the revolution than villagers in Colotenango, Ixtahuacán, or Chupol, and abandoned it soon after the massacres and the civil patrols, many nonetheless regarded democracy in light of the failure of prior struggles and as explicitly excluding the revolutionary demands that they shared.

Kay Warren (2002) suggests that Mayas engage in politics outside of state and political parties because of long histories of mistreatment. Perhaps this helps explain regional abstention rates of about 40 percent and the large number of null votes. Many indigenous Sampedranos avoided party politics altogether, while others drew the line at voting for Ríos Montt. But many saw such principled stances as luxuries they could not afford. Many null votes for president were refusals of the farce of neoliberal democracy.

Felipe Gutierrez was a teacher in his late thirties in 2004, whose father ran as part of the FRG ticket. After emphasizing that the people had strongly supported the guerrillas' fight against discrimination, he explained why he thought people who had participated in the guerrillas had turned against them, and then moved to the FRG:

Gutierrez: Almost everyone was in favor [of the guerrillas]. Some have the pride, the older ones. But when we talk about the present . . . '82 and after were tremendously hard. The people closed themselves up.

   [During the campaign] every person had to think [about] whom they were going to support. They say that it is true that Ríos Montt killed people in '82, but that the war can't come back again. It's not so easy that the war will come back again. So it's OK to join the FRG.

NC: Many say that he wasn't responsible for the violence, that it was Lucas García.

Gutierrez: I imagine it was Ríos Montt who killed the people. I know the history. He gave the order in the [military] zone. The soldiers were under the order. I didn't vote for him. I told my father clearly, "I'm not going to vote for Ríos Montt. For Mariano Díaz, yes." I marked a "null" for that reason, because I didn't agree.

After the popular guerrilla movement was crushed, people closed up, and, for most villagers, pride turned to silent shame and self-recrimination. Gutierrez sadly recalls preelection debates that turned on the fact that, although everyone knew Ríos Montt was a murderer, voting for him was unlikely to make the war return. Gutierrez found Ríos Montt too repulsive, so he voted null, even though Ríos Montt's victory would help his family. His was a vote of conscience, a mix of heartbreak and principle that showed respect for what he thought the ritual should mean: choosing what was right over personal interest, a refusal to be duped or to dupe others. Voting for the URNG was so futile as to go unmentioned.

Jennifer Burrell (2013) describes uncertainty as a central part of a postwar structure of feeling in Guatemala, and many scholars have noted the unpredictable nature of social life in an age when capital flows are reorganizing local lives and livelihoods. And although uncertainty was also pervasive in San Pedro, it was accompanied by numerous certainties: surfaces deceive, far-reaching political change was off the table, institutions benefit the wealthy at their expense, the state works with corporations to

exploit and harm indigenous people, accepting resources from these entities comes with strings attached, indigenous villagers are singled out for
discriminatory and harmful treatment by interlinked sovereigns that hide
their true motives behind humanitarian pretenses, and indigenous life can
be extinguished without consequence.

Harry West (2005) describes how rural Muedans in Mozambique used
discourses of sorcery to scrutinize successive regimes of state power. He
sees sorcery as a language of power that is a kind of anti-knowledge: an
ever-present, proactive suspicion of people who exercise power by entering into an invisible domain. Pessimism bleeds into skepticism and mistrust of any institutions and individuals claiming to improve and protect
local lives. Muedans, then, are like cynics who maintain a "permanent
negative and critical attitude towards any kind of political institution, and
towards any kind of *nomos,*" or law-making entity (Foucault 2001, 105).
Noting the prevalence of discourses of *engaño* (deception) among rural
Mayas and post-genocidal Guatemala in general, Nelson (2009) argues
that a habit of suspicious accusation born out of decades of manipulation guides interpretations of the nontransparent actions and intentions
of various groups and institutions in the postwar moment. Sampedranos also perceive hidden self-interested motives behind most discourses
of truth they encounter in the postwar terrain. Although some may read
skeptical expressions as resistance—and there is little question that they
reveal highly sophisticated critical understandings of the workings of
power—these do not typically translate into radical political agency. Pessimism and mistrust can inform engagement as well as disengagement.

Defending Territory against Neoliberal Extractivism

Free market reforms were promoted alongside the peace process as a path
to prosperity and modernity after Guatemala's long war.[18] Foreign investment capital was believed to create jobs and free trade to lower the cost
of imports and increase exports. Planners predicted that entrepreneurial-
ism and new economic opportunities would transform the countryside
and that decentralization would encourage rural villagers to govern themselves according to traditional cultural values as austerity and privatization reduced the state's responsibility for social welfare.[19] Instead, the

result was sharper inequality and expanding financial and physical insecurity. Unemployment and violent crime rose precipitously, fueling unprecedented migration to the United States. Rural communities felt increasingly left out of new opportunities and abandoned by the state, left to fend for themselves in a hostile landscape.

Amid a rising level of precariousness in the decade after the peace accords, changes in the global political economy that increased global demand for land-based resources coincided with free market regulatory frameworks to set the stage for Guatemala's extractivist boom.[20] Conflict over the extractive industries soon overshadowed contestation over the stalled accords. The World Bank had made multimillion-dollar loans for rural roads, conservation projects, and land titling programs (through market-led agrarian reform) that would literally and legally prepare the ground for extractive industries, while making other, more-sustainable projects untenable. Eric Holt-Giménez (2008) describes how the exorbitant costs of creating a mine shed through "territorial restructuring" were borne by Guatemalan taxpayers, while the 1997 Mining Law required mining companies to pay an astonishingly low 1 percent of royalties to the state. Private interests responding to rising energy prices grabbed up large swaths of land to plant African palm and sugar cane, "flex-fuel" crops that could be marketed as food or fuel. These chemical-intensive crops displaced thousands of subsistence farmers who found themselves on the outside of the extractive economy, unlike national elites who profited immensely.[21]

Many rural communities have organized to stop the advance of neoliberal reforms. In 2005 regional social movements in rural Huehuetenango blocked the Inter-American Highway at the Naranjales Bridge in Colotenango to protest the ratification of CAFTA, a Pandora's box of pro-market reforms that was never voted on by the population. The National Police advanced and fired live rounds at the protestors, wounding over a dozen and killing a Mayan teacher, Juan Lopez Velásquez, demonstrating an aggressive disregard for Mayan lives and rights to free assembly. Fabiana Ortíz and Anna Maria Ramos, indigenous women from *Asociación* Ceiba participating in the march, stood up to the army and were joined by several other women. Their courageous stand ended the shooting, and retellings of Fabiana and Ana Maria's bravery evoked stories about CONAVIGUA's confrontation of civil patrollers on that same bridge in 1993.[22] But the National Police had also made its point.

By far, the most contentious aspect of neoliberal reforms has been min-ing, which most communities see as a clear and present danger of per-manent damage to the environment from which they would benefit little, despite the government's and the mining companies' promises of employ-ment and proper safeguards. In 2005 the town of Sipacapa, San Mar-cos, held a highly publicized community *consulta* (consultation) vote in which 98 percent of the population opposed the operation of an open-air gold mine, setting off a string of *consultas* in the region.[23] The right to *consulta* is based in International Labor Organization Treaty 169, which recognizes the rights of indigenous peoples to make decisions regarding development and policies that affect the natural environment in their ter-ritories. This right is also enshrined in many municipal codes. When sur-veyors began work on dozens of mining concessions and machinery was put into place, communities began to organize to defend their territories.[24] Since 2005, more than a hundred communities have carried out *consultas,* and all of them have rejected mining, as well as other mega-development projects such as hydroelectric dams, which rural residents see as dedicated to providing energy for mining operations or remote sale rather than local consumption. These efforts have stalled many, but not all, projects. In response, the state and the mining companies have tried to undermine the right to consultation and have claimed that the constitution grants the state subsoil rights. Stuart Kirsch (2014) calls efforts to prevent new mines before they start the "new politics of time," made possible by activists in collaboration with international NGOs (the "politics of space"), a strategy that is much more effective than fighting to mitigate environmental harms once they are allowed to exist.

Activists have united the various strands of resistance to the neolib-eral project—increasingly called "neoliberal extractivism"—under the "defense of territory" umbrella, the dominant movement frame since the peace accords.[25] The defense of territory draws on language from ILO 169 and discourses of indigenous rights and sovereignty. Proponents frame the movement against mining, land grabs, and megaprojects as a "continua-tion of resistance against colonialism, genocide, and neocolonialism" and as a "new way of practicing citizenship," a form of direct democracy with connections to the radical politics of the late 1970s (Rasch 2012: 161).[26] The defense of territory frame represents a local resignification of democ-racy, defining it as the popular will, manifested through *consultas* and ancestral authorities, outside of party politics, rooted in a fundamental right to indigenous territorial self-determination in pointed contrast to the sovereignty of the Guatemalan state. The *consulta* process has reinvigorated indigenous forms of self-government, such as the *Alcaldías Indígenas* (indigenous mayoralties) that are recognized in the peace accords, and the movement proposes an alternative territorial project rooted in conceptions of sustainability and indigenous cosmovisions, known as Buen Vivir. It is a form of "indigenous cosmopolitics" that exceeds the terms of traditional leftist discourse by refusing a division between humans and Mother Earth, embraced here as a sentient being (see de la Cadena 2010, Escobar 2016), and also by insisting on the primacy of indigenous authority and governing structures. The defense of territory in Guatemala emerged as a dialectical reaction to the aggressive expansion of an extractivist project in a context where indigenous-rights discourses had recently gained official recognition in the wake of genocide and where peace accords and state multiculturalism had failed to resolve fundamental social contradictions. Indigenous environmentalism provides a language from which to politicize the social and environmental harms externalized by extractive industries that would not be profitable otherwise. It draws attention to trade-offs, such as the fact that growing sugar cane requires so much water that rivers are diverted, subsistence farmers go without, and fisher folk lose their livelihoods.

Activists in the journalist and social scientific collective Prensa Communitaria, have made good use of social media to garner national and international attention to local struggles against state repression, such as arbitrary arrests and the imprisonment of "territory defenders."[27] Movements for the defense of territory enjoy widespread support among rural residents, social movements, and progressive NGOs. The defense of territory unites Ladinos and indigenous interests despite historic antagonisms by focusing on their shared need for clean water and attachments to place. Assertions of indigenous territorial rights and the sentience of nature transcend the territorial boundaries of nation-states as well as the logic of capital that reduces nature to exchange values.

In 2014 the Guatemalan Congress passed the "Monsanto Law," which extended intellectual-property-right protections to genetically modified vegetables. This incited wide-scale indigenous protests that shut down the country and forced the law to be revoked (Grandia 2017).[28] Given this potential to challenge the political order, it is not surprising that the defense of territory has provoked a strong counterreaction. As community opposition to the neoliberal project became more vocal, it was met with state violence, reaching its worst (so far) under former President Otto Perez Molina (2011–2015). The army hard-liner declared states of siege in numerous communities throughout the country to repress local opposition to mining and mega-development. When, in 2011, leaders in Santa Cruz Barillas burned the equipment belonging to a hydroelectric company, the army arrested dozens of residents and leaders during a state of siege.[29] Protestors who block roads and work areas are frequently dislodged in violent *desalojos* (evictions), and a growing number of community opposition leaders have been assassinated. The army and national police opened fire against indigenous residents of Totonicapán, Sololá, whose autonomous government organized a blocking of the Inter-American Highway to protest rising electricity costs. The attack killed seven and wounded dozens. Territory and human rights defenders denounce this pattern of violence and repression as the "criminalization of protest," an attempt to silence and intimidate dissent. Repression continued even after Perez Molina's regime was overthrown because of corruption revelations from the International Commission against Impunity in Guatemala (CICIG).[30]

The defense of territory faces many challenges, foremost of which is translating it into an alternative territorial model with a relevance to a wide range of working people and also taking concrete steps toward building durable alliances with existing movements for redistribution and against neoliberalism (Reina 2008). The 2016 March for Water was one effort to raise awareness about and build broad-based opposition to the common practice of diverting rivers to irrigate private plantations, which results in water scarcities downstream and contamination. The 250-kilometer march was a response to the poisoning of the Passion River in Sayaxche, Petén, with agrochemical runoff from African palm plantations. It drew thousands of participants from dozens of communities and organizations and garnered significant urban support for a rural-led initiative.

The defense of territory in Guatemala and elsewhere parallels the formulation of alternative projects within La Vía Campesina, the global peasant movement, whose influential conception of food sovereignty centers around the significant redistribution of land-based resources, understands local access and control as human rights, and draws heavily on indigenous worldviews (Desmarais 2007, Nyéléni Declaration 2007). Food sovereignty and the defense of territory overlap significantly, but also differ, with the former more committed to traditional peasant struggles and demands and the latter to indigenous tradition and worldviews. Activists are engaged in ongoing dialogue around alternatives to neoliberalism. Finding a movement frame and programs of action with wide relevance is no small task given the fragmentation of the peasantry through decades of market integration that have increased social stratification and displacement.[31]

How long can communities keep up the fight against corporations lured by visions of mega-profits and prepared to use a combination of violence and incentives to gain access? Communities can be worn down by constant threats. Pessimism is one of the greatest obstacles to the defense of territory. I was in Huehuetenango in July 2009 as popular organizations planned anti-extraction roadblocks nationwide. A few weeks prior, I watched as the crowds in the Sunday market listened closely to the URNG Party members perched atop the municipal building with a bullhorn, criticizing mining and urging Sampedranos to join the protests. Several people I spoke with that morning said they planned to attend, which was not surprising because Sampedranos had almost unanimously rejected mining in a recent community *consulta*. When the day arrived, however, only members of URNG and the CUC (small and heavily overlapping groups) showed up. Even though most villagers in San Pedro opposed mining and austerity, few showed up at the protests or at the following demonstrations against the attacks on protestors. Many were worried, for good reason, about retaliation. I interviewed Anastasio Bravo again soon afterward and asked him why he did not participate. He explained, "It's already decided; we can't stop it," and rehearsed the defeated interpretation of *Nunca Más* that had become familiar. His sister, a local women's leader, put it more bluntly: "We don't go because we are afraid of getting shot, like what happened at Naranjales." Violence pitted the desire for self-preservation against the desire for social justice. Insidiously, collective conformity in the face of imposed policies creates an appearance of consent and frames dissent as a minority opinion, further legitimizing the use of violence.

Despite widespread opposition to extraction, villagers vote for parties whose leaders fully support it, parties that will side with extractive corporations and use violence if necessary. Through elections, resource extraction gains a claim to democratic legitimacy and the force of law, however lawless and antidemocratic mining appears to local residents. Leaders of the anti-extractivist movement worry about losing momentum during political campaigns when participants are distracted by local contests and bought off by party bosses. Even though pessimism limits the defense of territory, the movement frame helps communities learn to trust and rely on one another, see connections between their local struggles, gain regional and international support, and feel the power of their actions reverberate while they imagine a common future: a greener and more inclusive economy resonant with indigenous cosmologies, under indigenous authority, and out of the shadow of extractive industries and the state that supports them.

The Politics of Pessimism

Sampedrano political imaginaries demonstrate the failure of army and neoliberal hegemony and underscore deep affinities between Mayan and radical politics. But major elements of their political desires have been illegible in official democratic spaces, blurring the line between war and postwar. Rather than consider this a feature of failed democracy in a backward "elsewhere," indigenous imaginaries in San Pedro urge us to recognize dense, mutually reinforcing interconnections among the Guatemalan state, the US government, and national and multinational capital that constitute the unquestioned background to neoliberal democracy.

Many Sampedranos maintained their desire for collective rights and redistributive policies characteristic of the radical democratic imaginary of twentieth-century Latin America. Yet the distinctive demands and forms of political agency associated with that imaginary were missing, excluded a priori from neoliberal democracy. Mayan Sampedranos who engaged the state and other violent sovereigns were not dupes or "collaborators," and they did not vote for murderers such as Ríos Montt out of fear or straightforward ideological resonance. They mainly did so to survive and get by, but they felt far from strategic; they saw opportunities for individual and small-group gains without the possibility of radical reform. Pondering tensions between neoliberal restructuring and dreams of the good life in the North American context, Lauren Berlant (2012) describes "cruel optimism" as a tragic condition in which an object of desire undermines the possibilities for its own attainment. Although some are content with individual market advancement, desperate resignation, not false optimism, better summarizes Sampedranos' relationships with the violent sovereigns in their midst.

Powerlessness and resignation were the preeminent goals of counterinsurgency throughout Latin America. Benson and Kirsch (2010) describe how corporations strategically generate resignation when they respond to critique by reinforcing the belief that harm is inevitable and change is impossible. David Graeber (2013) sees the denial of alternatives as a central tenet of neoliberalism. Resignation in Guatemala is thus part of a global structure of feeling manufactured at different scales through distinct processes of state formation and capital accumulation in efforts to forestall organized dissent. Understanding specific configurations of pessimism and mistrust is critical to disentangling them and constructing alternatives, lest they become fodder for authoritarian populists, which appears to be the new global trend.

It is difficult to identify one specific kernel uniting the diverse expressions of pessimism on the neoliberal landscape, but post-conflict pessimism most frequently derives from a sense that official democratic spaces constitute the disappointing upper limit on social transformation, signaling change without delivering. Pessimism regarding neoliberal democracy in Western Europe and North America often grows from an inability to imagine a world beyond corporate control, as white North Americans in particular perceive a host of attacks on the American Dream from the "outside": minorities on welfare; immigrants stealing "American" jobs; liberal politicians and "big-government" regulations; the national debt; Barack Obama's alleged socialist, Muslim, and antigun agenda; and fears of Islamic terrorism.

White Americans in the United States tend to see economic and social problems as deviations from "true" capitalism, limited government, and the rule of law rather than as effects of capitalism, globalization, austerity, and deregulation, all of which are legally sanctioned. Most refuse to consider alternatives to capitalism, even as it victimizes them and conflicts with their moral sensibilities. Such aggrieved perceptions are evident in profound ambivalence toward avatars of free market capitalism, such as

Walmart, Wall Street, and insurance companies, which are suspected of hiding great harm beneath promises to do good (Copeland and Labuski 2013). Mistrust in the global North is produced by many of the same processes of nontransparent government and economic predation that inspire pessimism (and rebellion) among many poor, peasant, and indigenous communities in the global South, even as the harms, conceptions of justice, and histories of struggle differ.

Although many Mayas may have given up on radical change, others continue to fight for it, both through and against the system. Dissatisfaction with the deteriorating post-conflict state of affairs festers among Mayan youths who have grown up exposed to idealistic discourses of democracy, human rights, and universal religious brotherhood, positive images of Mayanness, and life in the United States. Their frustration and collective power animate national teachers' strikes, the anti-extractive movement, and protests against austerity, state violence, and corruption. New forms of agitation may reflect, and provoke, changes in political affect and a shifting of the political horizon beyond the thinly blunted oppression of neoliberal democracy. By drawing connections between long-standing injustices and common frustrations, challenging violent sovereigns and their proxies, and rejecting promises to protect life conditioned on the preservation of violent structures, new movements hold the potential for radical collective action as well as far-reaching redistribution and autonomy.

The Radical Organization of Pessimism

In an essay on the politics of poetry, Walter Benjamin (1999 [1929]) distinguishes the "absolute" pessimism informed by the surrealist profane illumination of bourgeois freedom and everyday life from the optimistic imagery that unites bourgeois and socialist poetics. He calls for an "organization of pessimism," with pessimism defined as follows:

> Mistrust in the fate of literature, mistrust in the fate of freedom, mistrust in the fate of European humanity, but three times mistrust in all reconciliation: between classes, between nations, between individuals. And unlimited trust only in . . . the peaceful perfection of the air force. (217–18)

Only pure pessimism, he wrote, could "expel moral metaphor from politics" and replace contemplation and "metaphysical materialism" with direct "contact with the proletarian masses," an encounter that changes circumstances rather than attitudes. He imagined surrealist art as a technology designed to make "body and image so interpenetrate that all revolutionary tension becomes collective innervation, and all the bodily innervations of the collective become revolutionary discharge" (56). He continues:

> The collective is a body, too. And the *physis* that is being organized for it in technology can, through all its political and factual reality, only be produced in that image sphere to which profane illumination initiates us.

Rural Mayas do not lack for "innervation" or profane illumination; mistrust of powerful and interlinked forces is a deeply engrained habit of social and political perception rooted in countless experiences of abjection. Rather than incite revolt, as it did in the 1960s and 1970s, this profane illumination is more often suffocated by repressive violence that generates pessimism about the very possibility of liberatory collective action. The affective force of violence overwhelms reactions against suffering and injustice by insisting that resistance only brings worse pain. But these reactions do not simply disappear; they remain a source of tension and conflict, and they continue to build, even though some individuals have found relief through market advancement. Many bottle up their frustrations in stress and worry; others prey on those more vulnerable. Systematic targeted violence clamps down the lid on the pressure cooker that is Guatemalan society, but it is not enough on its own to stop the eruptions, signs of which are everywhere.

Authoritarian organizations of pessimism through neoliberal democracy and development channel frustration with everyday violence and defeat into movements for the continuation of the political order.[32] In the following chapters I describe how electoral politics and authoritarian populism achieve this outcome. By contrast, the radical organization of pessimism channels frustration with suffering and exclusion into political movements to dismantle the structures that produce them and to create more-just and more-inclusive social arrangements. In Guatemala these structures are the liberal (and now neoliberal) economy and the Ladino state, the former systematically dispossessing and exploiting indigenous and poor people, the latter gracing this misery with the stamp of legality and excluding Mayas from positions of power (Cojtí 2007). Both were founded on violence and require violence to persist. Many Mayan Sampedranos, like many other poor and indigenous Guatemalans, fought for redistributive social democracy and suffered the consequences. Reorganizing pessimism in a society like Guatemala involves forming alliances across lines of difference—between Mayas and Ladinos, men and women, rural and urban populations—lines that are tense and difficult to cross in Guatemala's authoritarian political culture, where bodies are strictly mapped onto hierarchal social roles (Nelson 1999). It also requires overcoming increasing stratification and antagonism within Mayan communities.

Certain moments testify to the potential of this radical organization to come into being: the revolution of 1944, the guerrilla movement, and more-recent movements in defense of territory and against corruption. These examples also speak to the difficulties in forming cross-ethnic, cross-class alliances for meaningful and lasting social change, and also to the shape-shifting powers of forces that maintain injustice. Reorganizing pessimism in Guatemala also involves taking action despite the knowledge that resistance will sometimes be met with sheer brutality. In moments of rupture, the belief that resistance is futile is overwhelmed by the knowledge that maintaining the status quo guarantees incessant assaults on bodies and lives, as powerful interests will concede nothing without a fight. Everyday suffering and flagrant exposure to harm reach a point of unbearability, where even potentially futile action seems better than doing nothing.

Foucault (2001) discusses the courage of the *parahesiastes,* the truth teller, who places herself or himself at risk by saying "something dangerous—different from what the majority believes" or is at least willing to say such a thing (15). In Guatemalan democracy, dissident speech becomes coded as threatening when connected to concrete efforts to alter the political economic order that runs on the broken bodies and dreams of the indigenous majority, not only imagining but attempting to bring into existence a new set of social relations that is based in reciprocity and equality, and that directly challenges entrenched hierarchies of race, class, and gender. Embodied dissident speech beyond the fear of pain or death was on display in the defiance of the gunfire of the National Police at Naranjales Bridge and in the courage of many other Guatemalan activists who protest despite the risk of beatings, abandonment, imprisonment, and assassination. These examples of the radical organization of pessimism are enduring features of neoliberal democracy in Guatemala.

PARTIES AND PROJECTS

Democratizing Sovereign Violence

The past thirty years have witnessed a remarkable transformation in local politics in Guatemala's rural highlands. Previously excluded from municipal authority, Mayas with various political affiliations now dominate the political scene, holding the top positions in most municipal governments.[1] Elections feature about a dozen parties led mostly by indigenous candidates. At stake are development projects—infrastructure, valuable personal assistance, and even jobs—who gets what and when—and the prestige of those who broker them. When Mayan leaders in San Pedro won mayoral elections in 1993, projects began to flow to rural villages, breaking the previous monopoly of the mostly Ladino town center. Not long after, the peace accords brought a wave of national and international development institutions and NGOs whose assorted programs aimed to heal and rebuild Mayan communities, raise the standard of living, defend human rights, and preserve and restore Mayan culture.

Official public narratives and numerous NGO mission statements, which are repeated by most politicians, frame development as the route to Mayan inclusion in a multicultural nation; it is both the goal of democracy and the pathway to it. Large infrastructure projects symbolize concrete proof of social and political advancement, as well as the reformed state's commitment to protect and defend Mayan life, a departure from past discrimination. Development is the material manifestation of democracy's existence and promise and the highly fetishized cornerstone of a new world of postrevolutionary politics. Local candidates—almost all of them men—compete to demonstrate their commitment and ability to deliver projects procured through party and NGO connections to their patronage networks.

As the primary form through which democracy is lived in rural villages, party-led, project-centered development is a crucial site where rural Mayas imagine and construct the state, formulate concrete political demands and identities, and produce community relations. Despite the effectiveness of party politics as a conveyor of material goods, most Mayas in San Pedro have expressed deep misgivings about it precisely because of the manner in which it accomplishes this feat: by abandoning villagers who back a losing candidate. Clientelist party politics, often called machine politics, is a process in which Mayas exercise sovereign violence against one another and blame one another for this violence.

Most scholars are optimistic about community development since the peace accords, seeing access to resources as the fruit of decades of struggle, which is undeniably true.[2] These assessments coincide with favorable discussions of the "politics of distribution," a political strategy focused on the incremental accrual of resource-based rights for marginalized populations.[3] Similar sensibilities inform recent positive reevaluations of patronage networks that show how these perennial scapegoats for democratic dysfunction that are regularly targeted for dismantling by development institutions such as the World Bank can in fact coincide with local moral economies and forms of reciprocity, double as social-assistance networks, and even create conditions for collective action.[4] But clientelist party politics in San Pedro violated local moral economies and further disrupted local social relations that had long been divided by class, religion, and party; had been severely damaged during the war; and had been only partially reconstituted by force under the civil patrols.[5] Although clientelism delivered much-needed resources, the intermittent, insufficient, and competitive nature of the distribution undermined rights-based claims and fragmented local political agency.

This chapter examines how instituting party-led, clientelist, project-centered development in the context of extreme poverty, violence, and pessimism reconfigured political imaginaries, demands, and practices in ways that decimated capacities for collective action, thus achieving core counterinsurgency ends through democratic means. Projects refocused radical demands for collective redistribution on winner-take-all competition between party factions for insufficient projects, where personal interest demolished collective interest. Zero-sum competition and the intermittent delivery of projects multiplied the effects of state violence by exacerbating insecurity and powerlessness while also fomenting a bitter "war in the villages" that broke down bonds of trust. This process reinforced state assertions of scarcity and reframed poverty as a form of suffering that villagers inflicted upon one another and chalked up to individual greed and corrupt Mayan leadership.

Through electoral competition, Sampedranos came to participate in the maintenance of their neighbors' "slow deaths," defined by Lauren Berlant (2007) as "the physical wearing out of a population and the deterioration of people in that population that is very nearly a defining condition of their experience and historical existence" (754). I call this turning of the responsibility for deciding who may live and who can be left to die the "democratization of sovereignty," which is a central mechanism through which social exclusion is normalized in neoliberal democracies. In this way, Mayas played an active role in managing the potentially transformative inclusion of indigenous communities into a body politic founded on colonial violence. However, local criticisms of party politics revealed elements of an alternative democratic imaginary focused on reciprocity and collective well-being and that refused to normalize structural exclusion.

Embedded Understandings in Party Politics

A far cry from rights-bearing citizens in "civil society" engaging in free and consensual relations with the state, Sampedranos were a "governed population" grappling with economic and political coercion in "political society" (Chatterjee 2004).[6] Beneath narratives of democracy, development, and indigenous rights existed local meanings and experiences of democracy produced through mundane practices: primarily the ways that development projects and programs were pursued, administered, obtained, and contested by villagers. This section excavates the "tacit knowledge" (Elyachar 2012) surrounding the distribution of development projects, particularly infrastructure projects, in rural political society. This tacit knowledge, typical for the region, reflected the institutionalization of party politics under severely adverse conditions.

The first understanding is that development means projects. *Project* is an umbrella term for any kind of assistance—potable water, roads, scholarships, jobs, or medicine—precious commodities that most villagers could not otherwise afford. DIGESA programs, parties, and institutions trained Mayas to think of individual, familial, and collective development in terms of discrete projects and to create prioritized lists that include such items as mills, latrines, and stoves. Villagers were always on the lookout for projects. I once heard Mariano Díaz compare a project to a girl in a miniskirt, a sign of the extent to which they were desired and elusive. I was repeatedly asked if I could help get projects. Having no access and not wanting to take sides in interparty disputes, I always declined. With attention fixed tightly on the local distribution of development projects, national concerns became a distant issue.

Another characteristic assumption in formal as well as informal discourse about development was that most projects come from the "state." Although a significant number of projects were available through NGOs and international institutions after the accords, the municipal government was the main source for the most valuable projects. Moreover, under democracy, political parties were the primary gateway to development projects through the municipality, and parties and politicians were thus, alongside the police, the primary manifestation of the state in everyday life and also of the economic power of national elites. NGOs were not entirely separate; they administered public services, such as health care, and individual NGO leaders often used their connections and resources to build a political following. Furthermore, in mundane interactions with politicians and institutions, Mayas were depicted and often depicted themselves as dependent on public resources in order to survive and thrive. The chronic lack of projects was frequently attributed to their having been distributed to other villagers or villages rather than the state's refusal or inability to meet the needs of more than a fraction of rural citizens.

As it stood, projects were insufficient for community needs and arrived irregularly. Institutions and parties responded to village demands, or not, on their own timetables. It could take years for a project to go through institutional channels. The larger the project, the longer villagers must wait. Waiting is emotionally charged because the needs are real and false promises of aid are common. Waiting for uncertain benefits can be an enervating and demobilizing process in which villagers enact their subordination to an indifferent state.[7] This is why Jennifer Burrell (2013) insists, conversely, that the "refusal to wait may be a powerful counter-hegemonic subjectivity relative to the state" (166–67). The most common excuse given by politicians to impatient villagers for reneging on a promise was scarce resources, widely assumed to be a nonnegotiable fact beyond the reach of politics.

All of these understandings were illustrated when I accompanied Mariano Díaz on a routine trip to a village whose leaders had requested an audience. They wanted to ask why the projects he had promised during his campaign had not yet arrived, more than a year later. They were livid and were unwilling to accept his councilor as a substitute. Díaz was ready. He first told them that "the municipal budget does not have enough for everyone. Imagine, there are fifty-six communities in San Pedro." He said they could make a request: "But I can't tell you right away today, but perhaps we can help you in some part. I can't give projects like this, continuously, because other communities are also getting them and it depends on more urgent necessities in other communities."

Díaz had promised twenty *laminas* (corrugated tin roofing) to everyone who voted for him, a ridiculously expensive promise given that each *lamina* costs about Q75 ($10). There are simply not enough *laminas* for every community, he explained; the budget is too small, and Guatemala is poor. He then explained that a recent landslide in another village had to take precedence, justifying their long wait. The generalized condition of desperation in which they waited was framed as background information rather than a problem that should be addressed directly. Underscoring his generosity, he told the assembly that he had made coffee for the displaced families in the early morning when they came to his house seeking help. He then criticized the assembly for being childish: "We can help you depending on your necessities, but we don't want you to be *necios* [foolish] like a child, for example, that to *fregar* [cause harm] you get wet or you give your shoe to a dog so that the dog eats it and then come running to Daddy to ask for help. That's no good." He proceeded to lecture them that "projects are not the solution for poverty." For that, he counseled, everyone had to pray to God, work hard, and give their children a good education, saying in effect that they were on their own. This formulation meshed with the logic of *capacidad* that framed villagers as personally responsible for their welfare, independent of the state. The villagers then expressed their worries about crime and children stealers: several cases were rumored to have happened in the area, underscoring their vulnerability.[8] For this, the *alcalde* suggested—because ordering this would be illegal—that they reorganize civil patrols to fight the delinquents just as, one of his councilors emphasized, they had defended themselves from the guerrillas before.

In addition to rehearsing counterinsurgency dogma, these more "realistic" admissions highlight a fundamental ambivalence in development discourse within neoliberal democracy. Most promises of development are false; the major political complaint is that politicians promise everything but never deliver. In these moments the state, in the form of the municipal government, is depicted as weak, too poor to promote development, while the distant state is indifferent to villager concerns. Guatemala is full of poor people, each with their needs; the state won't fix this, and the *alcalde* certainly can't. Moreover, despite being heralded as the route to multicultural inclusion, projects are not a solution to poverty. Villagers' woes are part of a larger, intractable problem that democratic politics can ameliorate but cannot change.

After the meeting, which started and ended late, we bounced down the hill in the darkness, the slippery, steep trail illuminated by my flashlight. When we were out of earshot, the *alcalde* let his emotions fly: "Did we convince them, or did we convince them?" he exclaimed. One of his councilors, a young, high-school-educated Mayan man, exclaimed, "Yes, because we came with strategies!" These villagers were still waiting for their *laminas* three years later. A truism about elections holds that "he who lies most, wins," but it is really a matter of whose lies are the most believable. Although *alcaldes* get most of the blame when projects do not materialize, they are not solely responsible for false promises; they are all but required to make them in order to get elected and are structurally unable to fulfill them.

Such discussions were all predicated on the fact, as every village child knew, that development projects were exchanged for political support; villagers must affiliate. Francisco was a Ladino who owned a small hotel in the town center and was the local representative, or coordinator, for a prominent political party. One day I encountered him at Pollolandia, a popular roasted-chicken restaurant, in Huehuetenango, the department capital. Roast chicken was a luxury, unavailable in San Pedro at the time. Over a salty leg quarter, he told me that his party had planned projects in five villages. They would start by extending roads to each and then give the villagers *laminas*. With so many parties, he explained, each only needed solid support in several villages, so they focused on a small fraction. The FRG won with a little over 2,200 votes in 2003, less than one fifth of the total voters, roughly a tenth of the voting-eligible population. Providing for every village was never part of the equation.

Francisco preferred to recruit followers in remote villages "because the villagers who live close, lie. They promise you their vote, but at the last minute, they take it back. They take advantage. The people who live in distant villages, where there is more poverty, are more honest." Poorer villagers had better "character," meaning that they were more pliable, or so he hoped. His formulation framed docility and obedience, albeit rooted in economic vulnerability, as an ideal quality of a democratic citizen, in perfect harmony with counterinsurgency logic. When I asked if the parties were taking advantage of poverty by lying to get votes, Francisco looked a bit deflated. Then, chuckling with a sheepish look, agreed that they were.

There are several ways to direct projects. "Big" projects, such as a new municipal building or a major road, affect the entire town or large regions. One of the first megaprojects undertaken by Mariano Díaz was a retaining wall on the steep road from town to the Pan-American Highway. More typically, *alcaldes* promise projects to villages, village subsectors, and individuals. Common examples of the latter include good-paying jobs on a municipal infrastructure project or as a schoolteacher, potable water, or food assistance. Infrastructure projects were not simply given to villages; villagers were expected to provide *mano de obra*: a contribution of manual labor. For a school project, for example, village men would gather rocks and sand, excavate the foundation, mix cement, and lay cinder blocks, and women would prepare them food. *Mano de obra* builds community along with projects, but not everyone participates.

In addition to initiatives promoting Mayan culture, many projects specifically target Mayan women. After the peace accords, women's position in Mayan communities became a salient concern for a number of state institutions and national and international NGOs. Funders often require women's participation, but often only perfunctorily. It is now common for women to participate on development committees and oversee projects directed toward women, and the 2002 law of Community Development Councils (COCODES) required two women and two men on village councils.[9] However, in San Pedro between 2004 and 2014, all village representatives to the municipal council were men, and women who addressed these assemblies, however competent and well spoken, were not taken seriously, especially if they spoke about women's issues. Typical "women's" projects include stoves, mills, and food relief, reinforcing dominant gender roles. A few NGOs talked about women's rights, and even fewer programs seriously assisted women as economic actors or encouraged them to form organizations. Some women's programs framed traditional indigenous "culture" as sexist and in need of reform, a discourse common among Ladinos. *Asociación* Ceiba was an exception in all regards. It trained participants in women's rights alongside human and indigenous rights, denounced sexism and domestic violence in Mayan and Ladino communities, and promoted economic initiatives, skills development, and leadership formation for women. Although only a tiny number of Mayan women in San Pedro identify as feminists, a growing number believe in and advocate for women's rights.

Seeking Office: Amassing Projects and People

Long before Election Day in Guatemala, local electoral campaigns are at their heart a competition between candidates (always men) to prove that they have "more people." Nowhere is this obsession with crowd size more on display than in the spectacle of party caravans: public shows of strength in numbers. During the electoral season, party affiliates with pickup trucks volunteer to drive in a train formation through town on a market day, their beds brimming with party supporters dressed in party colors. Making villagers display their party affiliation in public is a check against the double-crossing of parties by villagers, who would otherwise have greater leeway in making multiple promises, and it is also a way for parties to gain new affiliates by demonstrating the probability that their party will win, which is the most common argument for joining a party in the first place. Parties strongly encourage anyone to whom they have promised something to attend these and other public party events and to paint their houses in party colors with candidates' names. In 2015 I accompanied the caravan of the Líder Party to a village that was a strong base of support for their local candidate, Julio Ambrocio. On the trip, the central topic of conversation was size: how many trucks, how many people? We hit a snag on a harrowing passage over a cable suspension bridge, which not all of the loaded trucks could cross. After walking the rest of the way, party affiliates watched *fútbol* and listened to a musical performance, while the party provided *pepián de pollo* (chicken pepián) and soda, and vendors sold beer and ceviche. Dozens of Mayan women sat on plastic chairs in the shade of a building overlooking the *fútbol* field, completely uninterested in the game, while men ate ceviche and drank beer on the back patio in the scorching sun. In demonstrating numbers, caravans showcased the candidate and party's wealth and generosity, a taste of things to come, or so it was hoped.[10]

Most politicians start off in their villages, working with committees, learning how to navigate institutions and NGOs, and developing relationships with parties. Men with political aspirations first build connections in the state and in development institutions and start sharing the benefits with other villagers. Parties select and sometimes groom men they think would make strong candidates. Effective leaders become local legends. At least one thousand people attended Antulio Morales' funeral in 2004, crowded among the colorfully painted raised cement graves. One of the eulogy speakers, a lifelong friend and ally, spoke of his generosity and service, proclaiming that "every community in San Pedro has a *recuerdo* [souvenir] from Chepe."

Mariano Díaz established himself as a development rainmaker before holding office, working on the board of the Community Development for Peace Program (DECOPAZ) in its second cycle of projects, when the World Bank–funded institution in charge of implementing large infrastructure projects, originally administered by the UN, was turned over to the FRG administration (1999–2003) and subsequently politicized. In a speech before the Municipal Development Council (COMUDE), composed of representatives from the COCODES, Díaz claimed to have personally spoken with Óscar Berger, the newly elected president, who had promised to pay for paving the dangerously switchbacked and dusty road into town. Although some did not believe that he had met Berger, many thought the project was possible. After all, Díaz had already procured roads, potable water projects, and schools for several villages. Although the law strictly prohibited development institution board members from holding office, it was this conflict of interest more than anything else that made Díaz a viable candidate. Not surprisingly, attacks from political opponents focused on candidates' weakness and inability to bring projects: how they procured them was irrelevant. Villagers held parties to celebrate the completion of major projects and commemorated them with placards posted near the project site, painted in party colors, often listing the names of the *alcalde* and his advisors, and the total project cost, broken down into government contribution and the value of *mano de obra*. These ubiquitous signs and painted houses last long after elections, creating a feel of constant and omnipresent campaigning, as well as a reminder of the public and private debts of individuals and their location in the web of local alliances and divisions. However, it would be a mistake to confuse a family's political convictions with those of the politicians whose names and colors adorn their house.

Legitimate and Illegitimate Corruption

Becoming an *alcalde* almost immediately (although not permanently) catapulted the candidate and his close advisors into *"superado"* status. If they were not already rich, they would soon have access to money, legal and otherwise. Antulio Morales got rich in office, investing in cattle, houses, and other businesses. Mariano Diaz's new, four-story house towered over his neighbors' rooftops and was filled with nice furniture. His clothes were new and stylish, and he wore silver chains and a fancy watch. Mayan leaders appropriated official discourses of multicultural progress, materialized through development, in pursuit of personal wealth and power. In the early years of indigenous control of the *alcaldía,* individual gain and collective advancement through electoral politics and development seemed compatible, but they soon came into conflict.

Residents were disgusted by signs of wealth and luxurious consumption among politicians, which they saw as fruits of corruption. Díaz's large house and shiny new red truck were taken as proof that he was dipping into the till. These accusations were standard fare in the *boletín* (bulletin), an incisive, crass, and usually sexist gossip sheet filled with juicy details about town residents (mostly Ladinos) and politicians that was distributed anonymously twice a year. Corruption rumors about Morales focused on his numerous homes: in his village (*with a terrace!*), in the town center (*two stories!*), and in Huehuetenango, where he spent most of his second term (*just like a Ladino!*). People also pointed to his potbelly, a rarity among indigenous residents, as evidence of his greed but also his power. Corruption was a huge temptation for the mayor and his cronies, who deftly bypassed new legal regulations. It was the main reason many individuals ran for office. Some said there were so many political parties because so many leaders wanted a cut, far more than the *alcalde*'s monthly salary—Q7,000 ($900) in 2004—already nearly three times a teacher's pay.

Corruption was inescapable; even politicians who never sought it out felt compelled to participate; it was how business was done. Insiders told me that it was hard for politicians and their teams to avoid bribes and "commission payments" from construction agencies.[11] A former municipal secretary told me that there was no control of funds whatsoever, and when he opened his wallet to hand me his card, I saw a stack of cards emblazoned with construction-company insignias. Not long after, the departmental *controlador* was murdered, prompting great speculation about what he *must* have been wrapped up in. Rather than the aberration implied in the term itself, corruption was a direct product of the way that electoral democracy and party politics were institutionalized in rural towns. Denunciations of individual corruption obscured its near unavoidability as well as the finer-grained ethical distinctions that villagers drew between kinds of corruption.

Alejandro was a micro-regional representative to DECOPAZ, a position he had obtained through the FRG, not a community vote, which was the official requirement. One day after a monthly meeting with the program representative in a small office in the central square, he told me he was angry with another board member:

Alejandro: But [the representative] is not good in politics either. He likes to get money from the *diputados* [congressmen] and the construction companies, to get his "tip." If a person works, the people are going to see it. This is possible but between everyone.

NC: You can take some of the money?

Alejandro: That's what I'm saying, but if it is between everyone, between all of the directors. He's not the only one there; there are five people legally authorized. One dialogue between everyone. But he does it alone. If there is a project, he likes to look for the contractors himself, alone. Why? So that in the very hour we make the decision to go with that contractor. But that is not right. It's better, if he wants to do it that way, that he does it between everyone. A certain contractor can do the job, but between everyone, not just one. Not only one person is hungry. Not only one person is thirsty. And we sign together.

Similar to Mbembe's (2000) description of postcolonial Africa, Sampedranos used the idiom of food and hunger and full bellies to talk about power and to critique the unequal distribution of wealth between individuals and groups. The eating metaphor informed Alejandro's explanation of a "moral economy of corruption" (de Sardan 1999): socially configured rules about moral and immoral forms of illegality. Alejandro felt that accepting money from powerful individuals like *diputados* and party leaders was ethical, as long as everyone on the bottom got an equal share. Rather than "socially ruinous" (Smith 2008: 5), he saw it as a way of maintaining social bonds, rooted in a redistributive principle in response to the hunger and thirst of the recipients. The emphasis on deprivation explained why corruption by wealthy individuals for personal gain and excessive consumption was seen as immoral, as did the fact that most villagers viewed the Guatemalan state itself as immoral and corrupt. Although much of the anthropological analysis assumes that people follow these moral codes,[12] in San Pedro, while widely shared, this moral rule was difficult to follow. Conditions strongly encouraged Sampedranos to engage in self-interested corruption, but it was still seen as harmful. Rather than see this reaction as part of a timeless Mayan ethic of reciprocity, this attitude emerged out of experiences with neoliberal democracy in which some individuals "ate well . . . but failed to feed others" (West 2008, 118).

Political life was defined by accusations of illegitimate corruption involving individuals who were already "full" capturing resources that "less fortunate" villagers "truly" needed. As the prime distributors of resources, *alcaldes* were at the center of these disputes. For example, tempers flared when hundreds of bags of government fertilizer turned up in the private storage houses of Mariano Díaz's allies. Fertilizer is not only expensive; it is also necessary for growing crops in the poor soils farmed by most villagers, a fact cementing its association with food, money, and life itself and explaining its high profile in public displays of patronage. Confronted at a COMUDE (municipal development council) meeting, Díaz blamed the local representative from the Ministry of Agriculture, Cattle, and Food (MAGA), who immediately replied, "Mr. Mayor, please do not involve me in your *sinvergonzadas* [shameless antics]," although it is possible that they had worked together. Trapped, Díaz quoted the Bible and called the angry crowd "devils" and said that they were chasing him. Although the person who recounted this event to me was laughing, this was serious business; many *alcaldes* have been killed or assaulted for stealing and for breaking promises to villagers. José Antulio Morales was once ambushed and beaten nearly to death. Despite a shared distinction between legitimate and illegitimate forms, there was no consensus about which acts fell within the local moral economy of corruption: individuals on the receiving end of patronage classified what they received as legitimate in the face of accusations to the contrary, even as they would criticize others for taking unfair advantage.

Preoccupied with consolidating patronage networks and getting reelected, *alcaldes* attempted to outmaneuver recent attempts to regulate their power through the COCODE/COMUDE system. The Law on Development Councils requires that each village elect their own representative committee, a COCODE (community council), which then sends a representative to the COMUDE.[13] The COMUDE, not the *alcalde,* sets development priorities for the town, such as which projects are the most needed, in what villages, following which design, using which construction company. This law, founded by the Law of Development Councils as part of state decentralization policies,[14] intended to substantially decrease the *alcalde*'s power to run patronage networks and to profit from projects, but it did not address the underlying motive or provide an enforcement mechanism.

In 2000 the United Nations Office for Project Services (UNOPS) completed a study of San Pedro, listing priorities and goals for development that had been collectively determined in workshops. José Antulio Morales ignored this document, preferring to decide alone, most likely at the insistence of the party leadership, but also because of his own will to survive. He knew that to get reelected he had no choice but to leverage promises of projects for votes: others would if he did not. Both he and Mariano Díaz, with the help of the nonfunctioning *controlaría,* evaded the new COCODE/COMUDE system. Because Díaz inherited the institution intact, he simply appointed his followers to the village COCODES, making the COMUDE a rubber stamp. Communities usually consented because they did not want to lose out on projects from the acting mayor. When Díaz faced criticism (which was at every session I attended), he would simply call for a "yea" or "nay" vote to close debate. Angry members of other parties also began to circumvent the COMUDE, blaming Díaz.

As a result, the COMUDES were a space for debate and oversight, constantly emphasizing that, legally speaking, projects "belonged to the people" and that *alcaldes* were public servants, not kings or project gatekeepers. All of these are important elements of municipal politics and critical democratic imaginaries. In many towns, COCODES and COMUDES have fostered critical dialogue and collective resistance. But calls for rules enforcement had no teeth, and criticisms typically faulted local political custom for their frustrations with the mayor's actions rather than the institutionalization of party politics as the mechanism for the distribution of scarce resources, in other words, neoliberal democracy itself.

Remaking the State-Community Relationship

Development projects reinforced a narrative in which the state was no longer simply an external threat to villager lives but also a vital resource provider that was encountered in various guises in everyday life.[15] From core infrastructure, such as potable water and housing, to basic grains, fertilizers, cooking oil, chickens, cereal, and jobs, state-provided projects were the basic ingredients of daily sustenance. Numerous villagers told me about projects that had improved their lives, sometimes tremendously. Imagine the difference between having water at home versus gathering it in buckets and carrying it a great distance, or an electrical hookup versus candles. But these resources were woefully inadequate and, when acquired from political parties, had strings attached. Party-led, project-centered clientelist development reorganized Sampedranos' affective perceptions and political behaviors in distinctive and consequential ways.

First, project-centered development established projects as the sole political objective and demand. Project procurement devoured the time and political energies of village governance, which was now organized around the development committee system rather than traditional authorities recognized in the peace accords. Village-level political discussion, committees, and organizing were almost completely dedicated to the pursuit of projects from the state and the occasional NGO.

Second, the simultaneous regularity and inadequacy of individual assistance programs transformed widespread economic insecurity into feelings of dependency on political parties for survival. When I asked rural farmers—and I asked many—what would happen if the state stopped subsidizing fertilizer, several said they would "just not eat." Despite these grave concerns, there was no discussion of changing the political economic structures that consign entire communities to poverty and dependency. This was caused primarily by decades of state violence, but electoral contests in search of projects created an entire domain of politics that sidestepped foundational inequalities. Most conversations focused on what individuals, families, and villages themselves should do to ensure their own well-being rather than uniting together to demand higher levels of state investment. Common answers were to seek a party affiliation or migrate to the United States. This was a far cry from the 1970s, when demands for infrastructure were connected to projects for deeper social transformation.

Third, it reinforced disempowerment, most notably through villager rituals of supplication in front of party representatives. When villagers visited Francisco—the Ladino party representative—hoping to get his assurances about specific projects, they held their hats in their hands. They spoke softly, respectfully, in overly formal language, with their eyes turned to the floor, performing submissiveness and a using a rhetoric of humility and necessity. People who approached me looking for projects, even some I had known for years, used the same impassioned tone. Petitioners evoked a sense of desperation. They were often proud village leaders but enacted uncommon deference because they were literally at his mercy. His tone in response expressed concern but remained noncommittal and aloof, conveying that he held all the cards in this relationship and was willing to turn his back. Francisco often subjected villagers to condescending lectures about following through on their end of the bargain.

The postwar state's carefully cultivated identity as protector and provider of Mayan life did not displace its identity as cold and indifferent to indigenous life. Conditioning aid on party affiliation reminded villagers of the looming possibility that assistance could be withheld. During a campaign visit to a village in the northern sector in 2011, after the candidate spoke, an elderly man raised his voice:

> If you win, are you going to come back? Are you going to help us? You speak so beautifully, but we don't know if you are going to win or another. Julio came here, and he also spoke beautifully. Now his term is almost over, and he hasn't come here, nor has he come near the people from here. We have called, and were told that he was not around, or that he was out. Who is against him, for the power that he has? And worse if this [candidate] is the same, when we look for him, he will never come here. Is this all right? An authority is like a father and should watch over all of his children. But if he has us in abandonment, I ask, "Is this acceptable?" Now you ask for our vote and then you do not make good on your commitment. Those are my three words to speak.

Abandonment epitomizes the sovereign power to "let die," in addition to taking life (Foucault 1980). Sampedranos know how little their lives matter in state calculations, realize how dependent they are on state resources, and recognize the ever-present possibility of falling into abandonment. Participating in social movements rendered some groups abandonable. When the neighboring *municipio* of Colotenango elected a URNG mayor in 2000, opponents warned that state assistance would stop.[16] But by far the most common way that communities become marked for abandonment was simply backing a losing candidate.[17] And as the villager eloquently explained, backing the winner was not always enough. Insufficient funds ensured that the vast majority would not receive assistance.

One man, a URNG member, said, "I have it analyzed, about the projects. On the one hand, they're good; on the other, they're bad. Maybe I'm mistaken, but I think the people sell themselves out for a gift. I accept [projects], but I'm not going to vote for their party." Guatemalan leftists criticize the exchange of projects for votes as an unethical and undemocratic. They see it as a problem of ignorance; villagers should be educated to cast a *voto consciente* (conscious vote), presumably for parties like the URNG that promise social transformation and on principle do not (typically) exchange projects for votes. Many villagers, not just URNG members, agreed that trading votes for projects was not correct. It is not that villagers do not know better but rather that these rules have been imposed on them by outside forces, and most see no other realistic method for acquiring resources.

Party-led, project-centered development is a coercive reminder of sovereign power. Rural Mayans measure the value or productivity of projects and electoral politics not in relation to other political alternatives—which were rendered unthinkable by violence—but to the threat of abandonment. Heightening this perception is the fact that the politics surrounding community development reproduce an image of the state, through political parties, as "vertically encompassing" Mayan communities, reinforcing its claims to dominate social force relations (Gupta and Ferguson 2002). These understandings were dramatized by the FRG's promise to pay $500 to party affiliates who had served in state-mandated civil patrols. Names were collected on a laptop computer. The FRG candidate assured them that the computer would "know" how they voted, adding that God would too. This was a very effective vote-getting strategy, the basis of which is linking a promise for resources to a threat of punishment, the certainty of which is guaranteed by a high-tech fetish: a laptop, a mobile panopticon, especially for people who know little about computers. The uncertain gift of resources was an unsubtle, if often unremarked, reminder of the state's indifference to indigenous life, knowledge that dampens the local sense of political agency. An FRG Party affiliate denied the computer ever went to the villages (although it had) but admitted that *"manipulación hubo"* ("there was manipulation").

Development committee leaders render village desires far more legible to parties and state bureaucracies than ever before, enabling them to address more acute ones while ignoring others. This nonconfrontational dialogue between rural indigenous communities and the state was similar to the vision of the planners of the Rural Cooperative Development Project in the 1970s.[18] In that model, communication would enable a rational management of resource distribution: no community would be left out completely, and no community should receive so many projects as to incite jealousy, yet both of these outcomes were compelled by the exigencies of patronage and electoral competition. In the 1990s the Antulio Morales coalition kept resources within its patronage circles and mostly ignored other villages and the impoverished northern sector in particular, leading to considerable resentment.

Democratizing Sovereign Violence

In addition to reinforcing the effects of sovereign violence and altering conceptions of development, party-led, project-centered development weakened trust and political unity in the villages. The scarcity of state offerings guaranteed that personal and familial gains entailed relegating other community members to abandonment. This political harnessing of visceral desperation fueled a cutthroat politics of self-interest that divided villages, communities, and families into numerous party factions. In this context, the only solution to corruption was more corruption. By the time I arrived in Los Altenses, villagers habitually looked upon many of their neighbors as threats, competitors for access to basic resources that everyone needs and wants.

A young Mayan man, Sergio, a recent high school graduate, captured this situation succinctly: "They say that politicians lie. Those than win, win for lies. For that reason, maybe it's better to just find a party for your own personal interests. Joining a party is how a person can find a job. If you don't join a party, you are left out of work." Several equated politics and sports, where you either win or lose with no in-between. This left little room for compromise. Local politicians follow the lead of party higher-ups, who encourage or even insist upon clientelist practices. However, the zero-sum perspective that guided these transactions relied on a questionable assumption of scarcity that conflated the amount of resources in the budget with the total amount of resources potentially available to communities.

Villagers divided into sometimes more than a dozen parties, fully aware that anything they gained would come at the expense of their neighbors. Parties increasingly courted village subsectors, rather than entire villages, further poisoning micro-relations between villagers. Divisions in San Pedro were never about ideology, which was widely shared.[19] The tentative political unity that emerged in the late 1980s in Los Altenses fragmented when all groups were not included equally in the distribution of projects: a direct effect of electoral democracy. After Antulio Morales took power, and especially after the peace accords, close friends, family members, and the most dedicated supporters of his coalition received noticeably more and more valuable development projects than other villages. This unevenness was not a result of the failure of some residents to "constitute themselves as deserving political society" (Anand 2011, 546); its source was the basic insufficiency of development funds managed by *alcaldes* exacerbated by the structural imperative to distribute those funds unevenly. Groups who were passed over even after their candidates won held grudges and sought their own parties, becoming the opposition. This pattern built over several electoral cycles to produce pervasive conflict. The air of these antagonisms lingered in the village, in personal encounters and in community meetings, or in absences and avoidances, sometimes long after the original event. Divisions between extended families layered over internal divisions among families.

This cycle of division motivated many villagers to support the FRG. Candelaria Ruíz was in her mid-forties, married to a freelance carpenter, with two children. She was an evangelical who earned money praying for people and faith healing, for which she had a particular skill, but one that some Catholics saw as either phony or witchcraft. Many criticized her for not wearing indigenous dress, but her services were in high demand. Candelaria campaigned hard for Mariano Díaz in villages across San Pedro. She prayed publicly for God to bless his campaign and painted her house blue and white with the FRG insignia. She told me that she was the "number one" for Díaz and that he had offered her a position in the corporation, which she had refused in order to continue her ministry.

She denied voting for Díaz because he was evangelical, however, explaining that "We don't make an exception for anyone. We treat everyone the same. I will support anyone as long as they are really Christian," presumably including nonevangelicals. Díaz attended a different church, but "it is the same word of God," echoing a common sentiment. Although Candelaria Ruiz loved Mariano Díaz, she disliked Ríos Montt, whom she said was a murderer, although she never said that on the campaign trail. She squinted when I asked why she joined the FRG, apparently annoyed that I had not already heard about the problem she had railed against for several years:

> They say that we're poor and don't work, but they only give *viviendas* [houses] to their family members and good friends. Only for them even though other people sign up for the projects. I signed up, I handed in my form, and afterwards I was told that it was not valid. "Yours didn't go through," even though it had a signature. They don't advise about most projects. Look at his friends' houses. They all got new ones, and they already had *viviendas*! Some of us others are using plastic and *ranchitos* (houses made of sticks). They signed up and didn't get anything. [*Viviendas*] should go to the most needy, everyone equally.
>
> There are *auxiliares* who are supposed to advise us. One came today to tell us that we would be doing work to maintain the road. But they don't advise about food, medicine, or vaccines for animals. When we don't know anything, their chickens are already vaccinated!
>
> We call him Chepe *chuch* [Chepe the dog] because he grabs everything for himself. His friends in our village are already taken care of. Ask where [person's name] got 300 cinder blocks! That is the village's money; it was what was left over on a village housing project! They grabbed it. That is why there is division. There is a war between groups. We don't go to reunions anymore. It's better to work with your own sweat. They don't do anything for us. It can be houses; it can be food assistance—all for them! With Natanael, he would give a little bit to everyone. But Chepe only gives to his supporters. We helped Antulio in the beginning, but he didn't give us any thanks. Not one cent. There were 150–200 houses [that were to be distributed] in the whole town. But they didn't give them to the poor people. Poor people are pushed to the side. Some people also don't like Chepe because he had *caseras* [mistresses]. But most were tired of the favoritism. *El hace excepción de personas.* [He distinguishes between people. He discriminates.]

Her religious fervor for Mariano Díaz was fueled by her anger over project favoritism during José Antulio Morales' administration. Candelaria Ruiz was incensed and felt that Antulio Morales' political methods violated a moral economy of material equality, especially attention to the vulnerable. Most galling was that his favoritism ignored *real needs* among villagers, such as people living in houses made of sticks, children without clothing or shoes, and lack of access to running water. People who already had more continued to take more, furthering existing disparities. Development committee members placed party allegiances above their duties to their community. She even questioned their faith: "They only say that they're Christians." Her belief that projects should go to the neediest villagers resonated far beyond her religious sect and was voiced by most Sampedranos, even as they flagrantly violated this ethical principle.

In this world of party politics, resource distribution was sorted out by competition between village headmen who represented a particular faction of villagers and who enjoyed individual access to the fruits of corruption from projects implemented under their stewardship. Sometimes this competition, driven in large measure by economic hardship and ever more noticeable inequalities, turned violent. I heard several reports of physical fights that erupted among some village men months after the elections were over, so bitter were the disagreements. Affiliating with a party was one of the best ways to get a job, or material aid, but it was no guarantee.

Party politics was widely disparaged as a wicked domain, controlled by personal interest, corruption, and lies, something that many individuals avoided in order to protect their reputations. Talk of personal interest spoke to a deep loss of faith in one another or in a better possible world. No one trusted politicians, and they barely trusted their neighbors. When projects did not arrive, or politicians acquired new luxury items, such as trucks, clothing, or houses, they were assumed to be thieves. When the second, postelection payment for the patrollers did not arrive, villagers were furious with Mariano Díaz. Many individuals privately admitted their own self-interested motives, even as they accused their neighbors of *interés*. McAllister (2003) argues that Chupolenses' perception of the Guatemalan state as fundamentally illegitimate did not impede their willingness to accept state resources. Sampedranos likewise welcomed state resources, needed them desperately, and deserved far more than they received, but they strongly objected to the way they were distributed.

This description of how Sampedranos relate to projects and parties runs counter the nostrum, common on the left, that ignorant rural villagers have been tricked by populist rhetoric or that greedy villagers sold their votes and collective futures for *regalitos* (little gifts). Earlier in his career, Antulio Morales likely viewed the pursuit of personal interest as consistent with the struggle for community rights on the new political terrain, although by the end of his tenure the local movement was deeply fractured. Most "sold out" because they saw individual benefits as the only thing politics could bring. In both cases, self-interested politics became thinkable relative to the absence of faith in meaningful alternatives, not ignorance or greed. Perversely, state and para-state policies that connected hopes for collective advancement to practices of political self-interest created division and disillusionment and further undermined their ability to imagine or build a collective future. Rather than a reflection of "true" human nature or "Indian backwardness," the politics of personal interest in San Pedro was a lamentable but in many ways predictable response to the perverse incentives created by the installation of a competitive, resource-driven form of electoral politics in a context of general abandonment and violence.

Widespread self-interest undermined the credibility of Mayan political leaders, who were almost universally seen as corrupt. José Antulio Morales' rapid economic advancement fueled rumors of malfeasance and even frustrated his supporters. Many of his family members abandoned his coalition to join the FRG.[20] When I asked Petróna Lázaro, a teacher and the only indigenous woman to participate in the municipal corporation (with José Antulio Morales), if she would consider running for *alcalde,* she quipped, "Why, so people can call me 'Ladróna?'" This is a play on the Spanish word *ladrón* (thief) and Petróna. The possibilities for corruption multiplied alongside Mayan political ascendance, as did its inevitability. Delivering development allowed Mayan politicians to be taken seriously as political leaders in the first place, but corruption surrounding development projects called Mayan leadership into question.[21]

It was disheartening that soon after Mayas won spaces of political power, they were discredited, even though corruption existed and racism flourished under Ladino *alcaldes.* An older man, one of the first indigenous catechists in the town and an early member of the Morales coalition, summarized the dilemma:

> The struggle now is that a Maya should govern. For years only Ladinos were in the government. Now there are indigenous, but perhaps it is the same as before, or even worse. We have an example with the *alcaldes* here in San

Pedro. The problem now is embezzlement of money. They just come to steal. Before there were only three candidates, and one would win. Now there are fourteen because everyone wants to get some money. That is why Guatemala is fucked. We don't know what to do to resolve this.

Corrupt, divisive politics have also emboldened critics of indigenous political ascendance, satisfied in the belief that this population was ill prepared for citizenship and governmental authority. Such critics undoubtedly include the leadership of political parties that snag millions of indigenous votes every four years. Their political success, and the negative local outcomes, circulate in diverse publics the false notion that Mayas lack the innate intelligence to self-govern, reinforcing the naturalness of their marginalization. But such dismissals mistakenly equate compromised democratic engagements in contexts of extreme violence and exclusion with innate proclivities.

Development shortfalls, poverty, and corruption persist not because individual politicians fail, which certainly happens; they are features of a political economic system founded on indigenous subjugation that is recognized as legal and defended through violence. Inadequate resources, loose regulations, and divisive party strategies make corruption and favoritism almost compulsory. Many individuals opt not to participate, but most feel compelled by necessity. The major limitation of common critiques of indigenous candidates and elected officials is that they obscure the fact that even if *alcaldes* were not corrupt, there would still not be enough for everyone under the current conditions. Mayas need guaranteed access to basic resources and should not be coerced to relinquish their right to organize politically and express their political beliefs in order to compete for them in what amounts to a lottery system. To demand that they do so is to violate their most basic human rights, recognized in Guatemala's constitution but rarely put into practice.

Foucault describes a shift in the exercise of sovereign power from classical society, in which sovereignty centered on the decision "to kill or let live," to modern biopolitics, where sovereignty involves interventions "to 'make' live and 'let' die" (2003, 241). Certain forms of life are invested and protected; others are allowed to die off. Unlike spectacles of sovereign power, which persist,[22] Foucault suggests that these permitted deaths appear to simply occur but are in fact made to happen, done purposefully.[23] In the cutthroat, competition for projects through political parties, the Guatemalan state's role as enforcer of an unequal system of property recedes, but structural violence does not remain faceless. Rather than directly attributing abandonment and *engaño* (deception) to the institutionalization of democratic competition in an exclusionary sociopolitical order, villagers blame their suffering on the greedy, corrupt, and undemocratic decisions of candidates and other villagers. These recriminations frame the sovereign power to "let die" not as something primarily exercised by the state or national elites, but by Mayas themselves. This democratization of sovereignty incites communities marked as disposable to use elections to determine who lives and who is allowed to die. This is not a robust conception of sovereignty, understood as self-determination and the development of self-governing capacity; it actively erodes those dimensions and grants Mayas only the power to administer the distribution of structural violence among themselves. Democracy furnishes local accomplices that, unlike the state, can be confronted directly. Inciting complicity with foundational violence among subordinated populations is a defining feature of democratic development politics in neoliberal San Pedro.

Sampedranos felt compelled to participate in party politics to obtain vital resources but had little influence over the terms of engagement. Electoral politics renders villagers complicit in violence against their neighbors, whose abandonment they lament, but feel compelled to condone as it is connected to their own well-being and suffering. If the aim of empowering Sampedranos to take municipal power and manage development after the violence was to create nationalist, state-identified Mayas, this failed. However, opening a limited space for the inclusion of a sanctioned route for Mayas to access to resources through elections extended the counterinsurgency by reorganizing village-level demands and fragmenting village solidarity. Villagers trusted each other even less than they had under the civil patrol system. Instead of united in a political movement to transform Guatemala's colonial political economy, or even to protect one another, Sampedranos competed for access to limited state and nonstate resources while their marginal status in apartheid-like Guatemalan society remained unchanged or grew worse. Sampedrano leaders' strategic decision to join big political parties to pursue collective advancement through development backfired in ways they could have scarcely anticipated and that few have publicly acknowledged.

Distribution of limited yet vital resources through electoral competition in conditions of extreme poverty and exclusion transformed politically active Mayas into agents of sovereign violence. Political parties, with Mayan personnel, harvest structural violence, offering temporary relief for poverty, exclusion, and abandonment while welding the victims into complicity with the very forces that cause them. As a result, despite sharing broad aspects of a decidedly antagonistic and oppositional subaltern political cosmology, Sampedranos found it increasingly difficult to trust one another and to speak with one political voice. This runs counter to the recent tendency among social scientists to view patron-client relations as consistent with grassroots conceptions of reciprocity and political agency. Fragmentation and resentment placed Sampedranos as a collective in a much weaker position vis-à-vis other sovereigns, such as parties, state agencies, development institutions, mining companies, and market forces, and in a weaker position to ally with social movements with which they share overlapping objectives. Mayan Sampedrano support for the FRG in 2003, even among evangelicals, was not primarily based on faith in the party or the national candidate; it was a tragic form of resistance to a violent system of competitive electoral politics that made villagers complicit in their own exclusion and consecrated this outcome as the will of the people, even as they fought to overcome it.

Almost everyone, including those who benefited, was critical of false promises, favoritism, self-interest, and division, and recognized the inability of projects to solve poverty. Many advocated prioritizing projects for the most needy. But the logic of party politics demands the former and does not allow the latter. Several towns have formed civic committees or joined parties such as the URNG that refuse to promise projects for votes, but these parties almost always lose, so strong is the pull of resources. Some Sampedranos have criticized party politics as an intentional strategy of divide and conquer, a new mechanism for thwarting Mayan political power.

This outcome should not be mistaken as Mayan backwardness or false consciousness, or blamed on individual moral failings, but seen as an effect of installing democratic procedures in conditions of structural and political violence. Most villagers I spoke with, from various parties, were quite concerned with the negative outcomes of party politics, but they also had very real needs, which were pressing enough to justify participating in

politics, as ugly as it was. Although these spaces were hard-fought concessions to long-standing grassroots struggles, the forms of resistance they
enabled were deeply contradictory and had become an obstacle to coalition building.

Through their disappointing experiences with electoral politics, Sampedranos have come to imagine an alternative form of democracy, one not
based on trade-offs between personal and collective interest, but instead
based on reciprocity, respect, and shared humanity, where the needs of
the most vulnerable are paramount. This "vision of a right order" (Ekern
2011) is not intrinsic to a timeless Mayan culture but is a dialectical inversion of actually existing democracy. Their alternative democracy can exist
only when its subjects have their basic needs met and can participate as
equals. Sampedranos are hungry for such an alternative, literally and figu-
ratively, but doubtful that one will emerge and remain entangled in webs
of power in ways that make it hard to organize.

A key question is whether democracy has established development as
more than an expectation in rural communities but as a *right,* a durable claim on resources. It was a positive sign that most political parties
competed to offer projects to rural villages and endorsed conditional
cash-transfer programs. But this redistributive mechanism was also heavily criticized. Neoliberals and many leftists fault them for reproducing
dependency, corruption, and clientelism.[24] Some warn of the deployment
of piecemeal reforms to palliate and normalize austerity and privatization,
and forestall broader claims to resources. Some may read the persistence
of development and the arrival of cash transfer as the successful end of
a long struggle for resources, an effort that Ferguson (2015) calls "distributive labor" and that is typically not counted. But development funds
tapered off after the post-accords boom and have always come with strings
attached. With cash-transfer programs, as with previous projects, many
Mayas point to contradictions between state promises to deliver the basic
necessities and the inadequacy of projects to meet their most basic needs.
One wonders how long the state can provide resources only for villagers fortunate enough to be included in patronage before enough abandon
parties in favor of less corrosive, if riskier, paths to deeper redistribution.

Building self-governance requires seeking ways to distribute scarce
resources without promoting division. The existence of structural inequality and dire need does not persuade everyone to give in to self-interest. Community leaders throughout the highlands have identified and attempted

various strategies to amend these problems by reforming the electoral system. The COMUDES offer one avenue for communities to devise "rules of engagement" with parties, specifying criteria for the distribution of projects; civic committees are another attempt to bypass the party system. Strengthening indigenous authority structures offers another potential hedge against atomization (Ekern 2011, Sieder 2011a). These strategies often presume the existence of a form of agency that is not disfigured first by counterinsurgency, then by neoliberal democracy and development, but can nonetheless be part of weaving alternative democracy from below.

Figure 4. UNE Party operatives distribute *laminas* to affiliates, 2011. Photo by author.

Figure 5. Líder political party caravan, 2014. Photo by author.

Figure 6. Julio Ambrocio on the campaign trail speaking with a group of village women, 2011. Photo by author.

Figure 7. Village men listening to a candidate respond to criticisms of false promises and abandonment lodged by village elder (right), 2011. Photo by author.

CRUEL POPULISM

Mutilating the People

When Efraín Ríos Montt's helicopter attempted to land at a presidential campaign rally in San Pedro Necta at the peak of the 2003 electoral season, he was greeted with hostility. Mayan FRG supporters congregated in the municipal *fútbol* field holding blue-and-white party banners were outnumbered by a swarm of angry villagers, mostly indigenous men, armed with machetes and hoes, and throwing rocks.[1] They forced Ríos Montt to make an emergency landing in a nearby town. The enraged crowd consisted of former civil self-defense patrollers ("ex-PAC"), the antiguerrilla paramilitary mustered by Ríos Montt and disbanded by the peace accords. Ex-PAC members were furious because although the FRG had promised them payment for their service—the ex-PAC movement's central demand—they had paid only the party affiliates, even many who never patrolled. Weeks later, the San Pedro ex-PAC kidnapped four journalists from the *Prensa Libre* when they arrived to report on an ex-PAC demonstration at Puente Cable, blocking the Pan-American Highway. The reporters were beaten, threatened with being set on fire, kept overnight against their will, then released when the FRG-led government promised to honor the ex-PAC payments. Despite betraying a significant portion of what many assumed to be his natural constituency, Ríos Montt and his party won the local election handily. Emblematic of a violent and chaotic electoral season, Guatemala's sixth since the democratic transition and the second since the peace accords, these events raise serious questions about the nature and sources of grassroots support for the authoritarian populists in the rural highlands.

A notorious former dictator who took power by coup just before the worst period of the armed conflict, key author of the scorched-earth campaign, supreme leader of the ultra-right, ultra-corrupt FRG, a noted evangelical who campaigned as a friend to the poor and humble, General Efraín Ríos Montt was an enigmatic presidential candidate to say the least. His vituperative rhetoric blended law-and-order themes with apocalyptic Christian moralizing and populist promises to defend poor indigenous communities against the rich.[2] Ríos Montt's campaign was resoundingly opposed by the national press, human rights organizations, the United Nations, the Catholic Church, and donor countries (including the United States), all of which saw his rise as a return to the violent past and a threat to democratic reforms.[3] Many Guatemalans, especially those on the left, hated and feared Ríos Montt and regarded him as a mass murderer—quite distinct from his populist persona.[4] Ríos Montt lost in the first round of the national election, but the FRG won a near sweep of the mayoral races in the rural highlands, ensuring his congressional seat and immunity from prosecution. What were Mayas who voted for Ríos Montt thinking? What did he, and other mafia-style politicians, mean to them? Did he represent hope, victimization, or both? Did widespread Mayan support for the far right, and the failures of the left, signal Mayan indifference to progressive politics, as some have suggested?[5] What did "support" and lofty ideals like "democracy" even mean after decades of counterinsurgency and centuries of colonization?

Guatemalan Populisms

Populism is widely recognized as an enduring feature of political life in Guatemala and most of modern Latin America, but it defies easy characterization because of its heterogeneous contents; the analytical slippage among populist politicians, movements, and discourses; gaps between rhetoric and policies; and its evolution over time. The entities most closely associated with Guatemalan populism in the mid-twentieth century were the nationalist governments of the Democratic Spring of 1944–1954—led by the Revolutionary Action Party (PAR)—and the various organizations of the revolutionary left after the 1954 coup:[6] peasant and indigenous organizations, labor unions, students, and armed guerrilla factions. It was part of a wave of Latin American nationalism that exploded with the Mexican Revolution in 1910–1917 and included Augusto Sandino's improbable stand against the US Marines in Nicaragua from 1927 to 1933. The PAR challenged the dictatorship, the oligarchy, and US imperialism, using mass organization of the peasantry and working classes to pursue democratic and redistributive policies. A philosophy professor guided by a moral vision of "spiritual socialism" (not actual socialism), Juan José Arévalo became Guatemala's first democratically elected president in 1944. He abolished forced labor, created social programs, and legalized unions, among other social democratic reforms. President Jacobo Arbenz, a military officer and Arévalo's defense minister, issued the bold Decree 900, a law that empowered local unions to claim uncultivated holdings of the United Fruit Company, Guatemala's largest landowner at the time.[7]

These reforms were vanquished but not forgotten during the decades of military dictatorship that ensued after the 1954 coup. Revolutionary nationalism spread among urban mestizo working classes, unions, university students, and the Guatemalan Worker's Party (PGT). Taking inspiration from the 1959 Cuban Revolution, these groups formed several armed Marxist Leninist organizations to fight for democracy, economic redistribution, and agrarian reform. Revolutionary and radical populist movements found eager adherents as well as detractors in rural indigenous communities, whose members perceived and responded to them according to their own moral economies, cosmovisions, economic conditions, and political struggles.

Human rights groups and popular organizations advanced cautiously in the miniature democratic space that opened in 1985. Leftist-style populism did not fully reemerge until leftist parties and social movements were legalized by the peace accords more than a decade later. By then, the social composition of the left had changed considerably: Mayanists and feminists had formed separate organizations because of both racism and patriarchy in the traditional left, as well as the need to better pursue distinctive agendas. In 1999 Álvaro Colom Caballeros—nephew of Colom Argueta, the popular reformist candidate assassinated right before the 1978 election—ran for president with the New Guatemalan Democratic Front (FNDG), a united coalition of former leftists, peasant and indigenous movements, human rights organizations, and feminist movements.[8] The FNDG placed third, with 12.36 percent of the popular vote in the first round.

Indigenous-rights activist Rigoberta Menchú, winner of the 1992 Nobel Peace Prize, ran for president in 2007 and 2011 with the Winaq Party, an alliance of leftist parties and peasant and indigenous movements. She called for full implementation of the accords, increased investment in rural development and education, taxing the rich, respect for human and indigenous rights, and ending impunity for organized criminals who had infiltrated the state. She also criticized austerity, privatization, and extractivism. However, Menchú won only 3 percent of the vote in both races, a sign that the crisis of the left had only deepened.[9] After the mid-2000s, the leftist movements expanded their opposition to free trade, austerity, mining, and other faces of "neoliberal extractivism" (see chapter 4).

Right-wing populisms have far overshadowed and outperformed left populisms since democratization, raising concerns about the health of Guatemalan democracy. Conservative movements' rejection of the peace accords and their violent implementation of neoliberal policies did not stop them from gaining a strong following in rural areas. In 1999 Alfonso Portillo, a former leftist who had joined the FRG, won the presidency. Portillo's candidacy also helped the FRG circumvent a constitutional ban against anyone who had taken power by coup, a provision written specifically to exclude Ríos Montt. Portillo espoused a populist discourse that favored poor, indigenous campesinos over the primarily Ladino Guatemala City in an election that centered on Ríos Montt even though he was not on the ballot.[10] Despite his association with the former general and reports that Portillo had murdered two students while teaching in Mexico, he won in a landslide, taking 63 percent of the vote against the conservative sugar magnate and free market conservative Óscar Berger. In office, Portillo gained a reputation and a durable following as a champion of the poor by raising the minimum wage, fighting monopolies to keep food prices low, launching antipoverty programs, and emphasizing citizen security, while keeping Ríos Montt, the party's supreme leader, in power with impunity.[11]

After a term defined by corruption, repression, impunity, a stalled peace process, and deepening neoliberal reforms, Ríos Montt ran for president himself in 2003 in open defiance of the constitutional ban. Like Portillo, Ríos Montt challenged entrenched elites, promised to expand pro-poor policies, and took a hard line on crime. His detractors denounced extreme corruption under Portillo and cited Ríos Montt's responsibility for geno-cide and warned of a return to the war if he was elected. Progressives, foreign observers, and the traditional elite breathed a collective sigh of relief when he placed third in the first round of voting. Óscar Berger, lead-ing the Grand National Alliance (GANA), an alliance of business-oriented parties, defeated Álvaro Colom in the runoff.

Álvaro Colom Caballeros was finally elected president in 2008 with the center-left National Unity of Hope (UNE) Party. A milquetoast populist, he campaigned on a promise to implement MIFAPRO, a cash-transfer antipoverty program similar to others in Latin America, which won him a strong following in rural communities.[12] He toned down leftist rheto-ric considerably, embracing the peace accords (the UNE Party symbol is a dove) and indigenous rights alongside mild criticisms of the economic elite. He defeated Otto Perez Molina, another former general turned presi-dential candidate who was accused of war crimes and who campaigned as a right-wing populist promising to use state violence to fight crime to restore order and promote development. Colom Caballeros governed as a pro-market liberal. He implemented MIFAPRO, while selectively repressing rising movements against land grabs and resource extraction, notoriously unleashing state security forces on Q'eqchi' lowlanders in the Polochíc Valley who had been displaced by sugar plantations. In 2011, Perez Molina, having lost to Colom Caballeros in 2007, won the presi-dency with strong support from the urban Ladino middle class in Guate-mala City, who were driven to outrage by a grisly epidemic of crime and violence.

Many Guatemalan neoliberals denounce populism as a threat to national stability, property, and the democratic rule of law.[13] They see populism as inherently divisive and illiberal, and denounce populist poli-ticians as *caudillos* (authoritarian strongmen). Yet even staunch critics resort to populist appeals in rural areas as they work to forge connections with poor people and in the process define who the people are and who they are not. In 2011, for example, I followed a mayoral candidate with the center-right Union of National Change (UCN) to a campaign stop in a remote village in the northern sector. To a crowd of mostly male villagers, he spoke of his credentials as a nurse ("Yes, I can save lives!") and his rural local origins ("I have lived in San Pedro all my life. I was born in [a specific village]. My father was Don X . . ."). His discourse reinforced his links to the area, his honesty, and his work ethic. And by addressing the audience in Mam and describing himself as an "eater of *chunch*," greens that were eaten mostly by indigenous villagers, he evoked his indigeneity.[14] His followers passed out warm cans of soda, luxury items in rural villages, assisting him in playing the role of benevolent patron.

Following Ernesto Laclau (1977, 2005), an eclectic body of critical research examines populism as a political discourse that antagonistically divides the social body between the people and the oligarchy, with "the people" understood as an interpellation, an articulation in the process of constructing hegemony, rather than a pre-given identity or set of demands. Analysis examines how "the people" are constituted and how their demands become linked in an imaginary "chain of equivalence," and follows the dialectical movement between political rhetoric and strategies and grassroots consciousness. Panizza and colleagues (2005) see populism as a "mirror for democracy" that reveals its deficits and exclusions. Populist leaders politicize social exclusions; claim to defend ways of life under attack; define the people, their grievances, and the threats they face in strategic ways; and pursue the people's agenda often with loose regard for the rule of law.

Building on these ideas, I ask what the configuration and reception of authoritarian populist appeals in San Pedro revealed about the exclusions and contradictions of neoliberal democracy and development. I also go beyond ideological theories to focus on the material and affective dimensions of authoritarian populist appeals, to reveal how they are constituted by political and economic violence, division, self-interest, and pessimism. This chapter is grounded in a close examination of Ríos Montt's campaign discourse and strategy in 2003, that of the local FRG mayoral candidate Mariano Díaz in the same year, and the populist campaign of Rony Galicia, a suspected narco-trafficker who won San Pedro's mayoral elections in 2011.

The combination of unmet political demands and a neutered left-ist politics in neoliberal Guatemala creates an opening for authoritarian populists whose appeals hint at structural inequality but focus instead on lower-level social divisions. Paradoxically, these three authoritarian populists combined a critique of the elite with attention to the poverty and suffering caused by and maintained for the benefit of that same elite. They excoriated the perverse effects of neoliberal democracy and develop-ment while perpetuating the same practices. Even as many Mayas rejected leftist candidates whose policies they actually endorsed, they supported right-wing populists whose national-level policies and politicians they did not necessarily like or respect but who were seen as far more likely to win and benefit them personally. Predictably, authoritarian populisms did little to resolve frustrations; even worse, they reinforced the lack of alternatives and exacerbated village divisions.

On Populist Resonance

Despite much discussion of the effects of neoliberal multiculturalism on indigenous politics, as well as several attempts to decipher the enigma of Ríos Montt, few have closely examined the specific efforts by parties and movements to compete for followers in rural villages and how villagers perceive and respond to these appeals. Most discussions focus on the reso-nance of Ríos Montt's populist appeals with grassroots moral economies, even as they interpret this resonance in different ways. David Stoll (2009) reads electoral support for Ríos Montt in the Guatemalan highlands as evidence that the revolution, which Ríos Montt notoriously defeated, did not and does not represent the desires of Mayan people. Conversely, Charles Hale (2006b) argues that rural Mayas found in Ríos Montt's pro-Maya populism a reflection of their progressive worldviews. The most nuanced explanation comes from the historian Virginia Garrard-Burnett (2010, 9–13). Along with favorable opinion polls and eyewitness reports, she cites anthropologists' accounts of Mayas who praised Ríos Montt as an upstanding vision of righteousness who protected their communities from the guerrillas rather than instigating the violence. Garrard-Burnett concludes that Ríos Montt used a combination of violence and moral dis-course to elaborate a symbolic universe inhabited by many and that "in some sectors generated outright enthusiasm for the regime." However, she claims that this universe imploded by 2003, when his party was implicated in corruption, leading to his poor electoral showing.[15]

Undoubtedly, each of these descriptions fits some subset of Ríos Montt's Mayan supporters, but even taken together, they do not tell the entire story. These interpretations all assume that the success of his populist appeals traded off with perceptions of him as a murderer or as corrupt, and that his support came primarily from people who viewed him positively; they assume a relatively straightforward connection between voting patterns and political desire. But is this relationship always so clear? And how exactly does violence become consent?[16] I found something more complicated in San Pedro, where Ríos Montt won the votes of many villagers who despised him, and he was not unique in this regard.

The authoritarian populist appeals of these three politicians in San Pedro framed the people as powerless, reinforced the effects of state violence on local agency, and fed on the resentments stemming from that sense of defeat. This authoritarian populism did not persuade villagers to share a value orientation with a political movement so much as it carved up political reality in specific ways, foregrounding local grievances and offering ways to even the score. Promising projects *or* abandonment, authoritarian populism operated directly on life processes and bodily anxieties, tapping into pessimism, structural violence, and resentment enjoining villagers into internecine competition with town Ladinos and with one another. Authoritarian populism promised conditional temporary relief for structural violence to poor villagers who had been excluded by patronage networks and were on the bottom of socioeconomic hierarchies of wealth and *capacidad*. It reified and inflamed these divisions and defined them as the primary focus of political contestation without ever questioning the legitimacy of these hierarchies or their structural causes.

In San Pedro the poorest villagers joined authoritarian populist parties to receive limited benefits from the state and to advance their position against local Ladinos and, increasingly, against neighbors who were somewhat better off and politically dominant. Authoritarian populism entrenched interethnic divisions and further disintegrated alliances and trust among a racially excluded class. I call authoritarian populism "cruel" because it promised solutions for poverty and inequality while obfuscating the systematic nature of these failures, blaming them on individual amorality, blocking national-level reform, and dispersing grassroots organizational capacities. It directly harmed the people whose interests it claimed to defend, and it rendered them complicit with harming others. Right-wing populism in San Pedro was a product of violence that gained traction without ideological resonance and merged democratic processes and counterinsurgency aims, mutilating the people whom it claimed to defend.

The Authoritarian Populism of the FRG

Mayan communities encountered populist discourses and performances through radio, television, billboards, newspapers, word of mouth, and speeches given by national politicians on whistle-stop helicopter tours through mountain towns. They also encountered them face-to-face when candidates visited their villages. Some received fertilizer, projects, cash payments, food, and jobs in advance, and even more were promised those things in exchange for affiliating, voting, helping with the campaign, participating in public demonstrations, and even running for office. National FRG discourse in the late 1990s through the mid-2000s consisted of several main elements: promises to promote the needs of Mayas against the oligarchy; a historical narrative that framed the revolution as a threat and erased Mayan participation in the revolution while responding directly to the criticisms of Ríos Montt, minimizing his role in the violence; a political analysis that foregrounded individual hard work and ignored radical alternatives; and a range of sovereign performances that transgressed the democratic rule of law, including attacks against activists and journalists during the Portillo administration.[17]

Ríos Montt presented himself to rural communities as a powerful general, a devout evangelical, and a defender of poor, indigenous Guatemalans against the elite.[18] His political speeches were thunderous sermons laced with calls for moral reform for a wicked country, to transform Guatemala into a New Guatemala, a City on the Hill and a beacon to the world. Billboards in Huehuetenango showed his immediately recognizable mustachioed face, with the words "El General, Sí," a direct assertion of his wartime identity. Another FRG billboard read "Forget the past; build the future," a not-so-subtle reference to Ríos Montt's wartime atrocities. Ríos Montt seemed eager to make every attempt to evoke his already well-known persona even as he denied responsibility for genocide. At the same time, he sometimes donned indigenous garb to highlight his humble rural origins and identification with poor Mayas. The meaning of the party slogan "Security, Well-Being, and Justice" was somewhat ambiguous but was often linked to anticrime policies and development assistance. These were accompanied by three promises: "I do not lie, I do not steal, I do not abuse [power]," indexed by their symbol of a hand with three fingers raised, the index, middle, and thumb, looking almost like a peace sign. Addressing the rural poor, he proposed funding development by taxing the rich until it hurt, but without ever questioning the general economic system in Guatemala.

Even in his most populist moments, Ríos Montt was explicitly *not* proposing to use his might to transform the political order in the manner once advocated by the guerrilla movement, but to fulfill the counterinsurgency mission. For example, in an interview with a national newspaper in 2003, in response to accusations of grave human rights violations during the war, he said, "What happened was that in the northwest of the country the guerrillas were in power and something had to be done. I armed the pueblo so they could defend themselves against the cruel guerrillas."[19] Furthermore, he denied any grassroots support for the guerrillas and framed the civil patrols as voluntary. As he had in the past, he called for reform of corruption, which he blamed on individual immorality. This is similar to the early 1980s, when Ríos Montt's vision of "La Nueva Guatemala required a return to security and the defeat of the guerrillas, but at the same time, the government, so long associated with repression and corruption, had to reestablish its own legitimacy" (Garrard-Burnett 2010, 58). Then and in 2003, this critique of the government was not to be confused with a call for serious economic or political reform. When asked if he thought the system should be changed, Ríos Montt equivocated, "I don't know, but what we want is to be citizens and stop being servants."[20]

Ríos Montt's populism unambiguously predicated a vision of national refounding on the repression and repudiation of the revolution *and* revolutionary demands. On the campaign trail, Rios Montt promised to defend "order" and invoked his "rifles or beans" scorched-earth campaign and the civil patrols' plan as defenses of the pueblo who were caught "between two armies." His daughter Zury Ríos, then an FRG *diputada,* also defended the rifles or beans program.[21] Furthermore, during the 2003 campaign, the FRG government continued to sanction human rights abuses, including the repression of reporters involved in uncovering army massacres.[22] Rather than addressing long-standing hierarchies of race and class, Ríos Montt framed Guatemala's myriad social problems as symptoms of spiritual failings and advocated Christian moral discipline as the path to redemption, an evangelical discourse that drained all historical content from poverty, inequality, and crime. Nothing underlined his reactionary, pro-military stance more than his promise to pay patrollers for their service defending "la Patria" (the Fatherland), which formed the cornerstone of FRG strategy. It is not a mistake that most Guatemalans viewed Ríos Montt's FRG unequivocally as the party of the army.

Ríos Montt dramatically reinforced the counterinsurgent orientation of his candidacy by orchestrating a major political spectacle in late July 2003. On June 6 of that year, the Citizens Registry of the Tribuno Supremo Electoral (TSE) barred Ríos Montt from registering as a presidential candidate, citing the constitutional rule against former dictators running for office. On July 14 the Supreme Court of Justice (CSJ) affirmed that decision, raising the case to the Constitutional Court (CC). Civil society organizations opposed to Ríos Montt's candidacy became alarmed, denouncing that the CC was filled with FRG supporters, and called for FRG members to recuse themselves. In response, Ríos Montt warned that the party leaders would lose control of their supporters, a backhanded call for riots. The FRG leadership, including Zury Ríos, organized a protest in Guatemala City on July 24 and 25 with the aim of pressuring the government to reverse its ruling. The party bused in supporters from around the country, paying for their travel and meals, and encouraging rural FRG leaders to send affiliates. Protestors wearing black ski masks and wielding machetes, sticks, and firearms surrounded the CSJ and the CC. They burned tires and cars, broke shop windows, and blocked roads, shutting down traffic in the capitol and in El Quiché, Jutiapa, and Chiquimula. They also threatened journalists. One, Hector Ramírez, died of a heart attack that he suffered after he was chased through town by a mob. Protestors doused two other reporters with gasoline and threatened to set them on fire. In the end the CC, with FRG loyalists unrecused, ruled in favor of

Ríos Montt's registration. Critics referred to these events as *Jueves Negro* (Black Thursday) and *Jueves de Luto* (Thursday of Mourning).

Jueves Negro, along with ongoing acts of repression of progressive journalists and indigenous political leaders, such as Antonio Pop Caal, who was killed under mysterious circumstances in 2002,[23] dramatized the willingness of the FRG to use fear and intimidation to get its way. Although Portillo and Ríos Montt officially denounced the protests, no one seriously doubted their involvement. Tellingly, this political performance—the centerpiece of the campaign—ran counter to Ríos Montt's moral discourse; the party had violated the law and had undermined one of the central rules of the new democracy with impunity. In this respect the campaign closely resembled the performances of sovereign power during the counterinsurgency, which transgressed the law to defend the social order. As a deliberate display of Ríos Montt's power above the law, *Jueves Negro* reminded many people of the war, which ironically made many in San Pedro believe his victory was inevitable, creating a reason to join the party.

Another highly visible public incident undermined FRG claims to represent Mayan peoples. In October 2003, when Rigoberta Menchú was attending a judicial proceeding appealing the CC's decision, she was accosted by hundreds of FRG supporters, several of who yelled, "Go and sell tomatoes in the Terminal, Indian woman!"[24] One of these was none other than Juan Pablo Ríos, Ríos Montt's grandson. This story was visible to villagers, who read the papers, listened to the radio, and discussed news. In 2005 the five individuals involved in those acts were the first to be tried and found guilty of racism under Guatemala's new antiracism law and sentenced to three years in prison or a $400 fine. The party never publicly disavowed their behavior.

Although Ríos Montt posed as a champion of the poor, Rigoberta Menchú identified him as a "symbol of genocide."[25] Many of Ríos Montt's followers in San Pedro remembered bitterly the suffering he caused in 1982, even while he denied it on the campaign trail. For many of his own supporters, his very existence as an unpunished leader and candidate inspired despair. Some reasoned that his violent past was not a reason to refuse to vote for him but indicated that he was invincible. Although I did meet a few individuals who said that Ríos Montt was more likely to help the poor than other candidates, I did not meet any FRG supporters who put much stock in his moral discourse and his plans for governance, or who believed that he would create a New Guatemala based on "a coherent moral vision of safety and order" (Garrard-Burnett 2010, 12).[26] This assessment was based on dozens of conversations with pro-FRG villagers in San Pedro in the months following the 2003 election and in subsequent years. In the following years, most had switched parties (Mariano Díaz joined the center-left UNE in 2007), and former FRG supporters spoke more candidly about their political attitudes and motivations.

FRG Populism in San Pedro

How did populist promises and moral discourses translate into local FRG political strategies at the grassroots? Mariano Díaz was in his early forties when he was elected as the FRG *alcalde* of San Pedro in 2003. After losing the 1999 election to José Antulio Morales, Díaz, acting as the leader of the FRG Party locally, was appointed to the board of directors of DECOPAZ, a World Bank–funded organization in charge of implementing infrastructural projects whose operation had been turned over to the state after the first round of projects was completed. The second round of projects was politicized when the FRG took control of the presidency and Congress in 2000. Díaz used his position and influence to build a political following.

Mariano Díaz was a thin man with longish, slicked-back hair, always sharply dressed, usually wearing a tie and expensive polished cowboy boots. He also sported a "soul patch" and wore a silver wristwatch whose sparkle was visible from a distance. Díaz was an enthusiastic and exciting public speaker; he addressed large audiences in the same tone and with the same intensity as an evangelical preacher delivering a sermon, self-consciously imitating Ríos Montt's distinctive verbal style. Díaz filled his speeches with jokes and humorous stories, and he was fairly self-aggrandizing, speaking at length about his proficiency in attaining projects and his closeness to God. Supporters saw him as a former teacher who had traveled to the United States, a *buena onda* (nice, cool man) who was connected to powerful groups. Several townspeople told me that the election was more about him as a person than the FRG as a party.

Díaz was reviled by most town Ladinos, who saw him as a disgrace to the *municipio*. Several prominent Ladinos expressed embarrassment that he was their mayor. They longed for José Antulio Morales, whom they had vehemently opposed. Likewise, most *capacitados* and professional Mayas

I spoke with strongly disliked Díaz and resented his political ascendance. Enemies spread vicious rumors in an attempt to sow contempt for his authority. Although he claimed to be a teacher, many swore that he never finished high school, never taught classes, and had simply purchased his diploma. Díaz hails from San Pedro, but he had lived and worked in Cancún for several years. One rumor alleged that he left for Mexico because he was implicated in the robbery and murder of a man who was traveling with cash after just having sold his land.

At several town functions I attended, almost no one in the primarily Ladino audiences applauded after he spoke, withholding a common courtesy. Jokes about his strange personal conduct were commonplace. He was frequently referred to as "Mariano *chiflado*" (crackpot) and also "Mariano *payaso*" (clown). Some used more vulgar words. Most assumed that he just wanted to be mayor for personal interest, calling him an opportunistic liar—a criminal with a taste for power. Many were embarrassed that an idiot like Díaz was their mayor, similar to how I felt about US President George W. Bush at the time, and later about Trump.

Despite the fact that he seemed too inexperienced to be mayor, the FRG Party sought Mariano Díaz out. Why? Several facts stood out. Díaz had sought political power in the *municipio* for several years but was not tapped for a leadership spot in José Antulio Morales' team, which was mainly composed of professionals and highly capacitated leaders. When Díaz joined the FRG in 1999, he lost his first mayoral race to Antulio Morales even when his own party won nationally. My assessment after observing his first year in office and again on visits during his second and third was that party bosses saw in him the perfect combination of characteristics. Díaz was Mayan, so he could speak in Mam and understood villagers' experiences and needs; he was ambitious, but mostly for personal gain, and eager to partake the fruits of corruption; he was too inexperienced to have political strategies or vision of his own; and last but not least, he was charismatic and energetic enough to attract attention as a candidate.

Mariano Díaz repeated Ríos Montt's discourse with some modifications. Díaz also played up his evangelical religion and advocated private acts of morality as the mechanism for social change. He also celebrated the populist policies implemented by the FRG under Alfonso Portillo. Moreover, as I described in chapter 1, FRG supporters, including Díaz, denied Ríos Montt's responsibility for extreme violence, blaming Lucas García, and argued that Ríos Montt's civil patrols "calmed things down." Both Ríos Montt and Díaz got a last-minute boost by politicizing the patroller payment, including promising payments to people who had never even patrolled. In addition to discourses that attempted to mitigate the negative aspects of voting for Ríos Montt relative to other parties and the politicization of the ex-PAC payment, Díaz crafted a range of positive incentives to persuade his neighbors to support him and the former general.

Most of Díaz's ground strategy was a fascinating tailoring of Ríos Montt's populist appeals into specific matters of local concern. He drew on his evangelical faith to reassure people that he was honest and would not steal once elected. He did not pit evangelicals against Catholics; instead, he successfully wooed blocks of Catholic and protestant supporters with offers of projects. Most significantly, he interpreted Ríos Montt's evangelical-sounding promise to not "make exceptions between people" to mean that no group or village should receive favorable treatment and that no groups should be excluded, especially the neediest. Specifically, he made extravagant development promises in the poorest, most remote villages that had been passed over by Antulio Morales' coalition. He won the most support from villages in *"sector norte,"* the *finca* zone, where villagers owned little or no land, and in villages at too high an elevation to grow coffee. Ironically, the regions where support for the guerrillas was the strongest also provided the base of FRG support in San Pedro, although their perceptions of both entities were quite different.

Additionally, although Díaz had a few Ladino advisors, several Ladinos complained that, when addressing communities in Mam, Díaz promised (or threatened) to cut Ladinos off from development entirely. They accused him of stirring up indigenous villagers' resentments and of provoking conflict, insisting that they, too, had necessities. This reaction overlooked the long history of discrimination by Ladinos that had created that anger, as well as inequalities between town and village. For its part, Díaz's anti-Ladino discourse ignored the fact that most Ladinos were also poor, isolated local antagonisms from national inequalities, thus erasing the origin of the Ladino-Indian divide in postindependence state formation.[27]

Revolt against *Capacidad*

Of the three main families in Los Altenses, the Ruízes were the strongest FRG adherents. Members of the Ruíz family were on the whole considerably less educated than the Bravo and the López families, and noticeably poorer. Economic divisions among these indigenous families had widened significantly over the last three decades; the Bravo and López families were increasingly professionalized and had family members in the United States, while the Ruízes were mostly subsistence farmers, often landless, and many traveled annually to the South Coast to work in the *fincas,* a practice that had been long abandoned by their neighbors. At the same meeting with the male members of the Ruíz family described in chapter 2, it quickly became clear that local divisions were not rooted in wartime allegiances but in a pattern of disrespect because of their lower level of *capacidad* and exclusion from leadership positions and patronage in Antulio Morales' political coalition. This was especially painful for Rodrigo, the family patriarch, but felt by all. Rodrigo's nephew, a farmer wearing muddy rubber boots and soiled work clothing, spoke angrily:

> They say that there is no one else can get projects like them. No one. Only they can do it. They say they're the smartest. Only they can. There is no one else. That is their pride. In the end when they changed their ways, when they began to take money from the community box. That's where the people separated, and they grabbed their roads, one for one side, the other for the other. The Ruíz family, we met—all 120 of us—and talked about how we could stop them from dominating.

It was not simply the Bravo family's corruption that angered him; it was their pride and arrogance. They seemed to believe that they were somehow smarter and better. Rodrigo's second oldest son, Eriberto, a teacher, continued, seething with resentment:

> And bragging too! Bragging that they have *capacidad* to do things! That's how the people realized, with they [the Bravos] getting drunk and saying that they know so much, that they are one way and that we're different. Insults. More than anything they talked about a family. . . . They talked about how more than anyone else the Ruíz can't—that they lack *capacidad.* Because [the Ruízes] lack money and go to the finca or go with a patron to work. That we don't do our own work. . . . With us the main leader of our family is my father. He organized the family. He struggled . . . for them to study. It was to answer them, so that they wouldn't go around criticizing. And the López are also proud. They still are.

NC: But you were divided long before, right, after the murder of Juan López?

Eriberto: Yes. But afterwards we were united to launch Pedro Ramírez [in his 1988 campaign]. Then the people were united again. It was after that that they started to say things about them being the only ones who knew anything. This year is the ninth year of division. In 1996 the division began. . . . We weren't able to win that day. Then we went with another candidate. . . . They have this saying that they're "political technicians" and when we don't win, they criticize us. And we, well, afterwards, we're never going with them. In the next election we helped Mariano Díaz. And Don Rodrigo's friends were in the muni. Then they shut up. That's when we got rid of the "zero." When they have their electoral campaign, only they want to participate. Only they get to be part of the municipal corporation. There's nothing for us. Only them. But not only they can do it.

He was vindicating the family against insulting comments that they were backward, incompetent, and less valuable people who were laughable and deserved disdain, and who did not have the capacity to participate in decision making. In addition to being cut out of resources, a desire to overcome or live down this disrespected identity played a determinative role in their decision to break from the Antulio Morales coalition and join the FRG, whose candidate, Mariano Díaz, offered them a credible path to victory and promised them leadership positions: a shot at respect. This, in addition to the economic windfall that a victory represented for the entire family, overwhelmed their ideological misgivings. The party itself—what it was and what it stood for at the national level—was a source of some guilt and embarrassment, but ultimately worth the sacrifice. Ironically, Eriberto's statement "not only they can do it" was the same criticism that Mayan Sampedranos lodged against Ladinos who had opposed "Indian" advancement in previous decades.

One day I met Rodrigo Ruíz while walking the road to the village, and he pulled me into a cantina that a family operated from behind their house. We ordered a drink, and as the tangy warm mix of *aguardiente*, soda, and lime burned my throat, Rodrigo said, "You have a lot of experience, a lot of studies. You're a *gringo licenciado*. You have more experience than me. I am illiterate. I never studied. But now, where am I? On top!" He then pulled out his FRG Party affiliate card, which named his job in the party:

> The gringos say that Guatemalans are only good for having children. I only have one daughter; the rest are boys. One time, José Antulio in a reunion in front of everyone, heard that I had had another boy. He said, "Good! Now I will have another *mozo* [peon]." But now you see, I have two children who are teachers, and another one who is going to be a teacher. All of them went out [*salieron*]. They're not farmers.

I asked him, "But being a farmer is honorable work, right?" His answer? "Yes, it is. But now I am working for development."

Rodrigo was ashamed about his family having less *capacidad* and education because it made them feel like less valuable people. Educating his children eventually paid off, but only after years of mockery. The FRG provided an opportunity for Rodrigo, as an uneducated, illiterate man, to be a leader like he had been in the 1970s, vindicating his own and his family's dignity. I detected a pattern: numerous FRG village leaders were former members of the Antulio Morales coalition who had been denied leadership positions and the spoils of corruption because they lacked *capacidad*. Their ascension was aided by the fact that projects had become much easier to acquire after the peace accords. With fewer bureaucratic obstacles and more sources, it required less experience and fewer technical skills. Implementing a strategy in close consultation with party bosses, Mariano Díaz built a coalition by offering leadership positions to village men who had been ignored by the Morales coalition. Díaz was selected by the party himself in part because of his lack of *capacidad,* which they associated with malleability.

This practice of targeting less-capacitated leaders who were also typically poorer than their counterparts in other parties added another dimension to the FRG and Díaz's pledge not to make exceptions between people. FRG populism defined exclusion from patronage networks—which roughly corresponded to class divisions and divisions over *capacidad*—as key foci of political contestation. Resentment about leadership hierarchies based on *capacidad* gave the FRG additional pull with some trusted local leaders, but the party never questioned the legitimacy of *capacidad* as a neutral measuring stick. Nor did they challenge in any meaningful way the root causes of the general condition of exclusion of indigenous villagers. Nor at the national level did the FRG go beyond superficial indigenous inclusion. Despite a few Mayan *diputados* and several Mayas in symbolic government posts, urban Ladinos controlled most high-level positions in the party, and the FRG ignored the Accord on Identity and Rights.[28]

At one level, excluded and less capacitated FRG supporters wanted resources and respect. At another, their criticisms of favoritism and exclusion questioned *capacidad* as the prerequisite for political and material inclusion. Douglas Brintnall (1979) described Mayan abandonment of traditional religion of ancestor worship in the 1970s to pursue cash cropping as a "revolt against the dead" that opened new opportunities for political and economic advancement. Decades later, many Sampedranos revolted against *capacidad,* not always explicitly and not rejecting the will to improve in itself, but objecting to its use as a justification for exclusion and interpersonal discrimination. The critique of *capacidad* formed part of a larger critique of neoliberal democracy and development from a standpoint of equality and fairness, which found expression in local FRG discourse and in FRG governing practices in limited and contradictory ways. Rather than resolve these issues, this temporary electoral inversion of the hierarchy of *capacidad* did not point to clear alternatives to neoliberal development and only hardened resentment and divisions between individual villagers and extended families.

My Needy People Who Have Been Deceived All Your Lives

The 2011 national election focused on a contest between Otto Perez Molina, campaigning as an anticrime hardliner, and Sandra Torres, the ex-wife of sitting President Alvaro Colom, from the UNE.[29] Torres was a neoliberal centrist best known for spearheading and administering the popular MIFAPRO program. Critics faulted Torres for politicizing MIFAPRO payments and for a scandalous divorce of convenience that intended but ultimately failed to render her eligible to run.[30]

I returned to San Pedro in June 2011, the peak of the electoral season, with the intention of observing local political processes. To my amazement, and to the amazement of many Sampedranos, Rony Galicia, a

Ladino widely suspected of being a narco-trafficker, was in the lead in the mayoral election and went on to win, representing, even more surprisingly, the URNG. Galicia's name was on everyone's lips when I arrived. Locals were astounded by how much he was spending. He had delivered an improbably large number of projects in the communities already, financing them out of his own pocket, they said. A friend told me that Galicia had spent over one million quetzals, a hefty sum that far surpassed previous campaigns. Most notably, he had procured dynamite to open a road to *Siete Cerros* (Seven Mountains), the village at the highest altitude, previously unreachable by car in the rainy season. Numerous houses were painted with URNG propaganda, yellow and green with an image of a *mazorca* (ear of corn). Such excessive expenditures fueled the narco rumors, according to which Galicia planned to use elected office to gain immunity from prosecution and to avoid police scrutiny. He dismissed this as a *campaña negra* (smear campaign). His involvement in the drug trade was the converse of Taussig's (1999) "public secret": it was something that no one knew for certain but that almost everyone believed and talked about, although few dared to say anything to his face. Narco-conspiracies are common in the remote border region, which is a major overland shipment point to the United States.[31] Narco-money flows through political campaigns, but it was rare for suspected narcos to win elections. These were not idle accusations. Several URNG members quit the party both because they believed the rumors and because they objected on principle to Galicia's project-centered, clientelist strategy.

Galicia's decision to run with the URNG, the revolutionary party that had never won in San Pedro, compounded the strangeness of his suspected drug dealing and the fact that he was the first Ladino to win local elections since 1990. In addition, Galicia beat a respected incumbent, Julio Ambrocio, a wealthy indigenous lawyer representing the UNE, whose solidarity programs were popular among poor villagers. Ambrocio was also the leader of Antulio Morales' coalition. Why in the world would thousands of indigenous Sampedranos choose a Ladino that almost everyone believed was a narco-trafficker above a leader of unquestionable ability? Was this politics driven by fear of crime or by something more complicated? Rony Galicia's populist discourse and strategy proved quite effective in building a bi-ethnic coalition that included many ideological opponents of the URNG. His success revealed how politicians can navigate a political field of *engaño* (deception), division, and mistrust to gain followers, and how this process further decimates local organizational capacities.

After several months, from an initial seven parties the local race had boiled down to a duel between Julio Ambrocio and Rony Galicia. Ambrocio was delivering five *laminas* to each supporter as promised, asking his supporters for patience, and promising new projects. His other major argument was that San Pedro would be cut off from the state solidarity program, MIFAPRO, if his party lost: a threat of economic coercion. Galicia insisted that MIFAPRO would continue regardless, and Ambrocio's warning undoubtedly meant less when Torres was removed from the national ballot late in the campaign. But as with most rural mayors, Ambrocio's main weakness was that he had betrayed and abandoned many communities to whom he had promised projects during his previous campaign. Galicia was attempting to capitalize on that resentment when I accompanied him and a caravan of followers to a remote village in July.

Galicia targeted his populist appeal to "humble indigenous people," whom he depicted as uniquely vulnerable. He took pains to demonstrate that he was on their side and that he respected them, even though he constantly referred to himself in the third person. He even lamented that he couldn't speak Mam, referring to "the desire that Rony Galicia has in his heart is to share with his humble people, his indigenous people, his people that speak Mam, his people that love him." These acts underscored the strength of this indigenous identification and the lengths to which politicians, including Ladinos, would go to demonstrate their desire to govern on behalf of the indigenous majority. This in itself was a sign of the way that social relations had changed in the past thirty years. However, Galicia contended that both Mayas and Ladinos could be crooked and argued that a candidate's respectfulness was more important than their ethnicity. Despite the third person, he lambasted politicians who "act like kings of the planet" and "drive around with their windows up": two thinly veiled jabs at Ambrocio, who had a reputation as somewhat of a snob. Similar criticisms were leveled at José Antulio Morales, who some villagers complained treated them with disdain like the Ladino *alcaldes* had in the past.

Galicia's discourse followed the definition of the political held by most parties: that helping indigenous people meant providing specific development projects, anything from potable water for a village, to a job, to corrugated zinc roofing. Development was at the heart of most populist appeals and was framed as what Mayan people lack and how politicians should show their care and concern. Development marked the horizon of indigenous political inclusion; discussion of structural reforms was non-existent. On this visit, Galicia gifted the villagers with an amplifier, worth several thousand quetzals, as a show of his wealth and generosity. He also repeated a laundry list of projects completed during his campaign and promised to build a *casa de posada* (guest house) where poor families could sleep when their loved ones visited the town hospital, instead of "on the cold street." The audience was impressed by his deeds and promises, although undoubtedly skeptical. The *posada* idea underscores how development populism involves regularly referencing the vulnerability of the villagers, a reminder of their status as "bare life": completely expendable as far as the state is concerned (Agamben 1998).

Galicia's campaign strategy upended standard URNG orthodoxy, which derided project-centered politics as a practice that tricked foolish villagers out of supporting revolutionary candidates who represent their "true" interests. Such criticisms, it should be noted, did not take into consideration the coercive forces that shape calculations of interest and hastily conflate these situated and overdetermined actions with political consciousness, or lack thereof. One longtime URNG member said that Galicia was winning because people "want honey in their mouths," adding that "this is no longer the URNG." Another man, amid snickers, blurted, "El URNG ya se chengó!" ("The URNG has fucked itself"). These supporters had given up the moral high ground. They thought it was impossible for the URNG to win on ideas, so they might as well win dirty if only for the opportunities for corruption, even if this ruined the party's prior reputation as uncontaminated by self-interest.

Rony Galicia framed his candidacy as a means for villagers to defend themselves from a variety of forms of *engaño*, stating, "I want to work for you, my needy people, my people that have been deceived all of your lives." He repeatedly warned the villagers not to let themselves be tricked, always referencing their vulnerability. He promised to defend the interests of poor, remote villages against closer-in villages and the Ladino urban center. Another aspect of his critique of *engaño* aimed at politicians who took personal credit for projects bought with public money. Galicia painted a strong contrast, claiming that the money he spent on projects was his own. In a shocking display, his wife stood by his side holding up a fistful of cash to emphasize the point. Here too, his double identity as a narco-trafficker gave him an edge.

Galicia's discourse and strategy reaffirmed the truth that party politics was a space of self-interest, deception, and corruption, a mix of *engaño* that gave it both a bad name and a compelling allure. His manner of defining *engaño* was contradictory, however, and his proposed solutions were limited. He naturalized the commonsense notion that politics was limited to competition with neighbors for scarce resources. His critique of abandonment focused on individual politicians, not the structural short-age of projects or historical inequalities. Like other politicians, Galicia engaged in divisive clientelist politics while simultaneously excoriating it as a *mala costumbre* (bad habit) and a "defect": the typical URNG line. Right before the election, he denounced Julio Ambrocio for attempting to "buy votes" by offering supporters a coupon worth Q400 that would be valid only if he won. But he himself offered projects and gifts in exchange for votes. The cynical double-speak was motivated by and reinforced the belief that this quid pro quo was simultaneously unavoidable and ethically problematic because family and personal interests contradicted with com-munity interests.

Galicia admonished villagers "not to be hypocrites" and said that if they did not help him get elected, they should not pretend they had, and that they could forget about any projects or favors if he won. His speech was laced with threats:

> If I lose, they're going to say Rony Galicia lost. But Rony Galicia is not going to lose. He's not going to lose his hands, his woman, his children, his mother, his family, or his house. You, the pueblo, are going to lose, if your sick family members go to the hospital, you're going to freeze to death, *"y que me importa?"* [and what do I care?] If the people from [a village] don't support me, their school can fall into the ravine.

With this speech, Galicia stoked and played upon villagers' very real fear of abandonment: the fate consigned to those who lose elections. He men-tioned specific bodily vulnerabilities typical among rural villagers, mak-ing clear that he did not share them and could cruelly disregard them. His threat was the instantiation of the sovereign power to let die by the withholding of development projects, violence that in this case would be carried out by him in his official capacity, for the benefit of his follow-ers with cold indifference to the rest. Galicia's populist discourse did not challenge the national oligarchy but the local political elite. He treated the everyday suffering and vulnerability of the villagers as background infor-mation, an inevitable fact that served as leverage for politics, not as some-thing to be addressed by politics. Galicia's candor about his willingness to sentence his opponents to abandonment perhaps made him seem more honest than other candidates because this was an accurate picture of what they had grown to expect from political parties.

Emphasizing the discursive construction of the social as a central aspect of politics, Ernesto Laclau and Chantal Mouffe (1985) describe new forms of conflictivity beyond traditional class politics produced by new forms of perceiving cleavages and lines of power. Their project for a new socialist strategy was to draw connections between diverse new (at the time) social movements (environmentalism, feminism, antiracism) to unite them into a counter-hegemonic project. Laclau (1977, 2005) argues that the central cleavage of populism is the people versus the powerful, and he focuses on the political construction of the people through discursively weaving aggregative linkages between discrete demands. Populist discourses in San Pedro invoke a range of intersecting lines of social division and politi-cal contestation: rich versus poor, indigenous versus Ladino, Mayas ver-sus the state, *capacitado* versus no *capacitado,* urban versus rural. Each presents unique risks of *engaño* and self-interest and serves as fodder for populist strategy. Sampedranos have varying feelings about each of these divisions, and also distinguish between axes of contestation worth pursu-ing and those that lie outside the realm of political possibility: actionable versus inactionable antagonisms.

In addition to his embrace of divisive, project-centered clientelism, Galicia's populism left out almost every recognizable element of leftist discourse. There was no coherent critique of the oligarchy, transnational corporations, free trade, or even extractivism, and no mention of human and material rights or even the peace accords. With all the talk about projects, there was no focused discussion on a lasting solution to poverty, malnutrition, and the general state of abandonment in which most villag-ers lived. In other words, it was as narrowly focused as most campaigns. Galicia's populism treated the economic and political order as inevitable and focused on tertiary divisions in the local body politic. This ignored the ultimate *engaño*—the nexus between the state and capital—recognized by many villagers as the one from which the others grow. It was not the people versus the powerful, but the people against one another.

Populist discourses navigate and reinforce a field of shared common sense and political affect shaped by decades of repression and zero-sum party politics. Villagers were interpellated by representations of themselves as deceived, vulnerable, and powerless to change the social order, and channeling these affects and perceptions was crucial to Galicia's success. His populism did not so much challenge state sovereignty as mimic it. The fact that he was rumored to be a narco inspired hope that he would actually be able to deliver projects, just as many villagers also saw Otto Perez Molina as a narco, despite his anticrime rhetoric. Such political thinking was not limited to rural communities. In 2014 I met a *Ladina* vendor in a market in the department capital. She was a no-nonsense, working-class woman in her sixties who lamented the recent capture of narcos in the border town of la Democracia: "They say they are bad people, but they are not. They are the ones maintaining us. They buy our products, and they give people jobs. Now the government arrested them, and we don't have anything." Perez Molina found support among middle-class Ladinos in Guatemala City who were fed up with crime and gang violence, also products of systematic social failures. His supporters felt betrayed when CICIG, the anti-impunity commission, uncovered that his administration had institutionalized unprecedented corruption and systematically looted state coffers, so much so that they launched a protest march and allied with rural and indigenous social movements that they usually opposed in order to remove him from office.

Powerlessness, pessimism, and vulnerability drove a corrupt, self-interested politics of development linked to the state. These violently restricted models of citizenship, vital to the reproduction of state order, were mediated in part through contradictory populist discourses. Neoliberals who deride populism as a threat to the social order disavow their active and violent reinforcement of the inequalities and exclusions that create conditions for populist politics. Laclau and other theorists (see Panizza and colleagues, 2005) treat populist appeals as primarily about interpellation: success means resonance that happens when populations come to imagine themselves as belonging to "the people" and as sharing a common stock of grievances and demands represented by the movement. This understanding equates political affiliation and voting with support, or belief in the populist message, however interpreted. This meaning-centered formulation misses the role of political violence in populist appeals in places like San Pedro, as well as the corporeal and affective dimensions that motivated otherwise radical-minded Sampedranos to support the FRG and a suspected narco-trafficker.

Beyond generating a political following, we must also understand populism as a potent mechanism of reinscribing effects of sovereignty and governance, accomplished in this case by denying Mayan political agency and history, focusing politics on projects, insisting that deeper change is impossible, and inflaming anger and division between poor villagers. Order-defending violence was the point of departure of authoritarian populism, a foundation that it did not question. Rather than threaten the oligarchy, the FRG and Rony Galicia selectively and symbolically addressed national and structural divisions—rich versus poor and Maya versus Ladino—and then divided indigenous people internally. Politicizing these secondary divides is not necessarily wrong and is in many ways integral to the project of organizing a counter-public out of a fragmented populace; the problem is evoking them as a means of obscuring shared forms of oppression that are more pressing in order to fracture community solidarity. Authoritarian populisms normalized and perpetuated trade-offs between forms of political agency: from active to reactive, collective to individual, class to ethnic, and national to local. These trade-offs were at the heart of ambivalent attachments to the FRG in San Pedro. Although this cruel populism worked to mystify and smooth out the contradictions of neoliberal democracy and to outmaneuver opponents, it left social problems unresolved and created new ones.

In San Pedro authoritarian populist discourses and strategies were crafted to appeal to subjects whose social worlds were shaped by material and symbolic exclusion, state violence, and inequality while disqualifying radical alternatives and pitting villagers against one another. FRG populism in 2003 promised to include Sampedranos as full citizens and provide "security, well-being, and justice" but instead provided partial, palliative solutions to the symptoms of structural violence while mustering grassroots energies into complicity with a political economic order that systematically exposed indigenous communities to disproportionate levels of harm. Rony Galicia followed a similar path in 2011 but with less pretense about justice and security, no veneer of evangelism, without an exclusive appeal to Mayan identity, and with the baggage of personal criminality rather than genocide.

Instead of framing local problems as expressions of structural contradictions in Guatemalan society, linking them together in a movement to challenge these realities, authoritarian populism addressed intrapersonal and familial resentments in isolation and as private concerns. Rather than resolving these concerns, it made them more rigid and reinforced the system that made them inevitable. Electoral antagonisms between excluded groups exemplifies what feminist theorist Christine Keating (2011, 1) calls "compensatory domination," a situation in which "political authorities seek to build consent to their rule by consolidating and/or enabling forms of intergroup and intragroup rule." But this is not consent; repressive violence rendered electoral politics the only feasible option. Even though villagers did not consent to the social order, they did consent to competition with their neighbors; in democratic politics, villagers appeared to one another as the enemy next door. Authoritarian populism shifted attention away from the forces that placed villagers into the antagonistic relationship that incited them to injure one another and toward a cycle of payback.

Lauren Berlant (2012, 1) defines cruel optimism as a relation in which "the object that draws your attachment actively impedes the aim that draws you to it initially." Building on this understanding, I highlight cruelty as a feature of authoritarian populism in that it mobilizes a following by promising partial solutions to problems generated by the constitutive exclusions and police mechanisms of the social order while striving to render the violence of that order invisible and more endurable, and actively working to repress or neutralize alternatives. Such populist appeals are increasingly common on the neoliberal landscape, do not require ideological resonance, and can also erode extant political imaginaries. Authoritarian populism is the reactionary organization of pessimism and social and political violence, but it is not the only way. In San Pedro the conditions that provided traction for authoritarian populism also inform reimaginings of democracy that promote large-scale economic redistribution, local control, and equality. What is missing is a populist appeal that would provide shape and force to these unmet desires in ways that might reverse the polarity of pessimism.

CONCLUSION

Reorienting Democracy

The Sampedranos who formed grassroots organizations in the 1980s and 1990s and who became the protagonists of electoral democracy during the peace talks were qualitatively different from the leaders of the late 1970s. Whereas the previous generation dedicated and sacrificed their lives for collective advancement, by the 1990s, avenues for personal interest expanded to the detriment of the common good. Survivors of state terror were obligated to publicly conform to the military's definition of the guerrilla movement as an illegitimate entity that was doomed from the start and to deny any shred of sympathy for that lost cause. They were also told that their leaders were guerrillas and deserved to die, an effort to suppress all independent activism of this period; this interpretation continued in the decades after the peace accords. Although many still idealized a radical or even revolutionary vision of social justice, most buried all trace of it. Post-genocidal leaders knew that if they were to survive and extend their struggles, they had to present a subservient face to the army and adopt democratic identities whose legitimacy was measured by their distance from the revolution. Throughout the 2000s, most Sampedranos were still afraid to talk openly about the past and had rewoven postwar identities in relation to official memories, tendencies that shrouded both the past and the present in a cloud of uncertainty.

The moral force of the "two-army" discourse is that it criticizes all violence equally. But upon closer inspection it frames counterinsurgent violence as illegitimate only when it was *excessive;* it held in reserve that some amount of state violence to repress an internal enemy was still necessary and legitimate. State violence also disqualified nonviolent organizing, the repression of which led to the formation of the guerrilla movement. Violence went beyond counterrevolution to vanquish all progressive aspiration, regardless of how it was pursued. After the peace accords, targeted violence against social movements that was previously enacted in the name of annihilating democratic desire was framed as a defense of democratic order.

State violence dramatized the asymmetry of force and reminded Sampedranos that the state was willing and able to kill indigenous citizens and movements that challenged oligarchic power or multinational corporations. It explicitly referenced counterinsurgent performances of violence as a reminder of the state's capacity for racial terror without reserve. The spontaneous recognition of this extreme foundational injustice and the refraction of this injustice through manifold practices of deception generated an atmosphere of pessimism that hung over everyday discussions of politics and infused villagers' engagements with state institutions, political parties, and other powerful forces in their midst. So stifling was this atmosphere that many Sampedranos found it nearly impossible to become invested in projects dedicated to building a brighter future. Even while most Sampedranos believed deeply that the prevailing political economic order was unjust and wicked, a violent colonial imposition, most were convinced that it was impossible and dangerous to challenge it. Demobilization in the post-accords era was not a product of a "culture of fear," but it occurred because social movements required significant effort, entailed real risks, and accomplished little, and because politics had been shifted to new domains. For a small but influential minority of successful villagers, structural change was no longer seen as necessary or as pressing.

Grandin and Klein (2011) argue that state terror during the cold war "trained citizens to turn their political passions inward, to receive sustenance from their families, to focus on personal pursuits, and to draw strength from faiths less concerned with history and politics" (197). State terror closed down the pursuit of collective well-being through political organizing and alliances, leaving only individual and familial spaces and market discipline. But terror alone was insufficient to describe the forms of agency within this privatized domain. Neoliberal democracy and development opened up a field of productive activity, an entire political and economic world, within the parameters defined by violence. As state violence became increasingly selective and targeted, indigenous citizens were trained to navigate new spaces for democratic agency and development that they helped construct. Violence, democracy, and development were mutually constituted: violence disqualified revolutionary politics while indigenous inclusion in market development and electoral politics made structural transformation seem less pressing and political violence seem increasingly less repressive.

By distinguishing a domain of "legitimate" democratic demands from "impossible" and "undemocratic" ones—especially far-reaching land reform—violence channeled preexisting struggles for resources into delimited spaces of memory, development, and electoral politics. In each area the state mimicked and partially acquiesced to grassroots desires and attempted to harness them into a restricted political field. Market-oriented individual capacity development provided a productive counterpart to repressive violence; it opened opportunities for individual economic advancement and trained villagers as democratic citizens. Capacity development empowered a new class of younger community leaders who led development committees and political campaigns. This reorientation of politics was not simply or even primarily ideological; it was framed by violence, materialized through projects, and taken up by an actively cultivated class of modernizing villagers who possessed the technical capacities to economically advance, win elections, and govern.

After a difficult struggle, these new capacities enabled the village organization to wrest control of town politics from local Ladinos and to procure and distribute hundreds of infrastructural projects. Because of these successes, with the signing of the peace accords and the larger democratic transition ongoing in the background, this post-1985 generation of leaders came to understand local elections, projects, and individual advancement through education and training as a more realistic, sophisticated path to indigenous empowerment. It was under these conditions, in the wake of genocide and in the context of new discourses about indigenous rights, that the leaders of the Antulio Morales coalition, who had worked hard in the past to stop being "Indians," came to identify and frame their politics as "Mayan." They even posited bilingualism and intercultural understanding as qualifications for town governance. The recognition of this developmentalist vanguard as the rightful leadership of the local Mayan population obscured growing class differences among villagers accelerated by market development.

In the late 1960s, developmentalist reformers in the Guatemalan and US governments dreamed of cultivating a modernizing, apolitical peasantry, oriented toward high tech and market agriculture and productively connected to state institutions. Army reformers imagined market democracy as the political field these "permitted" Mayas would occupy, as the completion of the counterinsurgency project. By the late 1990s, judging by Jose Antulio Morales' career and the wave of primarily local indigenous empowerment through the highlands, it looked as if the army had succeeded. But neoliberal democracy in San Pedro produced an outcome that army reformers never envisioned: an authoritarian, kleptocratic party gaining power on the strength of indigenous votes, driven by the intertwined failures of democracy and development.

Caught in the Democracy Development Machine

Attaining legitimate victimhood, market advancement, and electoral spoils required villagers to betray their reciprocal obligations to their neighbors and extended kin along with their hopes for national reform. Market integration replaced generally horizontal relationships of mutual support with antagonistic class divisions and increasingly blamed poverty on individual choices. *Capacidad* was a nearly unquestioned norm but also a source of frustration for the majority, whom it classified as lesser. In a grating, interminable electoral process that favored the more developed, dozens of political parties competed for Sampedranos' votes, each offering development, access to corruption, and political power. Clientelist electoral politics ramified shared concerns about poverty and discrimination into competing party factions focused on projects that succeeded only by excluding others. Elections were widely criticized as orgies of personal interest and deception in which most Sampedranos participated despite serious misgivings. Many simply opted out. Because neoliberal democracy and development required villagers to deceive and abandon their counterparts, it eroded the trust and solidarity required to engage in self-governance and collective action against the Ladino state and the transnational corporate allies that deceived and betrayed them all. Elected officials also sidelined indigenous forms of authority.

These observations echo critiques leveled by indigenous political organizations, such as the Council of the Peoples of the West (CPO), an alliance of ancestral authorities united in defense against extractivism. They view electoral democracy as a mechanism of colonial power that shatters indigenous communities:

> In election years, municipalities fill with shell and phantom parties shouting demagogic solutions, and often compete between nine and fifteen parties literally provoking the fragmentation of our communities and the atomization of the vote. And the vote becomes so local that we are left alone, without unity among indigenous peoples. (2014: 32–33)

Similarly, the Mayan Coordinator, Waqib' Kej, a convergence of indigenous authorities and organizations, women's groups, and indigenous youth, argues that the "system of political parties as a democratic medium to make incursions inside the state is vitiated and does not respond to the needs of the Pueblos" (2015, 63). The situation resembles Harry West's (2008) description of Muedan villagers in Mozambique, who after a transition from socialism to free markets, "experienced democracy as a regime that promoted irresolvable conflict in their midst and provided cover for dominant political actors to forgo the responsibilities of authority and to feed themselves at the expense of others" (118).

Although political inclusion and market advancement became a reality for some, most were left behind. Some migrated north, and many were landless, unemployed, and out of options. Most villagers lived in a constant state of vulnerability: exposed to economic downturns, rising prices, crime, natural disasters, and sickness, situations that could leave them without land, food, or shelter. They lived in a condition of semi-abandonment, where the threat of complete desertion was never far off. They worried that they could not afford to fertilize their crops or that they would have to sell their coffee for less than it was worth. They worried that their precarious houses might slide into a ravine in a heavy storm or that their tiny coffee plots would wash away, taking borrowed money with them. They worried that they could not afford medicine for their sick children and elderly parents, or an operation that they needed to survive. They worried that they would be forgotten and that they would have nowhere to turn, betrayed by politicians whom they had no choice but to trust. Post-accords optimism about political inclusion and development quickly soured when local needs outstripped patronage, campaigns were based in lies and corruption, and poorer, more remote villages were denied access. Many development-oriented villagers lost sympathy for their neighbors or saw no alternative while pursuing individual and familial well-being and controlling leadership positions and development funds, always speaking on behalf of community and indigenous rights.

Lubkemann (2008) argues that the commonplace use of the term *uncertainty* to characterize life during wartime "fail[s] to account for the sum of experiences that together make up war as a social condition" (249). The same holds true for neoliberal democracy. Although rural Sampedranos do live with a great deal of uncertainty, blanket assessments may obscure the "tacit knowledge" that informs their charged engagements with the sovereigns in their midst: that the state and corporations do not value indigenous people, that powerful entities deceive and control them, that democracy is limited to competition for scarce projects, that resistance is useless and dangerous (Elyachar 2012). For most Sampedranos, these truths were so obvious that they were usually left unsaid.

These unintended outcomes discredited the indigenous-rights movement that state multiculturalism had midwifed into power, smearing it with self-interest, divisiveness, and incompetence, and confirming long-standing racist platitudes casting indigenous people as incapable of self-governance. Neoliberal democracy staged a mockery of indigenous rights and inclusion, even though the democracy development machine actively undermined autonomous structures of communal governance. Mutual accusations of self-interest contained a potent critique of neoliberal democracy and development, but also rendered nearly every action and actor suspect, impeding trust and the search for alternatives.[1]

Why did villagers remain entangled in such a noxious regime and resigned to its products? Paley (2001) suggests that Chilean democracy rendered the people complicit with market policies that remained outside of democracy. For their part, Sampedranos played small, enabling roles in a machine that they viewed as malevolent. With their participation and votes, Sampedranos gave an official, if ambivalent and conditional, stamp of approval to parties that they knew would steal public money and endorse policies that actively harmed them, such as mining and austerity. Sampedranos did not confuse national policies with the popular will but saw it as the cumulative result of countless self-interested acts, including their own. Although Sampedranos were collectively abandoned by the state, democracy parceled out power to distribute the brunt of this abandonment—the sovereign power to let die—over to villagers themselves, who become intimately complicit in their neighbors' misery so that they themselves might live better. Electoral politics shared an elective affinity with market rationality because of the emphasis on self-interested competition among private individuals and factions in a zero-sum framework.

Tania Li (2007a) draws attention to the complex, multilevel operationality of governing assemblages, which produce subjects engaged in self-improvement, create alliances between governing institutions and target populations, render complex problems technical (e.g., apolitical and ahistorical) by using self-reinforcing official knowledge, smooth out social and operational contradictions, and reformat prior discourses and demands to fit new frameworks. Li's concept invites empirical specification regarding the composition of different assemblages and how they gain traction and produce effects among governed populations in diverse social and historical conditions. I have argued that the strategic appropriation of democracy and development by Sampedranos under highly difficult conditions helped to produce subjects who pursued circumscribed forms of freedom within a political economic order founded upon their continued and wholesale subjugation. In San Pedro, democracy and development tailored to the neoliberal terrain achieved counterinsurgency goals through both repression and empowerment without substantially legitimating the political economic order in the eyes of most villagers.

The reason that this was so effective was precisely because rather than bracketing political economic reform (Ferguson 1994, Li 2007a, 265), democracy and development were presented in San Pedro as ideal and safe modes of social transformation; they promised resources, empowerment, and dignity. They were designed to resemble, connect with, and absorb historical struggles, to appear as hard-fought victories (which they were) even if they eventually disappointed villager expectations. Meanwhile, democracy and development in San Pedro reorganized prior struggles—against discrimination and for land and social democracy—by reformatting them to fit an unequal market framework and by focusing them on local concerns and achievements, such as individual struggles in the marketplace, election to local office, and projects earmarked to specific villages, families, and sectors. Indigenous ascendance in municipal politics and the market was framed and experienced as a collective victory, but it primarily benefited individuals and private groups.

Democracy and development were celebrated as the solutions to Guatemala's deeply encrusted social contradictions; the path to prosperity, equality, and inclusion; and the foundation of a long and lasting peace. They opened a field of political contestation that excluded long-standing political demands yet were still framed as manifestations of popular desire. It is undeniably true that democracy and development constituted a major transformation of rural Guatemalan political society, despite its limitations. But they also defended national and international asymmetries and created new ones. My findings provide ethnographic specification to Susanne Jonas's prescient observation that "in a country marked by such extreme inequalities, even limited political democracy cannot be meaningfully obtained in the absence of structural reform" (1988, 28). They also demonstrate the suffering produced by the fact, noted by Mayan intellectual Demetrio Cojtí (2007) and others, that despite a transition to multicultural democracy, "the state, as well as the democratic system, remains structurally colonialist and racist" (124).[2]

Democracy and the Politics of Redistribution

These findings complicate interdisciplinary discussions of the "politics of redistribution" (Li 2014; Ferguson 2015): a global trend to provide basic income directly to poor populations that has emerged in the wake of the failure of free market reforms. The advance of democracy is a principal driver of this development, as politicians compete for votes among poor citizens harmed or left behind by free market policies. Cash-transfer programs "work" on their own terms to reduce poverty, but their acceptance requires new thinking about labor and productivity beyond the narrow, and increasingly obsolete, frame of jobs. Ferguson argues that unemployed people are not unproductive or lazy but are engaged in various forms of "distributive labor" (97), such as networking with political patrons. These theories resonate with the ideas of Marxist Indian economist Prabhat Patnaik (2010), who advocates a politics focused on the incremental accumulation of basic material rights as an alternative to growth-based development.

A different model of redistribution is central to the political program of La Vía Campesina, the transnational peasant movement that formed in reaction to the spread of free market frameworks, specifically the agenda that strengthened transnational corporate control to the detriment of peasant and indigenous subsistence. Unlike cash transfers, La Vía Campesina's alternative proposal—food sovereignty—is far more extensive, emphasizing local control over food production and a significant redistribution of land-based resources and state support to subsistence agriculture (Nyéléni Declaration 2007; Borras 2008). Food sovereignty involves putting productive resources into hands that will best use them and emphasizes ecological sustainability over extractivist development. It incorporates indigenous knowledges along with conceptions of territorial sovereignty and rights-based claims to universal access to resources (Borras, Franco, and Suárez 2015; McMichael 2015).

The guardedly optimistic assessment of the shift to provide basic income deviates from narratives of inexorable abandonment under neoliberalism. It also lines up closely with positive reassessments of patronage networks in the fields of political science and anthropology that frame such structures as a more or less benign means of accessing vital resources among marginal populations.[3] Writing about Zero Hunger programs in rural Brazil—an early, influential model for basic income programs—Aaron Ansell (2014) describes how the anti-patronage component of these policies disrupted "intimate hierarchies" in which "mutual sympathy and vulnerability between the partners becomes the basis of a shared humanity that transcends structural hierarchy" with the potential to "socialize the political class towards the challenges of a region's poor" (194). Ansell and others ask us to take seriously nonliberal claims to resources from patrons as a viable means to ameliorate economic brutality.

It is tempting to view the nontrivial redistribution associated with electoral democracy in rural Guatemala as an enshrinement of a basic right to resources mediated by intimate hierarchies oriented toward mutual care. Indeed, the pull of neoliberal democracy in rural Mayan communities, especially electoral politics, derives from its function as a mechanism of redistribution, typically framed in the language of the rights to state resources that "belong to the people." This was a marked improvement over previous decades when the state invested little in rural welfare, and the institutionalization of cash-transfer programs in the mid-2000s lends further credence to an incrementalist narrative. But cash-transfer programs in rural Guatemala are widely criticized—from the right and the left—for maintaining poverty and creating dependency, although they are popular at the grassroots. Unwilling to risk votes, Perez Molina promised to continue the program during the 2011 election, although funding dwindled under his administration and poverty rates increased.[4]

While preferable to exclusion, the conditions, degrees, and mechanisms of redistribution matter greatly. Despite the veneer of citizenship and rights, redistribution in rural Guatemala is one of the primary mechanisms through which "inequalities are socially institutionalized" (Ferguson 2015, 155), occurring via norms established by competitive electoral politics in which villagers play an active role. Rather than a right to resources, democracy extends a lesser "right"—if it can be called that—to compete for *access*. My findings support the contention that limited redistribution in conditions of scarcity and political violence may supplant substantive claims to resources by excluded populations asserting fundamental equality: the crux of what Jacques Rancière (2010) calls true democracy. Clientelist redistribution networks form important parts of governing assemblages that materially impede the emergence of organized transversal politics that challenge foundational inequalities. Vertical patronage structures can erode relations of horizontal reciprocity and the trust, sense of togetherness, and hope for a better future that they sustain: all key conditions for collective action.

The parallel between democratic redistribution and counterinsurgency becomes all too clear when one recalls that in 1982, Ríos Montt offered Mayan villagers a choice between "rifles or beans," slaughter or development, the latter a pittance conditional on surrendering revolutionary demands. As important as it is to "deal pragmatically with (rather than just deploring) the social world we have got" (Ferguson 2015, 155), we must also think idealistically, but no less pragmatically, about how to expand the political horizon beyond neoliberal democracy. In Guatemala this implies thinking beyond the limited vision of the peace accords while at the same time demanding their implementation.

Decolonizing Democracy and Development

Decentering normative neoliberal democracy and development means attending to three elements: the ways that they operate together in disparate historical and political conjunctures within different projects of rule; how they intersect heterogeneous forms of life, geographies, and political struggles; and how subalterns selectively rework and reimagine them for a range of ends. Ethnographic methods are ideally suited to show how democracy and development are taken up and operate in locations far removed from national politics, and to explore their narrative temporalities and material and affective dimensions.[5] I have described how democracy and development in Guatemala operate as a governing assemblage alongside state violence to fashion new political subjects and demands to extend counterinsurgency through a political and economic transition. I have also attempted to illuminate how Sampedranos occupied these spaces in pursuit of decolonized citizenship, how they were transformed as a result, and what they think about these processes today.

Mayas across the highlands are reimagining democracy through efforts to revitalize traditional indigenous governance structures that gained legal recognition through the peace accords and that have received support from a range of donors and institutions, national and international. Revitalization of indigenous governance is often driven by frustration with party politics and the rise of extractivism. They are exploring the extent to which traditional indigenous authorities can exercise sovereignty over their territories and interact on par with the monocultural Ladino state,[6] which continues to violently assert its supremacy (Cojtí 2007). In these spaces, democracy is reimagined through indigenous epistemologies. Stener Ekern (2005) describes how the actions and deliberations of the *alcaldía indígena* (indigenous mayoralty) in Totonicapán, known as the forty-eight *cantones* (districts), were guided by a "vision of right order."

In contrast to a state order focused on the supremacy of individual rights, this "right order" was based on a principle of respect and selflessness: "the Mayan community does not accept the idea that a person can put his/her own interests first" (289). They also embrace an understanding of territory as a space of identity and becoming rather than an extractable commodity, and they do not recognize a secular-spiritual division. Sampedranos expressed similar values, and in their criticisms they also advanced a shared conception of neoliberal democracy as the "wrong order": they decried the displacement of collective well-being for individual interest in the form of party competition and illegitimate corruption and growing divisions of class and relations of exploitation backed up by state violence.

Critical scholarship typically presents indigenous lifeways, cosmologies, and governing structures as antithetical to logic of capital and the state.[7] Similar to Ekern, Alpa Shah (2010) writes that in the newly autonomous indigenous state of Jharkhand, India, Munda villagers—the poorest of the poor—participate in a sacred democratic polity organized around notions of reciprocity, with rotating leaders, no status hierarchies, and consensus-based decision making. She describes how Munda villagers' shared allegiance to the sacred polity compelled them to avoid the state, and to access it only through local indigenous elites, even though this further marginalized them from the political process. Shah advocates building a postcolonial democratic ethics from the values and practices in these separate spaces. At the same time, she is critical of indigenous-rights narratives that depict indigenous peoples as environmentally conscious, egalitarian, and connected to place, and thus free from the contaminating entanglements of modern life, narratives that often ignore internal hierarchies in indigenous communities and can constrain indigenous lives and livelihoods. The same can be said for understandings of subaltern political imaginaries as radically divergent and wholly separate from Western practices.

West (2005) writes that indigenous villagers in Mozambique "enacted democracy" not by creating an alternative form but "by critically engaging with democracy in a language that differs profoundly from the one spoken by democratic reformers" (118). In San Pedro, as in many rural towns, the sway of electoral politics made it nearly impossible for the *alcaldía indígena* to wield meaningful decision-making power. Rather than being cordoned off from political society, it was through their engagement with state and corporate models of democracy and development that Sampedranos formulated alternative conceptions that emphasized ethics of redistribution and concern for the most vulnerable, local authority, collective rights, and connections to place. Unlike the revolutionary imaginary, the premier villains of grassroots democratic imaginaries were not exploitative Ladino landowners and abusive labor bosses but the corrupt politicians and the mining companies. The moral failure common to all was the pursuit of self-interest to the detriment of the collective. Such alternative democratic imaginaries are not pure survivals of indigenous cosmologies, but complex reactions to imposed realities, from refusals to creative reworkings, grounded in preexisting and heterogeneous forms of life and histories of struggle that are continually adapting. I propose grounding a postcolonial political ethics in the values expressed through experiences with the state and corporate sovereigns, social movements and NGOs, and different paradigms of democracy and development.

Rather than reject these concepts as colonial impositions, indigenous political organizations in Guatemala propose decolonized models of development and democracy. The CPO's vision (2014) of good municipal government and democracy focuses on free, prior, and informed consultation; active participation of communities through indigenous authorities; transparent budgeting; a fair distribution of public funds; more money for indigenous municipalities; and respect for indigenous sovereignty in a pluri-national state. The CPO's aim is to "create unity to change Guatemala from the municipalities to the national level, based on a principle that enhances democracy: municipal autonomy must respect the consultations of good faith and the open town council" (35, my translation). Waqib' Kej views corruption, exclusion, and violence not as aberrations of neoliberal democracy but as expressions of structural contradictions of a state and economy founded on the dispossession of the indigenous majority. It understands political democratization (fully implementing the peace accords, reducing the size of the army, and other reforms) as a necessary precondition for the creation of a pluri-national state founded on principles of Buen Vivir (living well): harmony between humans and with Mother Earth.

Buen Vivir is a concept of Andean origin that has spread through indigenous movements throughout the continent. It offers a civilizational alternative to capitalist forms of democracy and development in which individuals seek to "live better" through self-improvement, perpetual economic growth, private wealth accumulation, a model based on competitive individualism, consumerism, and the extraction of natural resources that threatens the ecosphere and life within it. Buen Vivir is the political proposal of the defense of territory, a form of social and economic relations rooted in interdependence, nonviolence, and respect. This indigenous anticapitalist vision articulates widely in a conjuncture defined by the aftermath of genocide, the recognition of indigenous rights and the rise of autonomous indigenous movements, the failure of market-oriented development and "green" revolution technologies that have contributed to a crisis of subsistence agriculture, and a wave of rapacious extractivist development that exposes indigenous lives, territories, and livelihoods to harmful contamination.

These considerations bear on the thinking of M'ek To'm Torres, a Mayan Ixil activist and agronomist who works in sustainable agriculture for FUNDEBASE, a progressive NGO.[8] Torres is a graduate of Ixil University and participates in Waqib Kej', the Social and Popular Assembly, and local and national defense of territory politics. He offered this reflection on the politics of development:

> There is much uncertainty about the political situation . . . that affects . . . our regions in the prelude to the election year, and the old partisan policies and politicking without us. And we worry, we worry but do not propose actions. If we began to generate proposals from our generation, to address the . . . issues of our region, always with our own identity, it would be a challenge from us. Offers come from many sisters and brothers who . . . practice the tricks of old politicians offering "changes and improvements" in our villages when we are not even clear on the term "development." Is this the development that we really want? Is it is based on our needs or just what they tell us must be done? Let us analyze before exercising that right and do it responsibly. It falls to us to make the present and future conditions we want (my translation).[9]

He believes that communities should define development for themselves and issue proposals based in their own needs and identity, rather than external agendas. He calls for communities to exercise the right and responsibility to imagine a type of development that would be a direct challenge to politics as usual. These proposals and analysis, part of ongoing decentralized efforts to decolonize democracy and development, are them-selves enactments of sovereignty directed toward the construction of indig-enous futures.

A key question in these reflections is the relation between the ances-tral authorities of the pluri-national state and the Guatemalan state. One reaction to widespread dissatisfaction with neoliberal democracy is for communities and movements to opt out altogether. The Zapatista experi-ence is instructive here, as is its desire to "change the world without tak-ing power," abandoning the state as a key objective for radical politics. Although opting out of party politics deprived Zapatista-aligned villages of state funds and projects, autonomous municipalities have pursued alternative paths to development, expanded self-governing capacities, promoted gender equality, formed new external alliances, taken con-trol of assistance from international solidarity organizations, and pre-served internal cohesion, allowing the autonomy movement to survive and grow.[10] The Zapatistas are well-known for decentered, horizontal organizing methods and rotating leadership positions; for weaving tradi-tional forms with Catholic social teaching, indigenous-rights discourse, and neo-Marxist and feminist perspectives; and for innovating politi-cal concepts such as *mandar obedeciendo* (leading by obeying).[11] They have made major contributions to the radical reinvention of democracy, inspiring and influencing a generation of activists. Although they have not defeated neoliberalism, they slowed its advance in their territories while still playing a role in national politics and sparking the antiglobalization movement.

It is worth recognizing, however, the significant advances in poverty reduction obtained by anti-neoliberal Pink Tide governments in Latin America through taking state power, even as they have posed new dilemmas for peasant and indigenous movements through their com-mitment to extractivist development. Avoiding the state in favor of self-sufficiency often leaves communities without basic resources with limited impact on the neoliberal project.[12] Holding the successes of the Zapatistas and Pink Tide governments in mind, especially as the latter face crises precipitated by imperial interventions and reactionary resur-gence, the lesson for radical movements is not necessarily to avoid the state as a site of struggle but of the importance of maintaining organiza-tional autonomy as they interact with states and to shape state policy in ways that can strengthen, or not obstruct, grassroots alternatives which demonstrate that another world is possible.

Populism without Hegemony

In less than a decade after the peace accords, lack of faith in mainstream parties to deliver resources to the poor; the routinization of corrupt, self-interested politics; and growing economic inequality created openings for authoritarian populists who peddled solutions for precisely these kinds of grievances, even as they defended the political economic order that drove local dissatisfaction and competition. For Laclau (2005), hegemony, populism, and politics are synonymous; politics is a struggle for hegemony, and populism is hegemony in action, the formation of the people through the education of consent and the articulation of demands.[13] The basis of authoritarian populism in San Pedro was not ideological resonance, not shared faith in a leader to deliver on the people's demands, not a unified popular identity, but raw need, pessimism, and resentment among a fragmented electorate. But its discursive components produced important effects. Populism asserted meanings, identities, and narratives as it distributed resources: it struck nerves, shaped understandings, and moved villagers to action. It mimicked commonly held criticisms of the political economic system and displaced them onto local divisions they expressly would not solve and would in fact make worse. It presented historical injustices as irresolvable, reinforcing the core counterinsurgency and neoliberal truth that no better future was possible and redefining neighbors as enemies.

These findings caution against reading subaltern participation in illiberal populist politics as straightforward resistance. Jeffrey Witsoe's (2013) examination of lower-caste politics in Bihar, India, suggests that political society, despite its naked violence and absence of rights, produces positive forms with the capacity to challenge dominant social relations. While defying liberal democratic norms, he describes how lower-caste support for the criminal Rashtriya Janata Dal Party challenged the developmentalist state and institutions that were used as mechanisms of caste domination and incapable of fairly delivering resources or protecting rights. Lower-caste Biharis, he claims, viewed this usurpation of class dominance as true democracy. Witsoe uncovers a radical ethics motivating behaviors that are often framed as pathological and antidemocratic. It is important to appreciate the many ways that subalterns exercise agency through subverting democratic politics in ways that violate liberal norms for citizenship. However, these alliances are premised on stark power imbalances and often entail profound misrecognitions, such as white, middle-class Trump supporters, who are hardly subalterns but often imagine themselves as racially oppressed victims of a corrupt establishment.

Mayan Sampedranos used authoritarian populism to challenge local hierarchies and to redirect resources to excluded groups. Along the way, they were obligated to use illegal means, which did not violate local moral economies as long as they benefited poor people. Support for Ríos Montt in San Pedro and later for Rony Galicia was driven primarily by desires to break the grip of an indigenous political elite on municipal power and state resources, not to challenge the power or property rights of national oligarchs and transnational corporations. These populisms offered a diminished appeal to a grassroots conception of democracy focused on redistribution, honesty, and care for the less fortunate, combined with a harsh promise to abandon nonsupporters. Authoritarian populisms did not meet the material needs of the vast majority of party affiliates or end the cycle of favoritism; they only intensified local competition for projects and corruption. FRG supporters in San Pedro celebrated their success and welcomed the resources they obtained, but did not view their victory as democratic fulfillment. Most Sampedranos were frustrated by party politics, worried about their livelihoods, deeply suspicious of the state and corporations, and cynical about the future. They lacked faith in alternatives and one another. Yet behind the division, many shared a sense of identity based in a common history of struggle and a pride in resilience. Many villagers longed for lost unity, which nostalgically overstated past harmony but also pointed to something that felt very real.

In the global North, authoritarian populism more closely tracks hegemonic ideology, even as it rails against the establishment. Right-wing populists' ability to channel anger against politically expedient scapegoats (e.g., minorities, immigrants, the government, and liberal elites) and to wedge issues, rather than foundational and widening inequalities, is aided by spontaneous faith in free markets and militaristic nationalism, especially among whites and shared by the Democratic Party #Resistance.

Authoritarian populists thus encounter few obstacles in an effort to present themselves as extensions of the law, common sense, and national culture, as an iconoclastic defense of familiarity or a "return to normalcy." Authoritarian populists displace the unintended effects of neoliberalism onto a perceived weakness of the physical and imaginary borders of the nation and onto liberal cultural politics, foregrounding national victimization and prescribing cultural reassertion and racialized violence (as if these were not already the norm). The revolt against *capacidad* in San Pedro mirrors resentment that many working-class whites in the United States harbor for the college-educated, technocratic elite: the liberal middle managers of neoliberalism who are shielded from its rough edges while chiding them for intolerance. Even in contexts with stronger ideological resonance than in San Pedro, authoritarian populist appeals still work on bodily desires, even if they exceed abstract rational calculations of interest and must be understood in relation to historically configured landscapes of memory and identity.

Because they defend the structures of power in the societies where they operate, rather than attribute scarcity as a problem of a vastly unequal distribution of wealth, authoritarian populist appeals almost always normalize private property and assume zero-sum logic. This is why the definitive affect of authoritarian populism is resentment of racialized and gendered others rather than class solidarity. Reports that racial resentment and cultural anxiety rather than economic hardship drove support for Trump tend to see such identifications as immutable, rather than effects of long-standing strategies of cultural governance that have encouraged whites to identify on the basis of their race rather than class.[14] The contradictory, unstable nature of political imaginaries and identities makes alliances with authoritarian populists at once more malleable and more deceptive than we might assume; at a minimum, critiques of the politics of white racial and masculinist resentment should recognize the deeply fragmented nature of political discourse[15] and how the absence of meaningful electoral options and leftist narratives and organizations kindles the flame of fascist politics.

In the global North, neoliberal democracy crowded out leftist populism by promoting multicultural diversity and adopting the language and symbols of radical grassroots movements while its free market and militarist policies exacerbated inequality, environmental harm, and migration (accelerated by free trade and wars on terror and drugs). Likewise, corporations used similar strategies to selectively include women, nonwhites, LGBTQ, and environmentalists—pink, brown, green washing—while legally blocking deeper reform and promoting corporate science to sow doubt about the harmful effects of industrial activities.[16] The rupture of neoliberal multicultural hegemony and the rise of reactionary movements in capitalist core nations may force liberals to redouble organizing, make common cause with radical groups, and rethink allegiance to capital. But it can also incite spirited defenses of the exclusionary model of neoliberal democracy that produced the reaction in the first place, and a concomitant hostility to left populism.

However abhorrent, the shocking success of Trump and Brexit and the weakening of the liberal world order remind us that neoliberal democracy contains deep contradictions and rests on weak foundations. The predictable failure of authoritarian populism to resolve widening economic inequality wherever it manifests, and the needless suffering it inevitably produces, could reinvigorate radical movements. Progressives in the global North should not feel constrained by conventional wisdom about the limits of politics, which must be transcended in order to develop coalitions powerful enough to implement just and lasting solutions to the interconnected problems of our time. The latter will require civilizational transitions away from imperialism, settler colonialism, militarism, socially and environmentally unsustainable economic growth, dependence on fossil fuels, and the nation-state as the limit on belonging and justice.

Democracy against Neoliberalism

Sampedranos find neoliberal democracy so perplexing in part because it confronts them with the unintended effects of a state of affairs they worked so hard to bring into existence, even if they did not decide its parameters. Neoliberal democracy and development have, alongside violence, transformed prior paradigms of political consciousness and solidarity; but hegemony existed only to the extent that they disavowed radical politics and viewed electoral politics and market development as reasonable avenues for advancement. Even as Mayas resignified new spaces, the conditions that led to decades of armed conflict remained unresolved, new threats emerged, and communities were poisoned by self-interest and divisionism. As a regime of control that relies neither on terror or consent but a mix of violence and participation, neoliberal democracy eludes criticism from a space of purity. This ethnography aims to further discussions among communities, activists, academics, and policy makers about what has been gained and lost through democracy and development in rural Guatemala and how to build alternatives.

I have argued against neoliberal democracy and development as a neutral or desirable basis for a post-conflict settlement by ethnographically depicting how they are predicated on the exclusion of wide-scale redistributive politics, and how they divert radical desire into sterile domains, deepening class divisions, eroding trust and social solidarity, and creating fodder for authoritarian populism. Divisions in rural towns mirror progressive politics at the national level, where divisions between sectors of the popular left and the Mayan movement,[17] among Mayan organizations,[18] and among peasant movement factions[19] impede the formation of alliances capable of challenging national elites. These fractures reflect ideological and strategic differences, battles for protagonism and leadership, NGO competition for international funding, the effects of state cooptation "divide-and-conquer" strategies, and the grinding toll of political violence.

Authoritarian populism constitutes the reactionary organization of pessimism, the victory of resentment and the substitution of revenge for empowerment. The radical organization of pessimism, by contrast, would harness disillusionment into movements for transformative goals such as territorial autonomy and far-reaching redistribution. How, practically, could the radical organization of pessimism come about? Rural Guatemalans are searching for ways to alter their relationship to political parties, the state, and corporations by attempting to revindicate identities, recover traditional institutions, remember ancestral authorities, use the law of community development councils, organize civic committees and community *consultas,* and engage in nonviolent civil disobedience. Sometimes these efforts prevail, and even when they fail, they push political limits; resignify democracy, development, and national identity; reweave community; and build collective power.

An important variable in neoliberal Guatemala is the political articulation of indigeneity. Discourses of indigenous rights initiated a reconsideration of social and political identities throughout the highlands, among Ladinos and mestizos as well as Maya, Xinca, and Garifuna, as many find value where they did not see it before. In the wake of a failed revolution, indigeneity provided a political language safer than Marxism to contest marginalization and largely compatible with dominant models of development and democracy. In San Pedro, notions of indigenous rights provoked shifts in ethnic identification and provided a moral language for Mayan advancement, even though it limited what advancement could mean. But attempts to cultivate a domesticated indigenous politics have proven unable to contain the expansion of political imaginaries and projects assembled under that sign, especially the opposition to extractivism.

Indigeneity is central to the "defense of territory," the master frame for a heterogeneous array of movements against extractivism. The defense of territory draws connections among diverse struggles against mining, hydroelectric dams, land grabs, and other spatializations of capital, recoding these markers of progress as expressions of an ecologically unsustainable development model led by a national and transnational elite. The defense of territory is a cosmopolitical populism that echoes revolutionary struggles but goes beyond the human to include Mother Earth as part of "the people." Guided by a conception of Buen Vivir, the defense of territory contrasts indigenous connectedness with nature to anthropocentric, extractivist neoliberalism and connects these cosmological ecopolitics to movements for human rights, feminism, and peasants' rights. By 2014, seventy-eight municipalities in Guatemala had held *consultas* against resource extraction under ILO treaty 169, overwhelmingly rejecting extraction, suggesting a wide resonance of this frame.[20] Territorial-defense movements have strengthened indigenous identifications and governing structures, and encourage Mayas and Ladinos to find common cause against corporate intrusions, often attracting people with no prior involvement in politics. Although the defense-of-territory rhetoric is sometimes ethereal, at its most concrete it connects peasant movements for land and for food sovereignty and articulates a compelling alternative vision of how to allocate and manage natural resources.[21]

The challenge is to build cross-sectoral organizations and alternative projects that include a wide range of working people and peasants. Beyond dividing radical from "sanctioned" Mayan politics, a central preoccupation of post-accords statecraft has been to prevent alliances from forming

among movements in defense of territory, teachers unions, peasant movements, labor, the urban poor, human rights organizations, and movements
against austerity and privatization. The political crisis unleashed by the
CICIG's revelations of corruption rising to the highest levels in the government created a unique opportunity to plant the seeds for precisely these
kinds of alliances with the potential to expand the political horizons. Protests in the capital led originally by the Ladino middle class were quickly
joined by rural and peasant organizations that shut down the country,
forcing the resignation and imprisonment of President Otto Perez Molina
and Vice President Roxana Baldetti, and the collapse of the candidacy
of Manuel Baldizón, a Peten-based businessman from the right-wing
Renewed Democratic Freedom (LIDER) Party, who was leading in the
polls. Outrage coalesced around the entire political system and all major
parties as the investigation uncovered a massive criminal network and led
to dozens of arrests. Protestors assembled in Plaza of the Constitution
and organized through social media under the hashtag #EsElSistema, and
issued coordinated calls to boycott the 2015 elections. Nevertheless, the
elections went forward, and Jimmy Morales, a comedian with no political experience, ran as a populist protest candidate against the corrupt
establishment. He represented the National Convergence Front (FCN), a
far-right party formed by ex-military officers who wanted to revindicate
their role in the armed conflict in response to the victims' rights movement. Morales narrowly defeated Sandra Torres from the center-left UNE
Party, prompting comparisons to Donald Trump's surprising victory the
following year. Not surprisingly, Morales was soon embroiled in scandals
over illegal campaign financing and bribery.

The organizations comprising Guatemala's Social and Popular Assembly believe that the path to the radical organization of pessimism is an
articulation of diverse movements rooted in the lives and experiences of
the poor and marginalized, all treated as equal partners (ASP 2016). It
formed in 2015 out of the movement for a constitutional convention as
an effort to unite the anticorruption uprising with rural political struggles. Rather than oppose identity politics to class politics, or urban to
rural, these organizations attempt to connect diverse movements within a
radically democratic, cross-sectoral alliance. Their ultimate objective is a
constitutional convention to refound the state as a decolonized, egalitarian, noncapitalist, and ecologically sustainable polity. Such a goal might

seem ambitious, but it is within reach if the reformist sectors of the urban middle class join rural demands for full implementation of the accords, territorial autonomy, real land reform and development, and the cessation of privatization, austerity, and extractivism.

As disillusionment with neoliberalism expands, alliances grow, and strategies sharpen, Guatemalan activists face intensified repression that attempts to sow pessimism about the prospects of even moderate social change, that aims to destroy hope itself. In closing, I want to return to the countless acts of defiance, big and small, to political and structural violence in Guatemala: rural villagers who fought for development and against discrimination during the dictatorship; those who joined the guerrilla movement; those who did not but fought to protect their neighbors from the army; human rights activists who denounced state violence and militarization, many who lost their lives; victims and survivors who testified in genocide trials; indigenous activists who demand recognition, respect, and self-determination as they revitalize traditional governing structures; women who fight for equality and respect in their homes, communities, workplaces, and national politics, and for an end to domestic violence; rural villagers from all over the country who block highways to oppose privatization and biopiracy or to stop the entry of mining equipment into their territories; farmers who squat land and face eviction; citizens who protest corruption; and rural workers who strike for better wages and conditions. In each moment, ordinary people are using nonviolence—and sometimes violence in self-defense—to achieve the collective good by putting their bodies on the line. Every refusal constitutes a counter-performance against the inevitability of politics as usual. Risking death and harm, they enact control over their own bodies and define themselves as legitimate sovereigns, avatars of the spirit of the people and a radical democracy against the neoliberal authoritarian state and its elite and corporate cronies, if only for a flash. Guatemalans from various social locations wonder what it will take to develop a form of democracy that does justice to these alternative visions.

NOTES

Introduction

1. For a discussion of the violence and its effects on indigenous communities, see Carmack 1988; Manz 1988; Falla 1992; REHMI 1998; CEH 1999; and González 2002.

2. See Black, Jamail, and Chinchilla 1984; Smith 1990b; and Schirmer 1998. The patrollers worked in tandem with the military to pacify rural communities, committing countless human rights abuses and tightening military control.

3. See Simon 1987 and Jonas 1991 for a discussion of human rights activism during the democratic transition.

4. For analysis of the Pan-Mayan movement, see Bastos and Camus 1996, 2003; Fischer and Brown 1996; Cojtí Cuxil 1997; Warren 1998; Nelson 1999; and Fischer 2001, 2009.

5. For a discussion of alliances leading up to the peace accords, see Warren 1998.

6. See Jonas 2000 on the gains and limitations of the peace accords. Burrell (2013) describes how Mayan villagers in Todos Santos Cuchumatanes, Huehuetenango, expressed that peace could not change the past or their poverty.

7. Feminist organizations forged out of wartime transformations of gendered divisions of labor promoted women's rights and equality against public and domestic patriarchy. See Hernández Castillo 2008.

8. This included a Ladino leftist, a Quiché feminist journalist, a Mam linguist, and a Catholic priest.

9. In the most high-profile example of state violence, Archbishop Bishop Juan Gerardi, the director of the REMHI, was bludgeoned to death in the rectory of San Sebastián days after

releasing the REMHI report in April 1998. Ricardo Sáenz de Tejada Rojas (2012) speaks of a "democratic malaise," and Edelberto Torres Rivas (2010) speaks of "bad democracies" that are characteristic of the Central America transition to neoliberalism, marked by top-down imposition, negative correspondence between political freedoms and reductions in poverty and inequality, increasing concentrations of power, and a tendency toward violence.

10. See Robinson 2000, 2003; USAID 2010; and Thomas, O'Neill, and Offit 2011. Of particular concern, the market-led agrarian reform program called for in the accords was underfunded and primarily benefited plantation owners. See Gauster and Isakson 2007.

11. Similarly, Ellen Moodie (2010, 2) describes how experiences of democracy in "post peace" El Salvador are shot through with anxiety and insecurity because of a rising crime rate commonly described as "worse than war."

12. See Solano 2005; Reina 2008; Yagenova and Garcia 2009; Holt-Giménez 2008; Fulmer, Godoy, and Neff 2008; Dougherty 2011; CALDH y CONIC 2012; Rasch 2012; Bastos and de León 2013; Nelson 2015; Alonso-Fradejas 2015; and Fultz 2016.

13. Mayan Nobel laureate Rigoberta Menchú won only 3 percent of the vote in her 2007 and 2011 presidential runs with a leftist-indigenous coalition. For further discussion, see Fischer 2009, 92; Velásquez-Nimatuj 2008, 2013; Bastos and Brett 2010; and Vogt 2015.

14. A rupture in postwar power structures occurred in the anticorruption protests of 2015. See Copeland 2015b.

15. For electoral results, see Tribuno Supremo Electoral 2003, 2007, 2011. See Kate Doyle 2013 for declassified documents from the National Security Archive tracing Ríos Montt's political career and actions during the armed conflict, and details about his genocide trial.

16. For example, Roxanne Dunbar-Ortiz (2014) describes a long history of "populist imperialism" in the United States, in which mass violence is narrated as necessary for the expansion of freedom and democracy. David Harvey (2005, 2) defines neoliberalism as "a theory of political economic practices that proposes that human well-being can best be advanced by liberating individual entrepreneurial freedoms and skills within an institutional framework characterized by strong property rights, free markets, and free trade." Neoliberalism refers to the post-Keynesian economic consensus led by the Chicago School of political economy that became dominant in response to the inflation crisis of the 1980s and became hegemonic through Reaganism-Thatcherism.

17. See Escobar 1995.

18. See Paley 2002 and Copeland 2018 for a review of anthropological approaches to democracy.

19. Many have observed how corporate deregulation and the influx of money into US politics have empowered an oligarchy that tramples public interests. Sheldon Wolin (2008) argues that American democracy "inverted" into a totalitarianism of corporate control, anti-unionism, media self-censorship, and militarism through the cold war and the war on terror.

20. See Dean 2009; Arias and Goldstein 2010; and MacLeish 2013.

21. See Escobar 2016.

22. Wendy Brown (2015) sees liberal democracy as withering in the face of neoliberal reason, a political rationality that entails the radical redefinition of human liberty on individual and market terms and has reshaped policies, institutions, and social relations, steadily eroding the domains in which popular sovereignty can be exercised (the public) and the cultural and educational spaces through which the deliberative capacities of the people are formed.

23. Autonomous Marxists Michael Hardt and Antonio Negri (2005) argue that the neoliberal empire is producing a decentralized, heterogeneous, democratic network united against corporate globalization, inequality, and "accumulation by dispossession" (see Harvey 2007).

In a similar vein, anarchist anthropologist David Graeber (2013) rejects electoral politics in favor of experiments with "horizontal" democracy such as the Occupy and the Zapatista movements. See also Zibechi 2010. Mark Purcell (2013, 2) calls for a "perpetual democratization" of experimentation and renovation to grapple with contemporary crises and concentrations of power. Latin America's "pink tide" governments used "vertical" electoral strategies to counter neoliberalism and launch projects of redistribution and decolonization, with varying levels of success. Vergara-Camus (2014) argues for development alternatives against rigid antidevelopment positions. I combine Deleuze and Guattari's (1983) insistence on the irreducible and multiple forms of desire within fascism and the possibility of their rearticulation with attention to the effects of political and economic violence on capitalist experiences of freedom and democracy.

24. David Gow (2008) describes the grassroots reappropriation of development as "counterwork." David Nugent (2008) writes of "alternative democracies."

25. See especially Schirmer 1998 but also Jonas 1988; Wilkinson 2004; Grandin and Klein 2011; Hale 2006b; and Way 2012. Schirmer conducted extensive interviews with General Hector Gramajo, the architect of the army's project for strategic democracy in rural villages, to be inhabited by docile "Mayas *permitidos*." Jonas (1988, 26) describes how the army made its intentions clear from the outset: "The ink was barely dry on the Central American Peace Accords signed in Guatemala City last August 7 when Guatemala's top military officials declared that the accords 'don't apply' to Guatemala. Five days later, in its first-ever public forum on '27 Years of Struggle against Subversion' army officials reiterated their view that 'politics is a continuation of war by other means.' Both in the forum and in an accompanying multimedia exposition, the army took a pointedly hard 'antiterrorist' line, leaving no doubt of its determination to pursue its counterinsurgency war in Guatemala amid the efforts for peace in the Central American region." Mona Bhan (2013) writes about democracy as counterinsurgency in Kashmir.

26. Similarly, Gramsci and Nowell-Smith (1971) described a transition from a war of maneuver on the battlefield to a war of position, a struggle for hegemony.

27. For a critical review of the various explanations of indigenous political alignments in the post-accords period, see Copeland 2007, 2014.

28. See Arias and Goldstein 2010.

29. Hale's point is that recognition of collective indigenous rights is not antithetical to neoliberalism, even though the classic subject of liberalism is the individual.

30. For discussions of democracy as socially and historically configured, see Coles 2007; Nugent 2008; Paley 2008; and Copeland 2018.

31. See Star 2010 for a discussion of the boundary object concept in actor-network theory. This concept has been fruitfully applied to the anthropology of development as an interactive process involving multiple groups and technologies. See Mosse 2005. I examine how different forms of development act as boundary objects within the democracy assemblage.

32. Phillips and Ilcan (2004) discuss capacity building as neoliberal subject formation.

33. Paul Farmer's (2005) conception of structural violence refers to conditions of material deprivation and inequality that create conditions for illness, death, rights violations, and political violence. For discussions of social suffering and the violence of everyday life in neoliberal Guatemala, see Benson, Fischer, and Thomas 2008; and Thomas, O'Neill, and Offit 2011. Protevi (2009) elaborates a theory of political affect and somatic politics.

34. For a discussion of the state as an ideological effect or reification produced through dispersed practices and in everyday encounters, see Abrams 1988; Gupta 1995; Gupta and Ferguson 2002; Coronil 1997; and Aretxaga 2000, among others. For a discussion of states as fetish objects that both repel and attract, see Brown 1995; Taussig 1997; Aretxaga 2003;

and Nelson 1999, 2009. For a discussion of sovereignty produced through performative enactments of violence on killable bodies, see Foucault 2012; Agamben 1998; Das and Poole 2004; and Hansen and Stepputat 2005, among others, who make the case for the continued relevance of sovereign violence in the contemporary political order.

35. Audra Simpson (2014) theorizes refusal of settler state sovereignty by Mohawks, who assert their membership in a polity that preexists the United States and Canada.

36. Anand (2011) describes a form of "hydraulic citizenship" produced in Mumbai as citizens pressure politicians to pull strings to increase their water pressure. My analysis extends beyond one infrastructural form to encompass how infrastructure operates as one element within a governing assemblage.

37. Berlant (2007, 757) moves away from a conception of sovereignty fixated on the drama of intentional acts of agency and toward "a shape made by mediating conditions of zoning, labor, consumption, and governmentality."

38. See Auyero 2001; Auyero, Lapegna, and Page Roma 2009; and Ansell 2014.

39. See Patnaik 2010; Li 2014; and Ferguson 2015. Patnaik (2010, 37) argues for a "rights-based" approach to development, as opposed to a bourgeois means-based approach focused on economic growth: "The acquisition of 'rights' on the part of the people, including 'rights' to minimum bundles of goods, services and security, amounts therefore to winning crucial battles in the class war for the transcendence of capitalism." He argues that establishing inviolable claims to basic resources is fundamentally antithetical to the spontaneous action of capital and argues for its place at the center of leftist politics. He views rights as "guarantors or welfare gains" that are not reversible, wholly distinct from "rights" that are intermittently and provided and withheld, and conditioned gifts from the bourgeois state. I found the latter in San Pedro.

40. I borrow the formulation of populism as a discourse that divides society into "the people" and the powerful from Ernesto Laclau (1977). His later work (2005) elaborates on the discursive constitution of the people and their demands through a process of articulation.

41. Laclau argues that conservative populism encounters an inherent limit because its ultimate aim is to absorb opposition to the political economic order, not transform it.

42. The department capital is also named Huehuetenango.

43. The hotels are used mostly by family members of hospital patients and occasionally state employees or development workers.

44. *Ladino* also means a swindler, a cunning and deceptive person. For a discussion of recent transformations of Ladino identity, see Hale 2006b.

45. Nearly 90 percent of Sampedranos live in poverty, 44 percent live in extreme poverty, and more than half are illiterate (SEGEPLAN, 2009).

46. I still return to San Pedro when I can, but I completed research for this book in 2014.

47. After the passage of CAFTA in 2005, Huehuetenango became a site of anti-mining protests. Sampedranos voted almost unanimously against mining in a community consultation in 2007.

48. See Hale's (2006a) definition of activist research. Calls for politically committed anthropology are one response to widespread criticisms of the irrelevance and unavailability of anthropological investigations from the typical subjects of this research: indigenous peoples. Indigenous activists increasingly lodge these criticisms directly and pointedly.

49. I presented Spanish translations of my initial findings and a history of town politics in San Pedro, and distributed copies. A local Ladino high school teacher used my early analysis of party politics as an example of how to write a "popular version" of a topic. As a result, dozens of teachers and students and community leaders read and discussed my analysis, and used it as a political reference.

50. Activist research focuses on alignment with groups with which one shares strong political affinities and their involvement in shaping the research questions (Hale 2006a). These methods can create productive collaborations but may present obstacles to engaged research in contexts where existing movements are deeply compromised, flawed, or nonexistent.

51. A number of scholars attempt to account for indigenous political participation in the FRG and other authoritarian movements without resorting to notions of false consciousness, binarized and essentialist conceptions of identity and culture, or universalizing teleologies while keeping violence and agency in the analytical frame and examining the contemporary relevance of long-standing political struggles. Garrard-Burnett (2010) emphasizes resonance between authoritarian and neoliberal discourses and changing worldviews in Mayan communities related to the rise of protestant religions, focusing particularly on Ríos Montt's reputation and rhetoric. Also focusing on religion, O'Neill (2010) suggests that a salvation-oriented Christian citizenship resonant with neoliberal ideologies has eclipsed wartime identities and political imaginaries. Hale (2002) and Nelson (2009) see democracy as a response to struggle and see Mayan engagement with democracy as strategic. Benson, Fischer, and Thomas (2008) attribute support for Ríos Montt and other hardliners to moralizing discourses about criminality that mystify structural violence.

52. See also Das and Poole 2004.

1. "They Committed No Crime"

1. My friends from Ceiba always found this story hilarious.

2. See Grandin (2013) for a summary of state-society relations in the rural highlands from the colonial era to the post-accords era, with their associated forms of political violence and their effects on ethnic identity and social relations. He documents the rise of intra-communal conflict dating from the late colonial period driven by the strain put on subsistence agriculture by population growth and the expansion of coffee plantation agriculture, and a corresponding sharpening of internal class divisions. He notes a dynamic in which increased community divisions "deepened appeals to ethnic solidarity" even as these divisions increased state power over communities (61).

3. See Handy 1984; McCreery 1994; and Taracena 1997.

4. See Grandin 2013, 63, on reformist politics and rural democratic movements in the 1920s.

5. See Forster 2001, 139, for a discussion of labor organizing prior to the Democratic Revolution of 1944. She argues that many indigenous workers viewed racism as the root of economic inequalities and pursued interethnic organizing.

6. See Handy 1994 on revolutionary processes in the countryside.

7. Events in San Pedro parallel regional processes that have been well documented. See, in particular, Falla 2001 [1978]; Brintnall 1979; and Warren 1989.

8. Pedro Morales, a union leader in San Pedro during the Revolution, was elected the first indigenous *alcalde* in San Pedro Necta in 1966, with the moderate Revolutionary Party (PR). Leading Catholic developmentalist Arturo Ramírez, an indigenous sacristan and a leader in the fight against *costumbre*, ran in 1974 with the center-left National Opposition Front (FON), a coalition that included the DC, the newly formed United Front of the Revolution (FUR), and the PR. FON's presidential candidate was Efraín Ríos Montt, then a young officer who had served as minister of defense under Arana Osorio. Ramírez won, but Ladinos prevented him from taking office. Francisco Domingo, an indigenous teacher from the village of Tecpán, confronted the Ladino *alcalde* to end the system of free indigenous labor. The brothers Jacinto and Alfonso Garcia led the fight to retain communal land and water titles. See Copeland 2007 for a more detailed discussion of town history.

9. The EGP was both a political and a military organization. Through a network of clandestine cells, the EGP raised consciousness and created supporter communities. ORPA was an exclusively military organization. Both groups focused recruitment efforts in the *finca* zones in the north of the township and in remote indigenous communities.

10. Understanding local presence and responses to guerrilla organizations was one of the central aims of my local historical research, but a difficult task for reasons I explore in this chapter. With persistence over several years of return visits, I was able to discuss this topic openly with more than a dozen individuals, mostly men but also women, both Mayas and Ladinos, who had firsthand knowledge of events during the revolutionary years. Most of these individuals identified as sympathizers, but one identified himself as a former combatant with ORPA. Like most of the village-level guerrilla leaders who had not been killed, he had fled with his family into Mexico. Others went to Canada.

11. CUC, the first Indian-led peasant organization, pushed for many of the same goals embraced by the cooperatives and made broader criticisms of conditions in the plantations and military power. See Grandin 1997.

12. The guerrillas were not responsible for other assassinations, kidnappings, or massacres of indigenous villagers in San Pedro.

13. ORPA, the more military-professional–oriented group, was increasingly dissatisfied with botched EGP military operations. Conversely, the EGP criticized ORPA's single-minded focus on combat and relative lack of interest in building support bases, which many thought left the communities behind.

14. The local candidate for *alcalde* was Jacinto García.

15. See Kobrak 2003. Sampedranos stayed informed of the guerrillas' military actions through radio, newspapers, and rumor.

16. Between March and April, the army killed seven in the aldea el Cable (CEH 1999, caso 5322). On August 2 in the aldea Ixnul, members of the army raped and executed six women, torturing two of them first, along with three other men from the village. A newborn infant, the son of one of the women, died shortly after of hunger (CEH 1999, caso 5052). On October 28, the army killed eleven people in the aldea Canoguitas. Two were tortured, and two were burned alive in their houses (CEH 1999, caso 5527). The García brothers were tortured all night long and killed the next day. Ten days afterwards, the army "disappeared" Tepán's Francisco Domingo, a leader of an Alcoholics Anonymous chapter suspected of being a front for guerrilla operations. Also in 1982, Arturo Ramírez was kidnapped while on a bus in Huehuetenango and was never seen or heard from again. Bodies of suspected guerrilla leaders, such as Natividad Ruíz Ramírez, were hanged under the bridge in Chimiche so that everyone could learn the fate of subversives. Abuses of power were built into the civil patrol system, the entire foundation of which was a human rights violation.

17. In the village of Niyá, the army, with the help of civil patrollers from the aldea, captured and tortured Olimpia Carillo and Yolanda Carillo for six days (CEH 1999, caso 5134).

18. See especially Krueger and Enge 1985 and Smith 1990b.

19. Their houses were often burned by the patrols or given to other villagers.

20. This was the situation in Aguacatán and Colotenango. See Kobrak 1997 and 2013, respectively.

21. See especially Hale 1997; REHMI 1998; CEH 1999; and Sanford 2003.

22. See Schirmer 1998.

23. Stoll (1993) reinforces the army's assertion that guerrilla commandos deliberately placed villagers in the line of fire.

24. See Arias 2001 for a compilation of perspectives on the Rigoberta Menchú controversy. See also Grandin 2010.

25. See Hale 1997.

26. See McAllister 2003; Konefal 2010; and Grandin and Klein 2011.

27. Sanford (2003) presents ample evidence that, in many cases, "Indian" meant "guerrilla" to the army and calls for a nuanced understanding of Mayan political allegiances during the armed conflict beyond the army-guerrilla binary.

28. Hale (2006b, 87) explains that "each narrative frame rests on certain categories of political consciousness (for example, a distinction between Mayan cultural rights and popular or class demands) and certain political distinctions (for example, separating the Mayan movement from the Left), which later became to appear entirely self-evident, but which had not come to predominate during the volatile and heady years between 1976 and 1981."

29. See especially Grandin and Klein 2011; Konefal 2010; and McAllister 2003.

30. This situation echoed Kobrak's (1997) findings about community acceptance of the civil patrols in Aguacatán, Huehuetenango.

31. Victor Montejo's (1987, 35) testimony describes the intense fear of living under military control in Tzalalá, Huehuetenango, and the excruciating emotional management required in a situation where "anyone can condemn to death their own neighbor with the slightest accusation or rumor."

32. However, the situation was distinct from what was described by Matilde Gonzáles (2002) in San Bartolomé, Jocotenango, where former civil patrol leaders still ran the town despite their role in the violence.

33. See Sanford 2003.

34. Even Sampedranos who were skeptical of the prospects of peace and democracy were glad that the peace accords had been signed and that the war had ended.

35. See Stoll 1990 and Garrard-Burnett 1998, 2010.

36. Garrard-Burnett 2010.

37. Nelson (2009) and Burrell (2013) describe a climate of historical uncertainty in the post-accords period.

38. Gill (2016, 223) writes about memories of "paramilitary takeover as peace" in Barrancabermeja, Colombia.

2. *Nos Falta Capacidad*

1. On the promotion of NTX by USAID as the cornerstone of rural development strategy in Guatemala in the 1980s, see Barham et al. 1992 and Fischer and Benson 2006.

2. I discuss these issues in more detail in chapter 3 and in Copeland 2015a.

3. Sol Tax (1953, 17) described Mayas in Panajachel, Sololá, and nearby regions as "penny capitalists" who participated eagerly in market activity and were steeped in the rational disposition and acquisition of services and resources according to cost-benefit ratios, "weighing choices in accordance with the economic principle," and who were divided by class.

4. Ricardo Falla (2001 [1978]) offers extensive observations of the traits and characteristics of a new merchant class in San Antonio Ilotenango, Quiche, many of them leaders of Catholic Action. He described new consumption patterns, including increased interest in leisure items and luxury goods, especially associated with dress and personal hygiene. He organized his descriptions on class strata, based on levels of available capital. Nowhere in his extensive categorizations does Falla mention the term *capacidad*. This was not predominant in the lexicon at the time he was working as a priest and taking ethnographic field notes. Forty years later, this term is one of the most common ways that Sampedranos distinguish between people and identify themselves. See also Goldin 2011 on the relationship between work and cultural transformation in Mayan communities.

5. Similarly, Anagnost (2004) describes *suzhi* as a perceived quality of populations and persons in China related to development, education, and consumption patterns.

6. Evangelicals also talked about *capacidad* with their followers during this time period. Virginia Garrard-Burnett, personal communication.

7. Cooperative organizing repressed after the counterrevolution was slowly re-legalized between 1956 and 1959 by President Peralta Azurdia. Cooperatives thrived in the late 1960s in the limited political openness of the Montenegro presidency; there were nineteen in Huehuetenango by 1972. The national cooperative movement was left-leaning, progressive, and pragmatic.

8. The goal of training cooperative leaders was that "the campesino or the cooperativist worker will turn into a new man. Discover their own *capacidades* (capacity, capabilities) and work to liberate himself from traditionalism, demonstrating that he is capable of responsibly assuming the challenge that we all confront underdevelopment, ignorance, and misery" (Gaitan 1972, 58).

Cooperative ideas were presented as in harmony with indigenous culture, while at the same time voicing a strong criticism of certain elements of indigenous tradition.

9. Town Ladinos whose larger land holdings better situated them to benefit from economies of scale often took over cooperatives.

10. One of the first was the Society for Strengthening the Indigenous Economy (SFEI). SFEI promoters—there were three for the entire department—went from town to town in Hueuhetenango from the mid-1950s to the late 1960s promoting chemical fertilizers and market agriculture. See Manz 2005. SFEI's coverage was miniscule, however, covering perhaps 1 percent of the population.

11. See Ortiz and Meneses 1989 and Ortiz et al. 1991.

12. One Ladino reportedly complained angrily that these programs would take away his peons. Some denounced DIGESA as communist because villagers sometimes worked in groups.

13. These rates are changing with more youths graduating from high school and becoming teachers.

14. Kay Warren (1998) identified *superación* as a shared goal among Mayan movement activists.

15. For details about the *cofradía* system, see Smith 1984, Warren 1989, and Watanabe 2010.

16. Concepción and her sister, also unmarried, had previously raised one of their brother's daughters, who had grown up to be a teacher.

17. For more detailed history of the emergence, activities, and ideologies of various Mayanist organizations up to and including the Pan-Mayan movement, and the changing economic and political situation that shaped them, see Fischer and Brown 1996; Cojtí 1997; Warren 1998; and Bastos and Camus 2003. Much Pan-Mayan activism occurred in urban centers (Quetzaltenango and Guatemala City) and among college-educated professionals, particularly a group at Rafael Landívar University.

18. These have been central concerns for Mayanist anthropologists for decades. See, for example, Wagley 1949 and Watanabe 2010.

19. See Fischer 2001.

20. In her preface, Warren (1989, ix) writes that she "never would have guessed that, along with successful careers in rural development and education, some of these questioning youths would become more, rather than less, active in indigenous cultural politics."

21. See Cojtí 1997; Warren 1998; Nelson 1999; Fischer 2001; and Bastos and Cumes 2007. Fischer argues that neoliberal decentralization and foreign aid directed to indigenous communities and informed by indigenous-rights discourses opened up new space for local activists who made new uses of these ideas. Rather than "permitted Indians" (Hale 2002), he sees these identities and politics as tactical improvisations.

22. Pan-Mayan activists contest this constructivist conception of identity, emphasizing an enduring core of Mayanness (Warren 1998, 74–78).

23. She was identified as a Ladina, but I do not know how she self-identified.

24. Rachel Sieder (2011a, 23–24) observes that "the efforts of Maya-K'iche' communal authorities to strengthen and 'recover' their own forms of law are primarily a response to insecurity, violence, and the structural exclusion and racism that impedes indigenous peoples' access to justice. They also constitute part of wider political processes of ethnic revitalization which have occurred in Guatemala since the end of the war. These processes have generated new forms of communal government and justice, combining Mayan epistemologies with discourses and practices grounded in human rights."

3. The Capacity for Democracy

1. See Foucault et al. 1991 and Rose 1996.

2. See especially Edelman 1999; Moore 2005; and Gow 2008.

3. See IDF 1968; USAID 1970; Fledderjohn 1976; and Copeland 2012.

4. See IDF 1968 and Copeland 2015a.

5. The Guatemalan army repressed even state-supported cooperatives. See Brockett 1990.

6. See Schirmer 1998.

7. The army attempted to resume "normal" life after the extreme violence, often through (largely symbolic and underfunded) efforts to promote economic development and build roads, houses, and schools, along with continued ideological indoctrination. See Krueger and Enge 1985, 29; Simon 1987; Smith 1990b; Nelson 1999; and Schirmer 1998.

8. Antulio Morales blamed this on the ANN's failure to invest in the departmental campaign. He began looking for another party and was leaning toward the newly formed National Unity of Hope (UNE).

9. Faith in a development fix rationalized continued US military assistance by assuaging US qualms about state-supported death squads, tipping history toward genocide (Copeland 2012).

10. Even fewer efforts were made to challenge long-standing monopolies on commodity markets, both internally and for export (Copeland 2012).

11. Brintnall (1979, 149) writes that "the fall of the hierarchies, in short, represented more of a negative statement about the character of the new order than a positive one—the old will not dominate the young, nor the Ladinos the Indians, and the ethnic groups will not be united as in the past. In retrospect, it is clear that the churches actualized this new order only partially, and other institutions were soon to take root among the Aguacatecs, creating a new public framework for Indian social life."

12. The concept of respect is important here because of its centrality within Mayan cosmovisions. See Ekern 2005. This quotation speaks to the way that respect became woven into counterinsurgency objectives.

13. See Copeland 2007 for a discussion of town politics in the 1960s and 1970s.

14. A friend of Antulio Morales told me he never intended to keep that promise because "the Ladinos would never permit a statue of an ex-guerrilla."

15. See also Escobar 1995 and Chakrabarty 2009.

16. Given the individualist orientation, Mayan Sampedranos typically understood their personal development as entailing familial responsibilities. Many immigrants sent back money to support their families, including many who left long ago and had no intention of ever returning. Young professionals often helped their parents with emergency and mundane expenses. Many helped support their younger siblings' education. Many used *capacidad* to help their village—for example, by coordinating with outside institutions and authorities or

serving on development committees. For their part, *superados* made a point of sharing wealth with family members.

17. Li (2014) describes a tragic situation in Indonesia, where the cacao boom led villagers to privatize communally held land. Some got wealthy and bought land and hired workers, but only through displacing and exploiting their neighbors. Her analysis speaks to a gap in modernizing narratives in which hundreds of millions of peasants do not advance into other fields but remain superfluous to the global market. She also contends that such concerns are invisible to indigenous-rights discourses that ignore contradictions between indigenous people and organizations.

18. This shows how the local power of the civil patrol was linked to the authority of local patrol leaders, who had obtained their power through assimilationist development programs and policed the boundaries of their authority through racism.

19. See also Fischer and Benson 2006. The association between free trade and mining was not clear to villagers in 2004.

20. Before the previous two elections, *Asociación* Ceiba led a *voto consciente* (conscious or informed-vote) campaign, which emphasized that the vote should remain secret, is an individual decision, and should not be sold. As Fernando suggests (indeed, Fernando might be paraphrasing from one of Ceiba's reunions), they say that votes are not for sale; that they are private, individual decisions; and that they need to be cast based on who a person thinks might be the best leader.

21. W. E. B. Du Bois (2017 [1935]) argued that freed Africans after the Civil War required education to become functional democratic citizens. However, he also believed that the black vote was urgent to prevent the reconstitution of a racist white power structure and could not wait for training.

22. See Carletto et al. 2010 on the disappointing long-term effects of NTX adoption.

23. See Camus 2008 for a discussion of migration in Huehuetenango.

4. Radical Pessimism

1. Nearby, I knew that two core FRG villages in Colotenango, Barranca Grande and Barranca Chiquita, had sided with the civil patrols against guerrilla-aligned villages during the war and were still bitter about a landmark conviction and incarceration of village patrol leaders for killing Juan Chanay during a protest against the patrol system (Kobrak 2013).

2. Philpot-Munson (2009) found exuberant agreement with the FRG among Pentecostal Ixil villagers in Nebaj who believed that Ríos Montt had saved them from the guerrillas and echoed his signature concoction of evangelical moralizing and counterinsurgency doctrine.

3. See Le Bot 1995; REHMI 1998; CEH 1999; Stoll 2003; Hale 1997; Zur 1998; Green 1999; and Remijnse 2002.

4. These expectations were shaped by my experience studying indigenous women's organizing in Colotenango with *Asociación* Ceiba. After the peace accords, Ceiba activists proudly, if painfully, remembered their revolutionary past and were eager to continue the struggle after the war by promoting human rights, democracy, women's equality, local health care, economic initiatives, and political organizing in the countryside.

5. See Green 1999 and Sanford 2003.

6. See Foucault 1980 and Rose 1999.

7. Poststructuralists question the commonsense view of the state as a seamless whole existing outside and above society and try to understand how this understanding is produced and what it accomplishes in distinct contexts. They point to the fragmented nature of institutions and view the perception of unification as one effect of decentered policies

and performances (Abrams 1988; Gupta 1995; Taussig 1997; Aretxaga 2000). Many see the state's peculiar magic as a product of the ways that it operates as a fetish and comes to be widely imagined as an object of fear and desire (Brown 1995; Taussig 1997; Coronil 1997).

8. See Nelson 1999, 2009; and Burrell 2013.

9. Nelson (2009) argues that the state's new role as a defender and protector of Mayan life, while coupled with the power to kill, opens new spaces for political agency that should not be discounted or treated as always already neutralized. She further contends that many Mayas have benefited individually and collectively from productive aspects of state power and that, as a result, many or most no longer understand themselves as living in opposition to an evil state. Rather than docile "indios permitidos" of "neoliberal multicultural governance" (Hale 2002), she views Mayas as creatively striving and producing new futures, with new resources, on a new terrain, despite the persistence of many old obstacles and new challenges. Writing about how Mayan Todosanteros turned to state authority in the wake of the lynching of a tourist, Jennifer Burrell (2013, 121) describes how "Todosanteros actively sought out and solicited the state's capacity to promote resolution. They did this because the state held an emergent and unrealized power—in that early moment of after-war promise—to exercise forms of authority that Todosanteros envisioned as potentially beneficial."

10. "Personal interest" is an ethnographic fact of immense concern throughout postwar Guatemala and in numerous post-conflict and postcolonial settings. See Smith 2009; Metz, Mariano, and Garcia 2010; and Nelson 2009.

11. See de Tejada Rojas 2004 for a discussion of the ex-PAC movement.

12. Few Sampedranos were in a position to export NTX crops.

13. This alliance ended when the leaders of the teachers' union made a pact with the Perez Molina government, after which they were considered sellouts by many leftist organizations.

14. Sampedranos have good reason to worry about baby thieves and adoption rings, as well as criminals and narco-traffickers. See Adams 1998 and Nelson 2009.

15. See Copeland 2014.

16. Simpson (2014) discusses Mohawk refusals of settler state sovereignty as an assertion of their own preexisting sovereignty.

17. This is similar to the way that Yonggom people in Papua New Guinea call the Ok Tedi mining company a sorcerer because, like a sorcerer, it hurts people and denies any responsibility (Kirsch 2006).

18. See Jonas 2000 and Robinson 2000.

19. See Guatemala's Decentralization Law, Government of Guatemala 2002b.

20. See Bastos and de León 2013; Grandia 2012, 2013; and Alonso-Fradejas 2015.

21. See Solano 2005 and Alonso-Fradejas 2015.

22. Patrollers opened fire on the protestors, killing an elderly man, Juan Chanay, seriously wounding two women, and injuring others. The Interamerican Court of Human Rights heard the case and ruled for the plaintiffs in a landmark decision that resulted in the removal of the civil patrols from most of the town. See Human Rights Watch 1994 and Kobrak 2013.

23. See Yagenova and Garcia 2009.

24. See Fulmer, Godoy, and Neff 2008; Dougherty 2011; CALDH y CONIC 2012; and Rasch 2012.

25. See Mérida and Krenmayr 2008; Reina 2008; Bastos and de León 2013; Nelson 2015; Alonso-Fradejas 2015; Fultz 2016; and Copeland 2019.

26. In 1978 striking miners from Ixtahuacán marched to the capital and found outpourings of support along the way.

27. See prensacomunitaria.org.

28. See also Klepeck 2012 and REDSAG 2014 on grassroots opposition to GMO maize.

29. See Bastos et al. 2015.

30. See Copeland 2015b.

31. See Copeland, forthcoming.

32. Tough-on-crime policies constitute another mechanism of authoritarian populism. See Benson, Fischer, and Thomas 2008.

5. Parties and Projects

1. Ladinos remain overrepresented in professional administrative positions such as secretary (treasurer) and justice of the peace, although this situation is also changing.

2. Stepputat (2001) sees a genuine openness to indigenous rights in state programs in Barillas. McAllister (2003) writes that the people of Chupol see no contradiction between a potable water project and their conscience. Nelson (2009) views development projects as products of struggle rather than counterinsurgency traps and see grassroots participation in the conservative parties that provide them as a strategic form of political engagement.

3. See Li 2014 and Ferguson 2015 about universal basic income programs in Africa. See also Patnaik 2010.

4. Ansell (2014, 194) describes how the anti-patronage component of Zero Hunger programs in Brazil conflicted with "intimate hierarchies," an arrangement in which "mutual sympathy and vulnerability between the partners [of clientelist exchange] becomes the basis of a shared humanity that transcends structural hierarchy" with the potential to "socialize the political class towards the challenges of a region's poor." Auyero (2001) describes clientelism as a survival strategy among poor communities rather than as an imposition. Auyero, Lapegna, and Page Roma (2009) contend that clientelism is consistent with, and can be a driver of, collective action. Fox (1994) argues that "authoritarian clientelism"—the exchange of resources for votes—evolves as poor communities assert their rights.

5. See Grandin 2013.

6. Elaborating on Gramsci's concept of the same name, Chatterjee (2004, 2005) develops the term "political society," as opposed to civil society, to describe political interactions between subaltern and elite sectors that are not structured around bourgeois rights and norms but are driven by the need for resources, from below, and political expediency among state officials. In this domain of clientelism and economic coercion, Chatterjee contends that populations (not "citizens") attempt to persuade leaders that they deserve resources, deploying distinct conceptions of democracy as they undergo a process of internal transformation.

7. See Auyero 2012 on the politics of waiting.

8. Child stealing rumors are prevalent in Mayan communities, fueled by a lawless and often predatory adoption industry. See Adams 1998 and Nelson 1999.

9. See Government of Guatemala 2002a.

10. The event lasted all afternoon. Halfway through, party affiliates handed out a few hundred *chuchitos* (tamales). The speeches were vague, with no reference to actual political matters, instead emphasizing Julio Ambrocio's personal qualities: his honesty, his dedication to work for the town, and his commitment to promoting sport, which he claimed was an alternative to delinquency. A candidate for *diputado*, a Ladino from Huehuetenango, had joined Ambrocio on the caravan. In what was perhaps the main event, he took the microphone and expressed solidarity with the community, and said that Julio was a great leader and that Manuel Baldizón, a businessman from El Petén and the party's presidential candidate, was committed to San Pedro Necta. He was there to reinforce the link between Julio Ambrocio and powerful individuals, and to generate name recognition. However, he rarely interacted with ordinary residents, but stayed in the small circle of local party leaders and

personal assistants. Meanwhile, Julio Ambrocio conversed with a long line of affiliates, hearing requests and making promises.

11. An indigenous activist who had worked in the *alcaldía* of Sololá, the capital of an indigenous-majority department in the central highlands, told me that outside institutions often required bribes and that construction companies routinely give them as a favor to *alcaldes* for awarding their company a contract, even if it was entirely legitimate. Once, he claimed, members of the national *controlaría* (auditor's office) demanded that the *municipio* buy them an expensive property on the shore of Lake Atitlan, the tourist Mecca, in order to approve plans for a new municipal building. Buying the land required going off the books. I heard many similar stories in San Pedro.

12. See, for example, Shah 2010.

13. Government of Guatemala 2002a.

14. Government of Guatemala 2002b.

15. Nelson (1999) described the post-accords Guatemalan state as a piñata.

16. Although Colotenango continued to receive funds, many still believed that the town had been disadvantaged as a result. Returned refugees resettled in Chaculá Nentón told me the *alcalde* bypassed them for projects because of their association with the guerrillas. This complicates the popular, stigmatizing perception that *retornados* are pampered by international organizations and have come to expect that things be given to them.

17. *Alcaldes* sometimes did projects in communities of nonsupporters, but these received less than original supporters.

18. See Fledderjohn 1976 and Copeland 2012.

19. This idea contrasts with Smith's (2009) description of ideological divisions between parties in Sololá.

20. While complaining about favoritism, one of Antulio Morales' close allies said, "Chepe was only interested in working on big projects, with contractors, so he could take out his percentage. If there was an administrative project—a necessity—he didn't want it."

21. This echoes Cattelino's (2008) description of the double bind of native sovereignty. In her analysis of Seminole gaming, she argues that the exercise of sovereignty leads to attacks on sovereignty.

22. Agamben (1998) contends that spectacles of sovereign violence against bare life, life that is not politically valuable and thus expendable, remain central to the constitution of biopolitical communities. See also Hansen and Stepputat 2005.

23. See also MacLeish's (2013) discussion of the power to kill or let live in the context of war.

24. Regarding MIFAPRO, the first cash-transfer program in Guatemala, Dotson (2014) argues that the discourse of transparency surrounding these programs contributes to the criticism of recipients' behavior by their "taxpaying" neighbors, who see themselves as possessing rights and responsibilities as auditors. See Sandberg and Tally 2015 for analysis of the programs' politicization.

6. Cruel Populism

1. "Huehuetenango: Ex-Pac frustran mitín con Ríos Montt," *Prensa Libre*, September 5, 2003.

2. See Garrard-Burnett 2010 for an in-depth description and analysis of Ríos Montt's rhetoric during regular radio addresses at the peak of the counterinsurgency.

3. The party was also accused of numerous acts of corruption and electoral malfeasances. Ríos Montt's eligibility to stand for election was a central concern. Guatemala's

constitution, ratified in 1985, prohibits anyone who has taken power by coup from becoming president, a law written specifically to block Ríos Montt.

4. In his testimonial description of living through the 1982 violence in the village of Tzalalá, Huehuetenango, Victor Montejo (1987, 55) recalls thinking that "what Lucas García had left undone during his brutal term in office was now being completed by his successor Ríos Montt. In all my thirty years I had not known darker days than the present ones." See Doyle 2013 for information about Ríos Montt's genocide trial, his conviction, and its reversal.

5. Stoll (2009) makes this assertion.

6. Grandin (2013) argues that the reforms of the 1920s and the Partido Unionista, often ignored by historians, mark the entry of rural communities into progressive mass politics and heterogeneous political alliances far beyond their hometowns.

7. See Handy 1994.

8. See Webber and Carr 2012 for a discussion of the Latin American left.

9. As with most political figures and events, Guatemalans viewed Menchú through a cloud of mistrust. Nelson (1999) argues that the plethora of dirty and disparaging jokes about Menchú are reactions to the anxieties about the very presence of an Indian woman on the national stage. Conservatives dismissed her as a violent guerrilla who was still advocating a failed leftist agenda that would harm both the rural sector and the country as a whole. Leftists criticized Menchú for selling out by joining the Berger administration as the goodwill ambassador for human rights. Many Guatemalans called her an opportunist for investing in a Farmacias Populares, a pharmacy specializing in generic and discounted drugs. In Huehuetenango, leftist leaders in Colotenango accused her and Rosalina Tuyúc of unfairly appropriating state *resarcimiento* (reparations) payments for war victims, but they still voted for Winaq.

10. See "Guatemalan Election Becomes Vote on Former Dictator," *New York Times,* January 7, 1996.

11. For a careful look at Portillo's populist record that compares rhetoric to reality, see Baires Quesada 2015.

12. See Dotson 2014 for details about local criticisms of MIFAPRO as a corrupt and nontransparent drain on taxpayers.

13. Guatemalan antipopulism has a conservative bias. The most noted recent Guatemalan anti-populist is Gloria Alvarez, a political scientist at the Youth Parliament of Ibero-America, whose academic condemnations of populism and her telegenic appearance have made her the darling of Guatemalan elites. However, rather than criticize Ríos Montt for his populism, she has defended him from accusations of genocide and claimed to respect him. See Martin 2018.

14. Long derided by Ladinos as primitive Indian food, greens had been recently revalued as a part of a healthier traditional diet. I often heard stories of ancestors who never got sick, lived long lives, and were physically much stronger than people today who eat fatty junk food with chemicals instead of herbs.

15. Garrard-Burnett (2010, 13) writes that since 2003 Mayas have come to participate in "an alternative symbolic universe, framed around the reports of truth commissions, forensic reports, 'recovered' historical memory, and the exigencies of new constructions of racialized politics that have emerged within civil society since the war's end."

16. Precisely how violence turns into consent is a riddle unanswered by theories of hegemony. Furthermore, Garrard-Burnett's description (2010, 11) of Ríos Montt's "heretofore unchallenged claim to moral rectitude" seems to understate long-standing criticisms of his role in the violence, as existed in San Pedro. Her account also cannot explain significant Mayan support for the FRG through 2003, long after FRG's corruption was abundantly clear.

17. See Human Rights Watch 2001 and Ruhl 2005.

18. See "El Pueblo Debe Juzgarme," *Prensa Libre*, October 17, 2003.

19. Milagros Leiva Galvez, "Ríos Montt proclama sus verdades," *La Nación*, October 26, 2003.

20. See "Ríos Montt, moralista y contra oligarquía," *Prensa Libre*, November 2, 2003.

21. See "Zury Ríos justifica la politica de 'balas y frijoles,'" *Prensa Libre*, October 7, 2003.

22. See Human Rights Watch 2002.

23. See Adams 2009.

24. *Prensa Libre*, October 10, 2003, http://www.prensalibre.com/noticias/Agreden-Rigoberta-Menchu_0_76794015.html. See also EMOL, "Condenan a cinco guatemaltecos por racismo congra Menchú," 2005, http://www.emol.com/noticias/internacional/2005/04/04/178089/condenan-a-cinco-guatemaltecos-por-racismo-contra-menchu.html.

25. See "Ríos Montt es símobolo del genocidio," *Prensa Libre*, November 20, 2003.

26. Garrard-Burnett (2010) argues that a new moral imaginary elaborated by Ríos Montt had shaped Mayan consciousness and captured genuine support since the 1980s but that by 2003 it had been supplanted by the new discourses from the peace accords and truth commissions. My findings suggest a more ambivalent relationship toward Ríos Montt that would remain invisible in opinion polls.

27. In the Liberal era, planter-class elites established rural Ladinos, who were poor and marginal, as a buffer class to help govern indigenous communities at a distance. See Smith 1990a.

28. Writing about the years after the 1999 FRG victory, Santiago Bastos (2009, 9) notes that "nevertheless, in those same years, the Accord on Identity and the Rights of Indigenous Peoples was the accord that advanced the least. Mayan public figures were promoted to relatively high government posts—Ministry of Culture, Secretariat of Peace, General Directorate of Bilingual Education—and specific spaces were created for policy management for the Maya, managed by Maya" (my translation).

29. Guatemalan presidents can serve only one term.

30. Perez Molina went on to defeat Manuel Baldizón, a businessman from Petén who had founded the Líder Party.

31. Narco-trafficking had become a growing phenomenon in Huehuetenango ever since Andean shipments to the United States shifted from water to overland routes in the mid-2000s. The department was a prime location because of its distance from state authority, its rugged terrain, and its large and almost-impossible-to-police border with Mexico, as well as a cash-starved population willing to take risks: many of the same reasons that Huehuetenango was an ideal place to launch the guerrilla movement. See UNODC 2012. Drug gangs operate secretly, but signs (or suspected signs) of their cash are visible everywhere.

Conclusion

1. Accusations of self-interest are similar in this way to Harry West's (2005) analysis of sorcery accusations among Muedans.

2. Cojtí (2007) notes the white supremacist and assimilationist biases of legislation, the scarcity of nonindigenous personnel, the lack of concern for or funding to meet the needs of indigenous people, and the racist attitudes of state workers, among other endemic problems.

3. See Englund 2008 and Auyero 2001.

4. See Geovanni Contreras, "Solo hay una entrega de Bono Seguro," *Prensa Libre*, September 25, 2015, https://www.prensalibre.com/bono-solo-hay-una-entrega, accessed November 7, 2018; and Manuel Rodríguez, "Programas sociales siguen envueltos en clientelismo y corrupción," *La Hora*, July 2015, http://lahora.gt/programas-sociales-siguen-envueltos-en-clientelismo-y-corrupcion/, accessed June 10, 2017.

5. See Nugent 2012 for a discussion of democratic temporalities.

6. For an analysis of indigenous sovereignty in Guatemala, see Sieder 2011a, 2011b.

7. See Scott 2009 and Zibechi 2010.

8. FUNDEBASE is the Foundation for the Strengthening and Development of Grassroots Organizations.

9. Personal communication, 2017.

10. See Mora 2017 for a discussion of Zapatista autonomy politics.

11. Zibechi (2010) discusses horizontal organization among indigenous movements in Bolivia.

12. See Nelson 1999 and Hale 2011 on convergences between indigenous autonomy projects and decentralized neoliberal governance in Guatemala. See Stahler-Sholk 2007 for a discussion of this dilemma in Chiapas.

13. See Arditi's (2010) review of Laclau 2005.

14. See Green 2017 for one of many examples of this argument.

15. See Greenhouse 2008 on the fragmentation of political discourse.

16. On corporate strategies to sow doubt and resignation, see Benson and Kirsch 2010; Copeland and Labuski 2013; and Kirsch 2014.

17. See Hale 1994; and Bastos and Camus 2013.

18. See Warren 1998; Nelson 1999; Esquit 2003; Bastos 2009; and Vogt 2015.

19. See Granovsky-Larsen 2013.

20. See Laplante and Nolin 2014. By the time of this writing, the number had passed 100.

21. On connections between the defense-of-territory and food-sovereignty paradigms in Guatemala, see Alonso-Fradejas 2015 and Copeland 2019.

WORKS CITED

Abrams, Philip. 1988. "Notes on the Difficulty of Studying the State." *Journal of Historical Sociology* 1 (1): 58–89. doi/abs/10.1111/j.1467-6443.1988.tb00004.x.

Adams, Abigail. 1998. "Gringas, Ghouls and Guatemala: The 1994 Attacks on North American Women Accused of Body Organ Trafficking." *Journal of Latin American and Caribbean Anthropology* 4 (1): 112–33. doi/abs/10.1525/jlca.1998.4.1.112.

——. 2009. "Revelation, Re-encuentro, and Retroceso in Post–Peace Accords Verapaz." In *Mayas in Postwar Guatemala: Harvest of Violence Revisited*, edited by Timothy Smith and Walter Little, 30–41. Tuscaloosa: University of Alabama Press.

Agamben, Giorgio. 1998. *Homo Sacer: Sovereign Power and Bare Life*. Chicago: University of Chicago Press.

Alonso-Fradejas, Alberto. 2015. "Anything but a Story Foretold: Multiple Politics of Resistance to the Agrarian Extractivist Project in Guatemala." *Journal of Peasant Studies* 42 (3–4): 489-515. https://doi.org/10.1080/03066150.2015.1013468.

Anagnost, Ann. 2004. "The Corporeal Politics of Quality (Suzhi)." *Public Culture* 16 (2): 189–208.

Anand, Nikhil. 2011. "Pressure: The Politechnics of Water Supply in Mumbai." *Cultural Anthropology* 26 (4): 542–64. doi/abs/10.1111/j.1548-1360.2011.01111.x.

Ansell, Aaron. 2014. *Zero Hunger: Political Culture and Antipoverty Policy in Northeast Brazil*. Chapel Hill: University of North Carolina Press.

Arditi, Benjamin. 2010. "Populism Is Hegemony Is Politics? On Ernesto Laclau's *On Populist Reason.*" *Constellations* 17 (3): 488–97.

Aretxaga, Begoña. 2000. "A Fictional Reality: Paramilitary Death Squads and the Construction of State Terror in Spain." In *Death Squad: The Anthropology of State Terror,* edited by J. Sluka, 46–69. Philadelphia: University of Pennsylvania Press.

———. 2003. "Maddening States." *Annual Review of Anthropology,* 393–410. doi/abs/10.1146/annurev.anthro.32.061002.093341.

Arias, Arturo, ed. 2001. *The Rigoberta Menchú Controversy.* Minneapolis: University of Minnesota Press.

Arias, Enrique Desmond, and Daniel M. Goldstein, eds. 2010. *Violent Democracies in Latin America.* Durham, NC: Duke University Press.

ASP (Asamblea Social y Popular). 2016. *Una mirada critica a nuestra conformación y fortalecimiento, Abril a Octubre de 2015.* Guatemala City: ASP.

Auyero, Javier. 2001. *Poor People's Politics: Peronist Survival Networks and the Legacy of Evita.* Durham, NC: Duke University Press.

———. 2012. *Patients of the State: The Politics of Waiting in Argentina.* Durham, NC: Duke University Press.

Auyero, Javier, Pablo Lapegna, and Fernanda Page Poma. 2009. "Patronage Politics and Contentious Collective Action: A Recursive Relationship." *Latin American Politics and Society* 51 (3): 1–31. doi/full/10.1111/j.1548-2456.2009.00054.x.

Baires Quesada, Rodrigo. 2015. *"Cuatro Razones para querer o no a Portillo."* Plaza Publica, May 5. http://www.plazapublica.com.gt/content/cuatro-razones-para-querer-o-no-portillo.

Barham, Bradford, M. Clark, E. Katz, and R. Schurman. 1992. "Nontraditional Agricultural Exports in Latin America." *Latin American Research Review* 27 (2): 43–82. www.jstor.org/stable/2503749.

Bastos, Santiago. 2009. "La movilización maya en Guatemala: exigiendo derechos y construyendo multiculturalidad en un contexto de postconflicto." *Cahiers des Amériques Latines* 60–61: 41–58.

Bastos, Santiago, and Roderick L. Brett. 2010. *El movimiento maya en la década después de la paz (1997–2007).* Guatemala City: F&G Editores.

Bastos, Santiago, and Manuela Camus. 1996. *Quebrando el silencio: Organizacion del pueblo maya y sus demandas.* Guatemala City: FLACSO.

———. 2003. *Entre el mecapal y el cielo: Desarrollo del movimiento maya en Guatemala.* Guatemala City: FLACSO.

———. 2013. "Difficult Complementarity: Relations between the Mayan and Revolutionary Movements." In *War by Other Means: Aftermath in Post-genocide Guatemala,* edited by Carlotta McAllister and Diane M. Nelson, 71–92. Durham, NC: Duke University Press.

Bastos, Santiago, and Aura Cumes. 2007. *Mayanización y vida cotidiana. La ideología multicultural en la sociedad guatemalteca,* 1. Guatemala City: FLACSO.

Bastos, Santiago, and Quimy de León. 2013. *Dinámicas de despojo y resistencia: comunidades, estado, y empresas.* Guatemala City: Colibrí Zurdo/Diakonía.

Bastos, Santiago, Quimy de Leon, Nelton Rivera, Dania Rodriguez, and Francisco Lucas. 2015. *"Despojo, movilizacion y repression en Santa Cruz Barillas."* In *Dinosaurio reloaded: violencias actuals en Guatemala,* edited by Manuela Camus, Santiago Bastos, and Julián López García, 271–304. Guatemala City: FLACSO.

Benjamin, Walter. 1999 [1929]. "The Last Snapshot of the European Intelligencia." In *Selected Writings.* Cambridge, MA: Harvard University Press.

Benson, Peter, Edward F. Fischer, and Kedron Thomas. 2008. "Resocializing Suffering: Neoliberalism, Accusation, and the Sociopolitical Context of Guatemala's New Violence." *Latin American Perspectives* 35 (5): 38–58. doi/abs/10.1177/0094 582X08321955.

Benson, Peter, and Stuart Kirsch. 2010. "Capitalism and the Politics of Resignation." *Current Anthropology* 51 (4): 459–86. doi/abs/10.1086/65309.

Berlant, Lauren. 2007. "Slow Death (Sovereignty, Obesity, Lateral Agency)." *Critical Inquiry* 33 (4): 754–80. doi/abs/10.1086/521568.

———. 2012. *Cruel Optimism.* Durham, NC: Duke University Press.

Bhan, Mona. 2013. *Counterinsurgency, Democracy, and the Politics of Identity in India: From Warfare to Welfare?* London: Routledge.

Black, George, Milton H. Jamail, and Norma Stoltz Chinchilla. 1984. *Garrison Guatemala.* New York: Zed.

Borras, Saturnino M. 2008. "La Vía Campesina and Its Global Campaign for Agrarian Reform." *Journal of Agrarian Change* 8 (2–3): 258. doi.org/10.1111/j.1471-0366.20 08.00170.x.

Borras, Saturnino, Jennifer Franco, and Sofía Suárez. 2015. "Land and Food Sovereignty." *Third World Quarterly* 36 (3): 600–17. doi.org/10.1080/01436597.2015. 1029225.

Brintnall, Douglas E. 1979. *Revolt against the Dead: The Modernization of a Mayan Community in the Highlands of Guatemala.* London: Taylor & Francis.

Brockett, Charles. 1990. *Land, Power, and Poverty: Agrarian Transformation and Political Conflict in Central America.* London: Unwin Hyman.

Brown, Wendy. 1995. *States of Injury.* Princeton, NJ: Princeton University Press.

———. 2015. *Undoing the Demos: Neoliberalism's Stealth Revolution.* Cambridge, MA: MIT Press.

Burgos-Debray, Elisabeth. 1985. *Me llamo Rigoberta Menchú y así me nació la conciencia.* Mexico City: Siglo XXI Editores.

Burrell, Jennifer. 2013. *Maya after War: Conflict, Power, and Politics in Guatemala.* Austin: University of Texas Press.

CALDH (Centro para la Acción Legal en Derechos Humanos) y CONIC (Coordinador Nacional Indigena y Campesino). 2012. *Revindicación política: doce comunidades maya kakchikeles en defensa del territorio.* Guatemala City: CALDH.

Camus, Manuela. 2008. *La sorpresita del Norte: Migración internacional y comunidad en Huehuetenango.* Guatemala City: INCEDES.

Carletto, Calogero, Angeli Kirk, Paul Winters, and Benjamin Davis. 2010. "Globalization and Smallholders: The Adoption, Diffusion, and Welfare Impact of Non-traditional Export Crops in Guatemala." *World Development* 38 (6): 814–27. doi.org/10.1016/j.worlddev.2010.02.017.

Carmack, Robert, ed. 1988. *Harvest of Violence: The Maya Indians and the Guatemalan Crisis.* Norman: University of Oklahoma Press.

Cattelino, Jessica. 2008. *High Stakes: Florida Seminole Gaming and Sovereignty.* Durham, NC: Duke University Press.

CEH (Comisión para el Esclaramiento Historico). 1999. Tomo IV. *Consequencia y efectos de la violencia.* Guatemala City: UNOPS.

Chakrabarty, Dipesh. 2009. *Provincializing Europe: Postcolonial Thought and Historical Difference,* 2nd ed. Princeton, NJ: Princeton University Press.

Chatterjee, Partha. 2004. *Politics of the Governed: Reflections on Popular Politics in Most of the World.* New York: Columbia University Press.

——. 2005. "Sovereign Violence and the Domain of the Political." In *Sovereign Bodies: Citizens, Migrants, and States in the Postcolonial World,* edited by Thomas Hansen and Finn Stepputat, 82–102. Princeton, NJ: Princeton University Press.

Clifford, James, and George E. Marcus. 1986. *Writing Culture: The Poetics and Politics of Ethnography.* Berkeley: University of California Press.

Cojtí Cuxil, Demetrio. 1997. *Ri Maya' Moloj pa Iximulew: El movimiento maya (en Guatemala).* Guatemala City: Editorial Cholsamaj.

——. 2007. "Indigenous Nations in Guatemalan Democracy and the State: A Tentative Assessment." *International Journal of Social and Cultural Practice* 51 (2): 124–47. doi.org/10.3167/sa.2007.510207.

Coles, Kimberley. 2007. *Democratic Designs: International Intervention and Electoral Practices in Postwar Bosnia-Herzegovina.* Ann Arbor: University of Michigan Press.

CPO (Consejo de los Pueblos del Occidente). 2014. *Proyecto Politico: Un nuevo estado para Guatemala: democracia plurinacional y gobiernos autonomos de los pueblos indígenas.* Guatemala City: CPO.

Copeland, Nicholas. 2007. "Bitter Earth: Counterinsurgency Strategy and the Roots of Mayan Neo-authoritarianism in Guatemala." PhD diss., University of Texas at Austin.

——. 2012. "Greening the Counterinsurgency: The Deceptive Effects of Guatemala's Rural Development Plan of 1970." *Development and Change* 43 (4): 975–98. doi:10.1111/j.1467-7660.2012.01783.x.

——. 2014. "Mayan Imaginaries of Democracy: Interactive Sovereignties and Political Affect in Post-revolutionary Guatemala." *American Ethnologist* 41 (2): 305–19. doi:10.1111/amet.12077.

——. 2015a. "Regarding Development: Governing Indian Advancement in Revolutionary Guatemala." *Economy and Society* 44 (3): 418–44. doi:10.1080/03085147.2015.1051848.

——. 2015b. "Repudiating Corruption in Guatemala: Revolution or Neoliberal Outrage?" NACLA, https://nacla.org/news/2015/05/19/repudiating-corruption-guatemala-revolution-or-neoliberal-outrage.

——. 2018. "Democracy." In *International Encyclopedia of Anthropology,* edited by Hillary Callan. London: Wiley.

——. 2019. "The Defense of Territory and Food Sovereignty: Two Paradigms for Radical Territorial Restructuring in Neoliberal Guatemala." *Journal of Agrarian Change* 19 (1): 21–40.

——. Forthcoming. "Meeting Peasants Where They Are: Assessing Agroecological Alternatives in Neoliberal Guatemala." *Journal of Peasant Studies.*

Copeland, Nicholas, and Christine Labuski. 2013. *The World of Wal-Mart: Discounting the American Dream*. New York: Routledge.

Coronil, Fernando. 1997. *The Magical State: Nature, Money, and Modernity in Venezuela*. Chicago: University of Chicago Press.

Das, Veena, and Deborah Poole, eds. 2004. *Anthropology in the Margins of the State*. Santa Fe, NM: School of Advanced Research.

Dean, Jodi. 2009. *Democracy and Other Neoliberal Fantasies: Communicative Capital and Left Politics*. Durham, NC: Duke University Press.

De la Cadena, Marisol. 2010. "Indigenous Cosmopolitics in the Andes: Conceptual Reflections Beyond Politics." *Cultural Anthropology* 25 (2): 334–70. doi. org/10.1111/j.1548-1360.2010.01061.x.

Deleuze, Gilles, and Félix Guattari. 1983. *Anti-Oedipus: Capitalism and Schizophrenia*, translated by Robert Hurley, Mark Seem, and Helen R. Lane. Minneapolis: University of Minnesota Press.

De Sardan, JP Olivier. 1999. "A Moral Economy of Corruption in Africa?" *Journal of Modern African Studies* 37 (1): 25–52.

Desmarais, Annette Aurélie. 2007. *Vía Campesina*. London: Pluto.

De Tejada Rojas, Ricardo Saénz. 2004. *¿Víctimas o vencedores? una aproximación al movimiento de los ex PAC*. Guatemala City: FLACSO.

——. 2012. *Democracia y Elecciones en Guatemala*. Guatemala City: Universidad Rafael Landivar.

Dotson, Rachel. 2014. "Citizen—Auditors and Visible Subjects: Mi Familia Progresa and Transparency Politics in Guatemala." *Political and Legal Anthropology Review* 37 (2): 350–70. doi.org/10.1111/plar.12079.

Dougherty, Michael. 2011. "The Global Gold Mining Industry, Junior Firms, and Civil Society Resistance in Guatemala." *Bulletin of Latin American Research* 30 (4): 403–18. doi.org/10.1111/j.1470-9856.2011.00529.x.

Doyle, Kate. 2013. "Indicted for Genocide: Guatemala's Efraín Ríos Montt." *National Security Archive*, http://nsarchive.gwu.edu/NSAEBB/NSAEBB419.

Du Bois, W. E. B. 2017 [1935]. *Black Reconstruction in America: Toward a History of the Part Which Black Folk Played in the Attempt to Reconstruct Democracy in America*. New York: Routledge.

Dunbar-Ortiz, Roxanne. 2014. *An Indigenous Peoples' History of the United States*. New York: Penguin Random House.

Edelman, Marc. 1999. *Peasants against Globalization: Rural Social Movements in Costa Rica*. Stanford, CA: Stanford University Press.

Ekern, Stener. 2005. "Visions of the Right Order: Contrasts between Mayan Communitarian Law in Guatemala and International Human Rights Law." In *Human Rights in Development Yearbook*, 265–91. The Netherlands: Martinus Nijhoff.

——. 2011. "The Production of Autonomy: Leadership and Community in Mayan Guatemala." *Journal of Latin American Studies* 43 (1): 93–111. doi.org/10.1017/S0022216X1000180X.

Elyachar, Julia. 2012. "Before (and after) Neoliberalism: Tacit Knowledge, Secrets of the Trade, and the Public Sector in Egypt." *Cultural Anthropology* 27 (1): 76–96. doi.org/10.1111/j.1548-1360.2012.01127.x.

Englund, Harri. 2008. "Extreme Poverty and Existential Obligations: Beyond Morality in the Anthropology of Africa?" *Social Analysis* 52 (3): 33–50. doi.org/10.3167/sa.2008.520302.

Escobar, Arturo. 1995. *Encountering Development: The Making and Unmaking of the Third World*. Princeton, NJ: Princeton University Press.

——. 2016. "Thinking-Feeling with the Earth: Territorial Struggles and the Ontological Dimension of the Epistemologies of the South." *Revista de Antropología Iberoamericana* 11 (11): 11–32. doi:10.11156/aibr.110102e.

Esquit Choy, Edgar. 2003. *Caminando hacia la utopía. La lucha política de las organizaciones mayas y el Estado en Guatemala. Colección Reflexiones, 4*. Guatemala City: Universidad de San Carlos (USAC), Instituto de Estudios Interétnicos (IDEI).

Falla, Ricardo. 1992. *Masacres de la selva: Ixcán, Guatemala, 1975–1982*. Guatemala City: Editorial USAC.

——. 2001 [1978]. *Quiché rebelde: Religious Conversion, Politics, and Ethnic Identity in Guatemala*. Austin: University of Texas Press.

Farmer, Paul. 2005. *Pathologies of Power: Health, Human Rights, and the New War on the Poor*. Berkeley: University of California Press.

Ferguson, James. 1994. *The Anti-politics Machine: Development, Depoliticization, and Bureaucratic Power in Lesotho*. Minneapolis: University of Minnesota Press.

——. 2015. *Give a Man a Fish: Reflections on the New Politics of Distribution*. Durham, NC: Duke University Press.

Fischer, Edward. 1996. "Induced Cultural Change as a Strategy for Economic Development: The Pan-Maya Movement in Guatemala." In *Maya Cultural Activism in Guatemala*, edited by T. Fischer and M. Brown, 51–73. Austin: University of Texas Press.

——. 2001. *Cultural Logics and Global Economies: Maya Identity in Thought and Practice*. Austin: University of Texas Press.

——. 2009. *Indigenous Peoples, Civil Society, and the Neo-liberal State in Latin America*. New York: Berghahn.

Fischer, Edward, and Peter Benson. 2006. *Broccoli and Desire: Global Connections and Maya Struggles in Postwar Guatemala*. Stanford, CA: Stanford University Press.

Fischer, Edward, and R. Mckenna Brown, eds. 1996. *Maya Cultural Activism in Guatemala*. Austin: University of Texas Press.

Fledderjohn, David. 1976. "Terminal Report: Agricultural Cooperative Project in Guatemala." Washington, DC: Agricultural Cooperative Development International.

Forster, Cindy. 2001. *The Time of Freedom: Campesino Workers in Guatemala's October Revolution*. Pittsburgh: University of Pittsburgh Press.

Fortun, Kim. 2009. *Advocacy after Bhopal: Environmentalism, Disaster, New Global Orders*. Chicago: University of Chicago Press.

Foucault, Michel. 1980. *The History of Sexuality*. New York: Vintage.

——. 2001. *Fearless Speech*, ed. Joseph Pearson. Los Angeles: Semiotext(E).

——. 2003. *Society Must Be Defended: Lectures at the Collège de France, 1975–1979*. New York: Picador.

——. 2012. *Discipline and Punish: The Birth of the Prison*. 2nd ed. New York: Vintage.

Foucault, Michel, et al. 1991. *The Foucault Effect: Studies in Governmentality*, edited by G. Burchell, C. Gordon, and P. Miller. Chicago: University of Chicago Press.

Fox, Jonathan. 1994. "The Difficult Transition from Clientelism to Citizenship: Lessons from Mexico." *World Politics* 46 (2): 151–84. doi.org/10.2307/2950671.

Fulmer, Amanda M., Angelina Snodgrass Godoy, and Philip Neff. 2008. "Indigenous Rights, Resistance, and the Law: Lessons from a Guatemalan Mine." *Latin American Politics and Society* 50 (4): 91–121. doi.org/10.1111/j.1548-2456.2008.00031.x.

Fultz, Katherine. 2016. "Economies of Representation: Communication, Conflict, and Mining in Guatemala." PhD diss., University of Michigan.

Gaitan, José Miguel. 1972. "El movimiento cooperativista de Guatemala: Desarrollo de la Federación Nacional de Cooperativas de Ahorro y Credito." *Estudios Sociales* (7): 33–62.

Garrard-Burnett, Virginia. 1998. *Protestantism in Guatemala: Living in the New Jerusalem.* Austin: University of Texas Press.

——. 2010. *Terror in the Land of the Holy Spirit: Guatemala under General Efraín Ríos Montt.* Oxford: Oxford University Press.

Gauster, Susana, and S. Ryan Isakson. 2007. "Eliminating Market Distortions, Perpetuating Rural Inequality: An Evaluation of Market-Assisted Land Reform in Guatemala." *Third World Quarterly* 28 (8): 1519–36. doi.org/10.1080/01436590701637375.

Gill, Lesley. 2016. *A Century of Violence in a Red City: Popular Struggle, Counterinsurgency, and Human Rights in Colombia.* Durham, NC: Duke University Press.

Goldin, Liliana R. 2011. *Global Maya: Work and Ideology in Rural Guatemala.* Tucson: University of Arizona Press.

González, Matilde. 2002. *"Se cambió el tiempo: conflicto y poder en territorio k'iche'1880 1996."* Guatemala City: Asociacion para el Avance de las Ciencias Sociales (AVANCSO).

Government of Guatemala. 2002a. *Ley de los consejos de desarrollo urbano y rural.* Congreso de la República, decreto número 11–2002. Guatemala City.

——. 2002b. *Ley general de descentralización.* Congreso de la República, decreto número 14–2002. Guatemala City.

Gow, David D. 2008. *Countering Development: Indigenous Modernity and the Moral Imagination.* Durham, NC: Duke University Press.

Graeber, David. 2013. *The Democracy Project: A History, a Crisis, a Movement.* New York: Random House.

Gramsci, Antonio Quintin Hoare, and Geoffrey Nowell-Smith. 1971. *Selections from the Prison Notebooks.* London: International.

Grandia, Liza. 2012. *Enclosed: Conservation, Cattle, and Commerce among the Q'eqchi' Maya Lowlanders.* Seattle: University of Washington Press.

——. 2013. "Road Mapping: Megaprojects and Land Grabs in the Northern Guatemalan Lowlands." *Development and Change* 44 (2): 233–59. doi.org/10.1111/dech.12020.

——. 2017. "Sacred Maize against a Legal Maze: The Diversity of Resistance to Guatemala's Monsanto Law." *Journal for the Study of Religion, Nature & Culture* 11 (1): 56–85. 10.1558/jsrnc.30666.

Grandin, Greg. 1997. "To End with All These Evils: Ethnic Transformation and Community Mobilization in Guatemala's Western Highlands, 1954–1980." *Latin American Perspectives* 24 (2): 7–34. doi/abs/10.1177/0094582X9702400202.

———. 2010, September 8. "It Was Heaven That They Burned: Who Is Rigoberta Menchú?" *Nation*.

———. 2013. "Five Hundred Years." In *War by Other Means: Aftermath in Post-genocide Guatemala*, edited by Carlotta McAllister and Diane M. Nelson, 49–70. Durham, NC: Duke University Press.

Grandin, Greg, and Naomi Klein. 2011. *The Last Colonial Massacre: Latin America in the Cold War*. Chicago: University of Chicago Press.

Granovsky-Larsen, Simon. 2013. "Between the Bullet and the Bank: Agrarian Conflict and Access to Land in Neoliberal Guatemala." *Journal of Peasant Studies* 40 (2): 325–50. doi/abs/10.1080/03066150.2013.777044.

Green, Emma. 2017, May 9. "It Was Cultural Anxiety That Drove White, Working-Class Voters to Trump." *Atlantic*.

Green, Linda. 1999. *Fear as a Way of Life: Mayan Widows in Guatemala*. New York: Columbia University Press.

Greenhouse, Carol. 2008. "Fractured Discourse: Rethinking the Discursivity of States." In *The Anthropology of Democracy*, edited by Julia Paley, 193–218. Santa Fe, NM: School of Advanced Research.

Gupta, Akhil. 1995. "Blurred Boundaries: The Discourse of Corruption, the Culture of Politics, and the Imagined State." *American Ethnologist* 22 (2): 375–402. https://www.jstor.org/stable/646708.

———. 1998. *Postcolonial Developments: Agriculture and the Making of a Modern India*. Durham, NC: Duke University Press.

Gupta, Akhil, and James Ferguson. 2002. "Spatializing States: Toward an Ethnography of Neoliberal Governmentality." *American Ethnologist* 29 (4): 981–1002. doi.org/10.1525/ae.2002.29.4.981.

Hale, Charles R. 1994. "Between Che Guevara and the Pachamama: Mestizos, Indians and Identity Politics in the Anti-Quincentenary Campaign." *Critique of Anthropology* 14 (1): 9–39. doi/abs/10.1177/0308275X9401400102.

———. 1997. "CA Forum on Anthropology in Public: Consciousness, Violence, and the Politics of Memory in Guatemala." *Current Anthropology* 38 (5): 817–38. doi/abs/10.1086/204669.

———. 2002. "Does Multiculturalism Menace? Governance, Cultural Rights and the Politics of Identity in Guatemala." *Journal of Latin American Studies* 34 (3): 485–524. doi.org/10.1017/S0022216X02006521.

———. 2006a. "Activist Research v. Cultural Critique: Indigenous Land Rights and the Contradictions of Politically Engaged Anthropology." *Cultural Anthropology* 21 (1): 96–120. doi.org/10.1525/can.2006.21.1.96.

———. 2006b. *Mas que un indio: Racial Ambivalence and Neoliberal Multiculturalism in Guatemala*. Santa Fe, NM: School of American Research.

———. 2011. "Resistencia para que? Territory, Autonomy, and Neoliberal Entanglements in the 'Empty Spaces' of Central America." *Economy and Society* 40 (2): 184–210. doi.org/10.1080/03085147.2011.548947.

Handy, Jim. 1984. *Gift of the Devil: A History of Guatemala*. Toronto: Between the Lines.

———. 1994. *Revolution in the Countryside: Rural Conflict and Agrarian Reform in Guatemala, 1944–1954*. Chapel Hill: University of North Carolina Press.

Hansen, Thomas Blom, and Finn Stepputat, eds. 2005. *Citizens, Migrants and States in the Postcolonial World.* Princeton, NJ: Princeton University Press.

Hardt, Michael, and Antonio Negri. 2005. *Multitude: War and Democracy in the Age of Empire.* New York: Penguin.

Harvey, David. 2005. *A Brief History of Neoliberalism.* Oxford: Oxford University Press.

——. 2007. "Neoliberalism as Creative Destruction." *Annals of the American Academy of Political and Social Science* 610 (1): 21–44. doi.org/10.1177/0002716206296780.

Hernández Castillo, Rosalva Aída. 2008. *Etnografías e historias de resistenciamujeres indígenas, procesos organizativos y nuevas identidades políticas.* Mexico City: Centro de Investigaciones y Estudios Superiores deAntropología Social (CIESAS).

Hernández Pico, Juan. 2005. *Terminar la guerra, traicionar la paz: Guatemala en las dos presidencias de la paz: Arzú y Portillo, 1996–2004.* Guatemala City: FLACSO.

Hirschauer, Stefan. 2006. "Putting Things into Words: Ethnographic Description and the Silence of the Social." *Human Studies* 29 (4): 413–41. https://www.jstor.org/stable/27642766.

Holt-Giménez, Eric. 2008. *Territorial Restructuring and the Grounding of Agrarian Reform: Indigenous Communities, Gold Mining and the World Bank.* TNI Land Policy Series 2. Amsterdam: Transnational Institute.

Human Rights Watch. 1994. *Human Rights in Guatemala during President de Leon Carpio's First Year.* https://www.hrw.org/reports/pdfs/g/guatemla/guatemal946.pdf.

——. 2001. *World Report: Guatemala.* http://www.hrw.org/legacy/wr2k1/americas/guatemala.html.

——. 2002, April 30. "Guatemala: Stop Violence and Intimidation of Rights Advocates." https://www.hrw.org/news/2002/04/30/guatemala-stop-violence-and-intimidation-against-rights-advocates.

IDF (International Development Foundation). 1968. *Case Study of a Pilot Project to Encourage Popular Political Participation in Guatemala.* New York: International Development Foundation.

——. 1970. *Progress Achievement Report: Rural Organization Development Program, Pilot Project—Guatemala.* New York: International Development Foundation.

Jonas, Susanne. 1988. "Contradictions in Guatemala's 'Political Opening.'" *Latin American Perspectives* 15 (3): 26–46. doi/abs/10.1177/0094582X8801500303.

——. 1991. *The Battle for Guatemala: Rebels, Death Squads, and US Power.* Boulder, CO: Westview.

——. 2000. *Of Centaurs and Doves: Guatemala's Peace Process.* Boulder, CO: Westview.

Keating, Christine. 2011. *Decolonizing Democracy: Transforming the Social Contract in India.* Philadelphia: University of Pennsylvania Press.

Kirmayer, Laurence. 1996. "Landscapes of Memory: Trauma, Narrative, and Dissociation." In *Tense Past: Cultural Essays in Trauma and Memory,* edited by Paul Antze and Michael Lambek, 173–98. New York: Routledge.

Kirsch, Stuart. 2006. *Reverse Anthropology: Indigenous Analysis of Social and Environmental Relations in New Guinea.* Stanford, CA: Stanford University Press.

——. 2014. *Mining Capitalism: The Relation between Corporations and Their Critics.* Durham, NC: Duke University Press.

Klepeck, James. 2012. "Against the Grain: Knowledge Alliances and Resistance to Agricultural Biotechnology in Guatemala." *Canadian Journal of Development* 33 (3): 310–25. doi.org/10.1080/02255189.2012.719824.

Kobrak, Paul. 1997. "Village Troubles: The Civil Patrols in Aguacatan, Guatemala." PhD diss., University of Michigan.

———. 2003. *Huehuetenango: historia de una guerra*. Huehuetenango, Guatemala: CEDFOG.

———. 2013. "The Long War in Colotenango: Guerrillas, Army, and Civil Patrols." In *War by Other Means: Aftermath in Post-genocide Guatemala*, edited by Carlotta McAllister and Diane M. Nelson, 218–40. Durham, NC: Duke University Press.

Konefal, Betsy. 2010. *For Every Indio Who Falls: A History of Maya Activism in Guatemala, 1960–1990*. Albuquerque: University of New Mexico Press.

Krueger, Chris, and Kjell Enge. 1985. *Security and Development Conditions in the Guatemalan Highlands*. Washington, DC: Washington Office on Latin America.

Laclau, Ernesto. 1977. *Politics and Ideology in Marxist Theory: Capitalism, Fascism, Populism*. London: New Left Books.

———. 2005. *On Populist Reason*. London: Verso.

Laclau, Ernesto, and Chantal Mouffe. 1985. *Hegemony and Socialist Strategy: Towards a Radical Democratic Politics*. London: Verso.

Laplante, J. P., and Catherine Nolin. 2014. "*Consultas* and Socially Responsible Investing in Guatemala: A Case Study Examining Maya Perspectives on the Indigenous Right to Free, Prior, and Informed Consent." *Society & Natural Resources* 27 (3): 231–48. doi.org/10.1080/08941920.2013.861554.

Le Bot, Yvon. 1995. *La guerra en tierras mayas: comunidad, violencia y modernidad en Guatemala (1970–1992). Sección de obras de sociología*. Mexico City: Fondo de Cultura Económica.

Li, Tania. 2000. "Articulating Indigenous Identity in Indonesia: Resource Politics and the Tribal Slot." *Comparative Studies in Society and History* 42 (1): 149–79.

———. 2007a. "Practices of Assemblage and Community Forest Management." *Economy and Society* 36 (2): 263–93. doi.org/10.1080/03085140701254308.

———. 2007b. *The Will to Improve: Governmentality, Development, and the Practice of Politics*. Durham, NC: Duke University Press.

———. 2014. *Land's End: Capitalist Relations on an Indigenous Frontier*. Durham, NC: Duke University Press.

Lubkemann, Stephen. 2008. *Culture in Chaos: An Anthropology of the Social Condition in War*. Chicago: University of Chicago Press.

MacLeish, Kenneth. 2013. *Making War at Fort Hood: Life and Uncertainty in a Military Community*. Princeton, NJ: Princeton University Press.

Manz, Beatriz. 1988. *Refugees of a Hidden War: The Aftermath of Counterinsurgency in Guatemala*. Albany, NY: SUNY Press.

———. 2005. *Paradise in Ashes: A Guatemalan Journey of Courage, Terror, and Hope*. Berkeley: University of California Press.

Martín, Karina. 2018. "Without Ríos Montt, Guatemala Would Have Succumbed to Communism." *Pan Am Post*, April 4. Online at: https://panampost.com/karina-martin/2018/04/04/without-rios-montt-guatemala-would-have-succumbed-to-communism/?cn-reloaded=1.

Mbembe, Achille. 2000. *On the Postcolony.* Berkeley: University of California Press.

McAllister, Carlotta. 2003. " 'Good People': Revolution, Community and Consciencia in a Maya K'iche Village in Guatemala." PhD diss., Johns Hopkins University.

McAllister, Carlotta, and Diane M. Nelson, eds. 2013. *War by Other Means: Aftermath in Post-genocide Guatemala.* Durham, NC: Duke University Press.

McCreery, David. 1994. *Rural Guatemala, 1760–1940.* Stanford, CA: Stanford University Press.

McMichael, Philip. 2015. "The Question of Land in the Food Sovereignty Project." *Globalizations* 12 (4): 434–51. doi.org/10.1080/14747731.2014.971615.

Mérida, Alba Cecilia, and Wolfgang Krenmayr. 2008. *"Sistematización de experiencias." Asamblea Departmental por la Defensa de Recursos Naturales Renovables y No Renovables de Huehuetenango.* Informe. Huehuetenango: Centro de Estudios de la Frontera Occidental de Guatemala (CEDFOG).

Metz, Brent, Lorenzo Mariano, and Julián Lopez Garcia. 2010. "The Violence after 'La Violencia' in the Ch'orti' Region of Eastern Guatemala." *Journal of Latin American and Caribbean Anthropology* 15 (1): 16–41. doi.org/10.1111/j.1935-4940.2010.01061.x.

Mitchell, Timothy. 2002. *Rule of Experts: Egypt, Technoscience, Modernity.* Berkeley: University of California Press.

Montejo, Victor. 1987. *Testimony: Death of a Guatemalan Village.* Willimantic, CT: Curbstone.

Moodie, Ellen. 2010. *El Salvador in the Aftermath of Peace.* Philadelphia: University of Pennsylvania Press.

Moore, Donald. 2005. *Suffering for Territory: Race, Place, and Power in Zimbabwe.* Durham, NC: Duke University Press.

Mora, Mariana. 2017. *Kuxlejal Politics: Indigenous Autonomy, Race, and Decolonizing Research in Zapatista Communities.* Austin: University of Texas Press.

Mosse, David. 2005. *Cultivating Development: An Ethnography of Aid Policy and Practice.* London: Pluto.

Nelson, Diane. 1999. *Finger in the Wound: Body Politics in Quincentennial Guatemala.* Berkeley: University of California Press.

——. 2009. *Reckoning: Ends of War in Guatemala.* Durham, NC: Duke University Press.

——. 2015. *Who Counts? The Mathematics of Death and Life after Genocide.* Durham, NC: Duke University Press.

Nugent, David. 2008. "Democracy Otherwise: Struggles over Popular Rule in the Northern Peruvian Andes." In *Democracy: Anthropological Approaches*, edited by Julia Paley, 21–62. Santa Fe, NM: School of Advanced Research.

——. 2012. "Commentary: Democracy, Temporalities of Capitalism, and Dilemmas of Inclusion in Occupy Movements." *American Ethnologist* 39 (2): 280–83. doi.org/10.1111/j.1548-1425.2012.01363.x.

Nyéléni Declaration. 2007. *Nyéléni Declaration.* http://www.nyeleni.org/spip.php?article290.

O'Neill, Kevin Lewis. 2010. *City of God: Christian Citizenship in Postwar Guatemala.* Berkeley: University of California Press.

Ortiz, R., and A. Meneses. 1989. "Increasing the Adoption Rates of New Technologies with a New Technology Transfer Model." *FSR/E Symposium Proceedings.* Fayetteville: University of Arkansas.

Ortiz, R., S. Ruano, H. Juirez, F. Olivet, and A. Meneses. 1991. "A New Model for Technology Transfer in Guatemala." The Hague (Países Bajos): Agricultural Research Indicator Series (ISNAR).

Paley, Julia. 2001. *Marketing Democracy: Power and Social Movements in Post-dictatorship Chile.* Berkeley: University of California Press.

———. 2002. "Toward an Anthropology of Democracy." *Annual Review of Anthropology,* 469–96. doi.org/10.1146/annurev.anthro.31.040402.085453.

Paley, Julia, ed. 2008. *Democracy: Anthropological Approaches.* Santa Fe, NM: School for Advanced Research.

Panizza, Francisco, ed. 2005. *Populism and the Mirror of Democracy.* London: Verso.

Patnaik, Prabhat. 2010. "A Left Approach to Development." *Economic and Political Weekly* 45 (30): 33–37.

Phillips, Lynne, and Suzan Ilcan. 2004. "Capacity-Building: The Neoliberal Governance of Development." *Canadian Journal of Development Studies* 2 (3): 393–409. doi.org/10.1080/02255189.2004.9668985.

Philpot-Munson, J. Jailey. 2009. "Understanding Evangelical Resistance to the Peace Process in a Postwar Guatemalan Town." In *Mayas in Postwar Guatemala: Harvest of Violence Revisited,* edited by T. Smith and W. Little, 42–53. Tuscaloosa: University of Alabama Press.

Pigg, Stacy Leigh. 1993. "Investing Social Categories through Place: Social Representations and Development in Nepal." *Comparative Studies in Society and History* 34 (3): 491–513. doi.org/10.1017/S0010417500017928.

Protevi, John. 2009. *Political Affect: Connecting the Social and the Somatic.* Durham, NC: Duke University Press.

Purcell, Mark. 2013. *The Deep Down Delight of Democracy.* West Sussex: Wiley.

Rancière, Jacques. 2010. *Dissensus: On Politics and Aesthetics.* London: Bloomsbury Academic.

Rasch, Elisabet Dueholm. 2012. "Transformations in Citizenship Local Resistance against Mining Projects in Huehuetenango (Guatemala)." *Journal of Developing Societies* 28 (2): 159–84. doi.org/10.1177/0169796X12448756.

REDSAG (National Network for the Defense of Food Sovereignty). 2014. http://www.redsag.net/index.php?option=com_content&view=article&id=132:comunicado-contra-ley-monsanto&catid=39:catnoticias&Itemid=53.

REHMI (Restoration of Historical Memory Project). 1998. *Guatemala Never Again!* Maryknoll, NY: Orbis.

Reina, Carmen. 2008. *"Retos de la participación ciudadana en la construcción democrática: un enfoque en el desarrollo local y la resistencia por los recursos naturales."* El Observador 3 (14): 47–82.

Remijnse, Simone. 2002. *Memories of Violence: Civil Patrols and the Legacy of Conflict in Joyabaj, Guatemala.* Indianapolis, IN: Purdue University Press.

Robinson, William I. 2000. "Neoliberalism, the Global Elite, and the Guatemalan Transition: A Critical Macrosocial Analysis." *Journal of Interamerican Studies and World Affairs* 42 (4): 89–107. https://doi.org/10.2307/166343.

———. 2003. *Transnational Conflicts: Central America, Social Change, and Globalization.* London: Verso.

Rolph-Trouillot, Michel. 1995. *Silencing the Past: Power and the Production of History*. New York: Beacon.

Rose, Nikolas. 1996. "Governing 'Advanced' Liberal Democracies." In *The Anthropology of the State: A Reader*, edited by Adrahana Sharma and Akhil Gupta, 144–62. Malden: Blackwell.

——. 1998. *Inventing Our Selves: Psychology, Power, and Personhood*. Cambridge: Cambridge University Press.

——. 1999. *Powers of Freedom. Reframing Political Thought*. Cambridge: Cambridge University Press.

Roy, Ananya. 2009. "Civic Governmentality: The Politics of Inclusion in Beirut and Mumbai." *Antipode* 41 (1): 159–79. doi.org/10.1111/j.1467-8330.2008.00660.x.

Ruhl, J. Mark. 2005. "The Guatemalan Military since the Peace Accords: The Fate of Reform under Arzú and Portillo." *Latin American Politics and Society* 47 (1): 55–85. doi.org/10.1111/j.1548-2456.2005.tb00301.x.

Sandberg, Johan, and Engel Tally. 2015. "Politicisation of Conditional Cash Transfers: The Case of Guatemala." *Development Policy Review* 33 (4): 503–22. doi.org/10.1111/dpr.12122.

Sanford, Victoria. 2003. *Buried Secrets: Truth and Human Rights in Guatemala*. New York: Palgrave.

Schirmer, Jennifer. 1998. *The Guatemalan Military Project: A Violence Called Democracy*. Philadelphia: University of Pennsylvania Press.

Scott, James C. 2009. *The Art of Not Being Governed: An Anarchist History of Upland Southeast Asia*. New Haven: Yale University Press.

SEGEPLAN (Secretaría General de Planificación). 2009. *Indices de pobreza y pobreza extrema*. Guatemala City: Government of Guatemala.

Sen, Amartya. 1999. *Development as Freedom*. Oxford: Oxford University Press.

Shah, Alpa. 2010. *In the Shadows of the State: Indigenous Politics, Environmentalism, and Insurgency in Jharkhand, India*. Durham, NC: Duke University Press.

Sieder, Rachel. 2011a. "Building Mayan Authority and Autonomy: The Recovery of Indigenous Law in Post-Peace Guatemala." *Studies in Law, Politics and Society* 55: 22–57.

——. 2011b. "Contested Sovereignties: Indigenous Law, Violence and State Effects in Postwar Guatemala." *Critique of Anthropology* 31 (3): 161–84. doi.org/10.1177/0308275X11409729.

Simon, Jean-Marie. 1987. *Guatemala: Eternal Spring—Eternal Tyranny*. New York: Norton.

Simpson, Audra. 2014. *Mohawk Interruptus: Political Life across the Borders of Settler States*. Durham, NC: Duke University Press.

Smith, Carol A. 1984. "Local History in Global Context: Social and Economic Transitions in Western Guatemala." *Comparative Studies in Society and History* 26 (2): 193–228. doi.org/10.1017/S0010417500010872.

——. 1990a. *Guatemalan Indians and the State: 1540 to 1988*. Austin: University of Texas Press.

——. 1990b. "Militarization of Civil Society in Guatemala: Economic Reorganization as a Continuation of War." *Latin American Perspectives* 17 (4): 8–41. doi.org/10.1177/0094582X9001700402.

Smith, Daniel Jordan. 2008. *A Culture of Corruption: Everyday Deception and Popular Discontent in Nigeria*. Princeton, NJ: Princeton University Press.

Smith, Timothy. 2009. "Democracy Is Dissent." In *Harvest of Violence Revisited*, edited by T. Smith and W. Little, 1–29. Tuscaloosa: University of Alabama Press.

Solano, Luis. 2005. *Guatemala: petróleo y minería en las entrañas del poder*. Inforpress Centroamericana.

Stahler-Sholk, Richard. 2007. "Resisting Neoliberal Homogenization: The Zapatista Autonomy Movement." *Latin American Perspectives* 34 (2): 48–63. doi.org/10.1177/0094582X06298747.

Star, Susan Leigh. 2010. "This Is Not a Boundary Object: Reflections on the Origin of a Concept." *Science, Technology & Human Values* 35 (5): 601–17. doi.org/10.1177/0162243910377624.

Stepputat, Finn. 2001. "Urbanizing the Countryside: Armed Conflict, State Formation, and the Politics of Place in Contemporary Guatemala." In *States of Imagination: Ethnographic Explorations of the Postcolonial State*, edited by T. Hansen and F. Stepputat, 284–312. Durham, NC: Duke University Press.

Stewart, Kathleen. 1996. *A Space on the Side of the Road: Cultural Poetics in an "Other" America*. Princeton, NJ: Princeton University Press.

——. 2010. "Afterword: Worlding Refrains." In *The Affect Studies Reader*, edited by M. Gregg and G. Seigworth, 339–54. Durham, NC: Duke University Press.

——. 2011. "Atmospheric Attunements." *Environment and Planning D: Society and Space* 29 (3): 445–553. doi.org/10.1068/d9109.

——. 2013. "Studying Unformed Objects: The Provocation of a Compositional Mode." *Cultural Anthropology*, June 30. https://culanth.org/fieldsights/350-studying-unformed-objects-the-provocation-of-a-compositional-mode.

Stoll, David. 1990. *Is Latin America Turning Protestant? The Politics of Evangelical Growth*. Berkeley: University of California Press.

——. 1993. *Between Two Armies in the Ixil Towns of Guatemala*. Princeton, NJ: Princeton University Press.

——. 2009. "Harvest of Conviction: Solidarity in Guatemala Scholarship 1988–2008." In *Mayas in Postwar Guatemala: Harvest of Violence Revisited*, edited by W. Little and T. Smith, 167–80. Tuscaloosa: University of Alabama Press.

Taracena, Arturo Arriola. 1997. *Invención criolla, sueño ladino, pesadilla indígena: Los Altos de Guatemala: de región a Estado, 1740–1850*. Antigua: Centro de Investigaciones Regionales de Mesoamérica (CIRMA).

Tax, Sol. 1953. *Penny Capitalism: A Guatemalan Indian Economy*. Washington, DC: US Government Printing Office.

Taussig, Michael. 1997. *The Magic of the State*. Chicago: University of Chicago Press.

——. 1999. *Defacement: Public Secrecy and the Labor of the Negative*. Stanford, CA: Stanford University Press.

Thomas, Kedron, Kevin O'Neill, and Thomas Offit. 2011. "Introduction." In *Securing the City: Neoliberalism, Space, and Insecurity in Guatemala*, edited by K. Thomas and K. L. O'Neill. Durham, NC: Duke University Press.

Torres Rivas, Edelberto. 2010. "*Las democracias malas de Centroamérica*." *Nueva Sociedad* 226: 52–67.

Tribuno Supremo Electoral 2003. *Memoria de las elecciones*. Guatemala City: Gobierno de Guatemala.

——. 2007. *Memoria de las elecciones*. Guatemala City: Gobierno de Guatemala.

——. 2011. *Memoria de las elecciones*. Guatemala City: Gobierno de Guatemala.

UNODC (United Nations Office of Drugs and Crime). 2012. *Cocaine from South America to the United States*. www.unodc.org/documents/toc/Reports/TOCTASouthAmerica/English/TOCTA_CACaribb_cocaine_SAmerica_US.pdf.

USAID (United States Agency for International Development). 1970. "Guatemala: Rural Development Loan." Capital Assistance Paper. Proposal and Recommendations for Review of the Development Loan Committee.

——. 2010. *Country Profile: Guatemala. Land Tenure and Property Rights Portal*. http://usaidlandtenure.net/sites/default/files/country-profiles/full-reports/USAID_Land_Tenure_Guatemala_Profile_0.pdf.

Velásquez-Nimatuj, Irma Alicia. 2008. *Pueblos indígenas, estado y lucha por tierra en Guatemala: estrategias de sobrevivencia y negociación ante la desigualdad globalizada*. Guatemala City: AVANCSO.

——. 2013. "'A Dignified Community Where We Can Live': Violence, Law, and Debt in Nuevo Cajolá's Struggle for Land." In *War by Other Means: Aftermath in Post-genocide Guatemala*, edited by Carlotta McAllister and Diane M. Nelson, 170–94. Durham, NC: Duke University Press.

Vergara-Camus, Leandro. 2014. *Land and Freedom: The MST, the Zapatistas and Peasant Alternatives to Neoliberalism*. London: Zed.

Vogt, Manuel. 2015. "The Disarticulated Movement: Barriers to Maya Mobilization in Post-Conflict Guatemala." *Latin American Politics and Society* 57 (1): 29–50. doi/full/10.1111.

Wagley, Charles. 1949. *Social and Religious Life in a Guatemalan Village*. American Anthropological Association.

Waqib' Kej. 2015. *Demandas y propuestas políticas de los pueblos indígenas de Iximulew*. Coordinación y Convergencia Nacional. Guatemala City: Waqib' Kej.

Warren, Kay B. 1989. *The Symbolism of Subordination: Indian Identity in a Guatemalan Town*. Austin: University of Texas Press.

——. 1998. *Indigenous Movements and Their Critics: Pan-Mayan Activism in Guatemala*. Princeton, NJ: Princeton University Press.

——. 2002. "Voting against Indigenous Rights in Guatemala: Lessons from the 1999 Referendum." In *Indigenous Movements, Self-Representation, and the State in Latin America*, edited by Kay Warren and Jean E. Jackson. Austin: University of Texas Press.

Watanabe, John M. 2010. *Maya Saints and Souls in a Changing World*. Austin: University of Texas Press.

Way, John T. 2012. *The Mayan in the Mall: Globalization, Development, and the Making of Modern Guatemala*. Durham, NC: Duke University Press.

Webber, Jeffery R., and Barry Carr, eds. 2012. *The New Latin American Left: Cracks in the Empire*. New York: Rowman & Littlefield.

West, Harry. 2005. *Kupilikula: Governance and the Invisible Realm in Mozambique*. Chicago: University of Chicago Press.

———. 2008. "'Govern Yourselves!' Democracy and Carnage in Northern Mozambique." In *Democracy: Anthropological Approaches*, edited by Julia Paley, 97–122. Santa Fe, NM: School of Advanced Research.

Wilkinson, Daniel. 2004. *Silence on the Mountain: Stories of Terror, Betrayal, and Forgetting in Guatemala*. Durham, NC: Duke University Press.

Witsoe, Jeffrey. 2013. *Democracy against Development: Lower-Caste Politics and Political Modernity in Postcolonial India*. Chicago: University of Chicago Press.

Wolin, Sheldon. 2008. *Democracy Incorporated: Managed Democracy and the Specter of Inverted Totalitarianism*. Princeton, NJ: Princeton University Press.

Yagenova, Simona, and Rocío Garcia. 2009. "Indigenous Peoples' Struggles against Transnational Mining Companies in Guatemala: The Sipakapa People vs. Goldcorp Mining Company." *Socialism and Democracy* 23 (3): 157–66. doi/abs/10.1080/08854300903208795.

Zibechi, Raúl. 2010. *Dispersing Power: Social Movements as Anti-state Forces*. Oakland, CA: AK Press.

Zur, Judith. 1998. *Violent Memories: Mayan War Widows in Guatemala*. Boulder, CO: Westview.

INDEX

Page numbers in *italics* refer to figures.